GROUCHO MARX

It is almost impossible to credit that Groucho Marx, the most verbally outrageous of the Brothers, would now be well over 100 if he were still alive, for the range of insulting wit he purveyed still seems timely. Born in New York, son of a tailor, he began his professional career in 1901 as a boy singer, brothers Chico and Harpo being beneficiaries of piano lessons. Their formidable mother, Minnie, launched her boys into vaudeville as a musical team, originally known as 'The Three Nightingales', but it was not until they switched to comedy that they clicked. It was in the mid-1920s that Groucho developed his unique style. He became identified with the crouched walk, the painted moustache, the leering eye, the steel-rimmed glasses, and the ever-puffing cigar.

The Brothers made their film debut in 1929 in *The Cocoanuts*, adapted with little alteration from their Broadway show four years previously. Its vitality, travesties of logic and lack of inhibitions (especially from Groucho) appealed to all brows – and it led to four more films from Paramount, culminating in what is probably their best from that period, *Duck Soup*. But there was an urge by the front-office men to alleviate their comedy with romantic sub-plots and some attempt at plot coherence – much to Groucho's dismay. The first film of this new, gentler order was *A Night at the Opera* for MGM, and in fact it did out-gross its predecessors. Its follow-up, *A Day at the Races* showed signs of deterioration in the interests of box-office, and, although the Marx Brothers continued to make films together until the final *Love Happy* of 1950, the later ones had moments of brilliance within minutes of dross.

Groucho, the youngest of the three best known Brothers, continued to make some films on his own, but achieved a new television fame by hosting a comedy-quiz show, *You Bet Your Life*, with anarchic irreverence and proving that he was still a master of the impromptu put-down that turned away wrath. *Groucho and Me*, the first of his three autobiographical volumes, has the very special quality of reading as he once spoke.

His last film appearance was in 1968, and his final, senile years were clouded by legal wrangles. An ironic end to a man who claimed that his life was full of yearning for the young – 'girls, but only when they are above the age of consent, and do a lot of consenting.'

GROUCHO AND ME

Groucho Marx

Foreword by James Thurber

Published by Virgin Books 2009

2 4 6 8 10 9 7 5 3 1

Copyright © Groucho Marx 1959
Foreword from a review in the *New York Herald Tribune*

Groucho Marx has asserted his right under the Copyright, Designs
and Patents Act 1988 to be identified as the author of this work

First published in Great Britain in 1994 by
Virgin Books
Random House, 20 Vauxhall Bridge Road,
London SW1V 2SA

Reprinted 2005, 2007, 2008

This edition published with permission of the original publisher,
Bernard Geis Associates

www.virginbooks.com
www.rbooks.co.uk

Addresses for companies within The Random House Group Limited
can be found at: www.randomhouse.co.uk/offices.htm

The Random House Group Limited Reg. No. 954009

A CIP catalogue record for this book is available from the British Library

ISBN 9780753519509

The Random House Group Limited supports The Forest Stewardship Council
[FSC], the leading international forest certification organisation. All our titles that
are printed on Greenpeace approved FSC certified paper carry the FSC logo.
Our paper procurement policy can be found at www.rbooks.co.uk/environment

Printed and bound in Great Britain by CPI Bookmarque Ltd, Croydon CR0 4TD

For What it's Worth
This Book is Gratefully
Dedicated
To These Six Masters
Without Whose Wise and Witty Words
My Life Would have been Even Duller

Robert Benchley
George S. Kaufman
Ring Lardner
S. J. Perelman
James Thurber
E. B. White

CONTENTS

CONTENTS

FOREWORD

More than twenty years ago my wife and I were entertained at dinner in London by an American diplomat and his wife. It was black tie, of course, and I had steeled myself for an evening of polite conversation. Instead, our host took us to see the smartest show in town and the hardest to get into, the Marx Brothers' *A Day at the Races*. Two years later, in Hollywood, I met the protean author of *Groucho and Me*, and I'll be darned if we were not, within five minutes, engaged in a serious discussion of Henry James' ghost story, *The Jolly Corner*.

There is nothing ghostly or ghosted about *Groucho and Me*. The 'Me' is a comparatively unknown Marx named Julius Henry Marx. Groucho and Julius are one, but not the same. The latter is a writer from way back. When the *New Yorker* was six weeks old, in April 1925, it printed the first of four short casuals that year, signed Julius H. Marx. In 1929 there were three more pieces in the magazine, this time signed Groucho Marx. I think Harold Ross had insisted that Groucho come out from behind his real name and admit, you might say, who he wasn't.

Julius-Groucho's *New Yorker* pieces consisted of anecdotes, dialogues, jokes and reminiscences. They dealt with vaudeville, Boston, the Middle West, and Press agents, and there was one entitled 'Buy It, Put It Away, and Forget About It'. It appeared in May 1929, and began like this: 'I come from common stock. I always planned to begin my autobiography with this terse statement. Now that introduction is out. Common stock made a bum out of me.'

This is the way the autobiography of Julius H. Marx actually begins: 'The trouble with writing a book about yourself is that you can't fool around. If you write about someone else, you can stretch the truth from here to Finland. If you write about yourself, the slightest deviation makes you realize instantly that there may be honour among thieves, but you are just a dirty liar.' Julius often cuffs himself about like that, and he takes Groucho in his stride. You learn about the comedian almost incidentally, for the book turns its brightest spotlight on the humorist, wit, essayist, philosopher and man of many worlds.

The twenty-eight chapters are, in part, the saga of the five sons of a Yorkville tailor and his wife, and of how they came out of the Nowhere into the Here, out of the small time into the big time, out of a dark obscurity into a luminous fame. Well, there was one spark of immortality in the family to begin with. A maternal uncle of the Marx boys was Mr Shean, who rode to undying fame in the company of Mr Gallagher.

In the song 'Fine and Dandy' there is a line that goes: 'Even trouble has its funny side', but Groucho, as I shall call him from now on, shows not only the funny side of trouble, but also the troublesome side of fun. Before the Marx Brothers became an everlasting part of our great comedic history and tradition, they ran the hard gamut of everything. The purely autobiographical chapters, in the swift, expert and uniquely witty style of the master, tell how the young Marxes – Chico, the eldest, was the only one to graduate from grammar school – survived the abuses, loneliness, crookedness and cruelty of small-time vaudeville without becoming disenchanted by show business, although they had to fight for a livelihood, learned to carry blackjacks and to hold their own with the monsters called theatre managers. The only hospitality they enjoyed in the awful early years on the road was supplied by sporting houses and pool rooms, for the actor was suspect, not glamorous, in those days.

Groucho's book might have been subtitled: 'How I Ran an Allowance of Five Cents a Week into an Income of $18,000 a Week, with a Vicuna Coat and Two Cadillacs Thrown in'. Money plays a big part in this, as in any other American success story, and in a chapter called 'How I Starred in the Follies of 1929' he tells how he lost nearly a quarter of a million in the stock market crash. (That May 1929 *New Yorker* piece of his was indeed prophetic.)

The stock market did not make bums out of the Marxes. It was a kind of godsend, for in 1931 they went to Hollywood where their guardian angel introduced them to Irving Thalberg, the man responsible for the screening of *A Day at the Races*, and that finest of all Marx masterpieces, *A Night at the Opera*. The book gleams and glitters with the names of show business and show art. George Kaufman is praised for his valuable contribution to the Marx success, and we meet, or rather Groucho met, Charlie Chaplin when the Little Man was making only fifty bucks a week in an act called 'A Night at the Club'.

Everything in this book is fresh and new, for neither Julius nor Groucho included any of his earlier writings. Those two share a cold eye, a warm heart and a quick perception. *Groucho and Me* is an important contribution to the history of show business and to the saga of American comedy and comedians, comics and comicality.

James Thurber

CHAPTER ONE

WHY WRITE WHEN YOU CAN TELEGRAPH YOUR PUNCHES?

THE TROUBLE WITH writing a book about yourself is that you can't fool around. If you write about someone else, you can stretch the truth from here to Finland. If you write about yourself the slightest deviation makes you realize instantly that there may be honour among thieves, but *you* are just a dirty liar.

Although it is generally known, I think it's about time to announce that I was born at a very early age. Before I had time to regret it, I was four and a half years old. Now that we are on the subject of age, let's skip it. It isn't important how old I am. What is important, however, is whether enough people will buy this book to justify my spending the remnants of my rapidly waning vitality in writing it.

Age is not a particularly interesting subject. Anyone can get old. All you have to do is live long enough. It always amuses me when the newspapers run a picture of a man who has finally lived to be a hundred. He's usually a pretty beat-up individual who invariably looks closer to two hundred than the century mark. It isn't enough that the paper runs a photo of this rickety, hollow shell. The ancient oracle then has to sound off on the secret of his longevity. "I've lived longer than all my friends," he croaks, "because I never used a mattress, always slept on the floor, had raw turkey liver every morning for breakfast, and drank thirty-two glasses of water a day."

Big deal! Thirty-two glasses of water a day. This is the kind of man who is responsible for the water shortage in America. Fortunes have been spent in the arid West, trying to convert sea water into something that can be swallowed with safety, and this old geezer, instead of drinking eight glasses of water a day like the rest of us, has to guzzle thirty-two a day, or enough water to keep four normal people going indefinitely.

I STILL CAN'T understand why I let the publishers talk me into tackling this job. Just walk into any bookstore and take a look at the mountain of books that are currently published and expected to be sold. Most of them are written by professionals who write well and have something to say. Nevertheless, a year from now most of these books will be on sale at half-price. If by some miracle this one should become a best-seller, the tax department would get most of the money. However, I don't think there's much danger of this. Why should anyone buy the thoughts and opinions of Groucho Marx? I have no views that are worth a damn, and no knowledge that could possibly help anyone.

The big sellers are cook-books, theological tomes, "how to" books, and rehashings of the Civil War. Their motto is, "Keep a Civil War in Your Head." Titles like, *How to Be Happy though Miserable*, *Cook Your Way into Your Husband's Heart* and *Why General Lee Blew the Duke at Gettysburg* sell millions of copies. How can I ever compete with them?

I don't know anything about cooking. On those frequent occasions when my current cook storms out, shouting, "You know what you can do with your kitchen!" only the fact that I have a fairly good supply of pemmican left over from my last trip to Winnipeg saves me from starvation. Oh, I have some men friends who can wrap a barbecue apron adorned with funny sayings around their waists, and in two shakes of a lamb's tail (or forty minutes on the clock) whip up a meal that would make Savarin turn in his bouillabaisse, but cooking is just not my cup of tea. If I had attempted to write a cook-book it would have sold about three copies.

I did toy with the idea of doing a cook-book, though. The recipes were to be the routine ones: how to make dry toast, instant coffee, hearts of lettuce and brownies. But as an added attraction, at no extra charge, my idea was to put a fried egg on the cover. I think a lot of people who hate literature but love fried eggs would buy it if the price was right. Offhand, this seems like a crazy idea, but a lot of things that seemed nutty at first have turned out to be substantial contributions to mankind's comfort.

Take mouse-traps, for example. Mice weren't always caught with traps. Only a few centuries ago, if a man wanted to catch a mouse (and many men did), he had to sneak up to a hole in the corner of the kitchen with a piece of cheese clamped between his teeth. Incidentally, this is where the expression,

"Keep your trap shut" (usually uttered by the wife just before retiring), came from.

THERE ARE many things sold on TV today that are fairly meretricious. People buy these products because they are merchandized with dogged persistence and more than a soupçon of deceit. This, of course, doesn't apply to any of the legitimate sponsors, but mainly to the local charlatans who stop at nothing.

Perhaps to merchandize this book wisely I ought to give away not only the previously mentioned fried egg, but as an added attraction (at no extra charge) I should give away with each and every book, a hundred pounds of seed corn. Not ninety pounds, mark you, not eighty pounds, but one hundred pounds. Where am I going to get the corn? I have already anticipated your question. I'm going to get it from the farmer. For years the American public has been getting it in the neck from the farmer and, in return, all we have received is a large bill for farm relief and rigid price supports.

The reason the farmer gets away with so much is that when a city-dweller thinks of the farmer he visualizes a tall, stringy yokel, with hayseed in his few teeth, subsisting on turnip greens, skimmed milk and hog jowls and living in a ramshackle dump with his mule fifty miles from nowhere. But what's the good of my trying to describe it? Erskine Caldwell wrapped it up neatly in *God's Little Acre*.

This kind of farmer may have existed years ago, but today the farmer is the best-protected citizen in the entire economy. As a city-dweller, I can assure you that there is no love lost between the urbanite and the farmer (unless the farmer has a daughter).

Each year the government is faced with the same problem—how to dispose of the corn surplus. They've tried everything: storing it on battleships, dumping it in silos (with the hope that the rats and squirrels will make away with some of it); they've even tried giving it away free to the moonshiners. But the White Mule business ain't what it used to be. The moonshiners now want potatoes because the American public has switched over to vodka. Well, the government's problem can be solved very easily. Just give me the corn my book so sorely needs.

The government's eternal solicitude for the rustic has got

the rest of the country gagging. Why don't they do something for the book publisher and the author? Why don't they do away with literary critics who, in three fine sentences, can cripple the sale of any book? Did you ever hear of a farm critic coming out and saying, "Farmer Snodgrass' corn is not up to his last year's crop"? Or, "Another year's crop like this one, and he'll be back digging sewers for the county asylum"?

The book publishers of America, you'll notice, have no lobby in Washington looking after their interests. They have a surplus of books they would like to plough under, but they haven't got enough money to buy the hole to bury them in.

The public is pretty angry at the farmer. No matter how many farmers we plough under, those fake rustics manage to gouge more money out of the government than all the other pressure groups combined. Now it's about time the American farmers did something for the people. So, if the publishers who sucked me into this job have anything on the ball, instead of hanging around Madison Avenue lapping up vodka martinis, they should be out hustling, putting pressure on the government and also on the farmers. If my publishers are successful in getting the free seed corn, this could easily become The Book of the Year. Just think what you would get for your lousy four bucks—a fried egg, a bag of corn, and the combined wisdom of Groucho Marx. And all for a poultry four dollars. And remember, this book wouldn't have to be sold just in the bookstores. It could be sold in supermarkets, lunchrooms, garden supply shops and drive-in theatres.

Nowadays things have to be merchandized. You can't just write a book and expect the public to rush out and buy it unless it's a classic. I could write a classic if I wanted to, but I'd rather write for the little people. When I walk down the street I don't care a hoot if people point a finger at me and say, "Look at him. He just wrote a classic!" No, I'd rather have them say admiringly, "What a trashy writer! But who else writing today gives away a fried egg and a bag of corn with each copy of his book?"

THEY SAY that every man has a book in him. This is about as accurate as most generalizations. Take, for example,

"Early to bed, early to rise, makes a man you-know-what." This is a lot of hoopla. Most wealthy people I know like to sleep late, and will fire the help if they are disturbed before three in the afternoon. Pray tell (I cribbed that from *Little Women*), who are the people who get up at the crack of dawn? Policemen, firemen, garbage-collectors, bus-drivers, department store clerks and others in the lower-income bracket. You don't see Marilyn Monroe getting up at six in the morning. The truth is, I don't see Marilyn getting up at any hour, more's the pity. I'm sure if you had your choice, you would rather watch Miss Monroe rise at three in the afternoon than watch the most efficient garbage-collector in your town hop out of bed at six.

Unfortunately, the temptation to write about yourself is irresistible, especially when you are prodded into it by a crafty publisher who has slyly baited you into doing it with a miserly advance of fifty dollars and a box of cheap cigars.

It all started innocently enough. Years ago, influenced by the famous diaries of Samuel Pepys, I too started keeping a diary. Incidentally, I think that the Peeps or Peppies or Pipes diaries would be much more popular today had there been a universal pronunciation of his name. Many times, at a fashionable literary dinner party, I have been tempted to discuss the Pepys diaries, but I was always uncertain as to the proper pronunciation of his name. For example, if you said "Peeps" the lady on your left would invariably say, "Pardon me, but don't you mean Pipes?" And the partner on your right would say, "I'm sorry, but you're both wrong. It's Peppies." If Peeps, Pipes or Peppies had been smart enough to pick up a name like Joe Blow, every schoolboy in America would be reading his diaries today instead of being out in the streets stealing hub-caps.

At this point during the party, if you are wise, you abandon the literary gambit and Pepys and plunge into some subject that you know something about, such as the batting and fielding averages of George Sisler. A discussion of George Sisler will quickly bring about the exodus of the two dumpy dowagers between whom your hostess has so thoughtfully planted you. This gives you an opportunity to smile tenderly at that cute little starlet across the table, the one whom nature has so generously endowed with the good things in life.

I don't know what TV and free love have done to the book

publishing business, but one of the biggest blocks to the launching of a literary masterpiece (which this unquestionably will be) is the miserly Scrooge known in bookish circles as "the browser." I'm sure you have seen him in many a bookstore. He reads a review in *The New Yorker, Atlantic Monthly* or *The Saturday Review* of some new book that sounds pretty tasty. Fortified with this briefing, he casually enters a bookstore, ferrets out a copy of the book, and if he is a rapid reader (or "skimmer," as he is known in the trade) he gets through it pretty thoroughly in forty-five minutes. He then scrams unobtrusively through a side door so that he can come back another day and help pauperize some other hard-working author.

In the event that the owner of the bookstore is foolish enough to ask if he can be of assistance, this creep (knowing he is trapped) will be crafty enough to ask for *Frangani's History of the Chinese Wall* or *A Comprehensive Compendium of the Argine Confederacy*. A man will think nothing of paying four or five dollars for a pair of pants, but he'll think a long time before he'll pony up the same amount of money for a book.

THIS OPUS started out as an autobiography, but before I was very far into it I realized it would be nothing of the kind. It is almost impossible to write a truthful autobiography. Maybe Proust, Gide and a few others did it, but most autobiographies take good care to conceal the author from the public. In nearly all cases, what the public finally buys is a discreet tome with the facts slyly concealed, full of hogwash and ambiguity.

Except in the case of professional writers, most of these untrue confessions are not even written by the man whose name is on the book jacket. Large letters will proclaim it to be THE AUTOBIOGRAPHY OF CHARLES W. MOONSTRUCK, and letters small enough to fit the head of a pin will whisper, "As told to Joe Flamingo." Joe Flamingo, the actual writer, is the drudge who has wasted two years of his life for a miserly stipend, setting down and embellishing the few halting words of Charles W. Moonstruck. When the book finally appears in print, Moonstruck struts all over town asking his friends (the few he has),

"Did you read my book? . . . You know, I've never written before. . . . I had no idea writing was so easy! . . . I must do another book soon."

He forgets that he hasn't written a word of this undistinguished epic and, except for the fact that he told his "ghost" where he was born and when (he even lied a little about this), his literary stooge had to ad lib and create the three hundred deathless pages himself.

THIS IS INDEED the age of the "ghost." Most of the palaver that emanates from bankers, politicians, actors, industrialists and others in the high-bracket zones is written by undernourished hacks who keep body and soul together writing reams of schweinerei for flannel-mouthed stuffed shirts. Like it or not, this is the kind of an age we're living in.

I'm really sticking my neck out with this blast at ghostwriting. I know damned well I'm no Faulkner, Hemingway, Camus or Perelman . . . or even Kathleen Winsor. As a matter of fact, I'm not even the same sex as Kathleen. But every word of this stringy, ill-written farrago is being sweated out by me.

The fact remains that most autobiographies don't have too many facts remaining. Ninety per cent of them are ninety per cent fiction. If the real truth were ever written about most men in public life, there wouldn't be enough jails to house them. Lying has become one of the biggest industries in America.

Let's take, for example, the relationship that exists between husband and wife. Even when they're celebrating their golden wedding anniversary and have said "I love you" a million times to each other, publicly and privately, you know as well as I do that they've never really told each other the truth—the *real* truth. I don't mean the superficial things like, "Your mother is a louse!" or "Why don't we get an expensive car instead of that tin can we're riding around in?" No, I mean the secret thoughts that run through their minds when they wake up in the middle of the night and see imaginary things on the wall.

If two people who have been happily married for fifty years

can be so successful in keeping their innermost thoughts to themselves, how in hell can you expect an autobiography, which theoretically is going to be read by thousands of people, to be anything but a long list of semi-fabrications? The private thoughts that percolate through the minds of individuals remain in deep, dark recesses and never come to the surface.

As far as I can recall, most of the incidents I've related are true, but actually you don't know me any better now than when you started reading this madcap adventure. I don't say that this is a calamity. My guess is, you're open to congratulations. What I mean is, you haven't the faintest idea of what goes on within me. Just remember, "Every man is an island unto himself." (This may not be the precise quote, but I haven't got time to look it up. I'm getting a massage at three o'clock, and besides, I'm running out of paper.)

I suppose one could write a factual, honest and truthful autobiography, but to play it safe it would have to be published posthumously. I, for one, believe I could write a sensational book if I were willing to reveal my innermost thoughts and feelings about life in general and me in particular. But what good would a posthumous book do me? Even if it turned out to be a best-seller and was picked up later and condensed by the *Reader's Digest*, I would get nothing out of it. So until they figure out some way that you *can* take it with you, what you're getting here is pure ersatz Groucho. You'd be much better off just reading the dictionary or pruning fruit trees.

CHAPTER TWO

WHO NEEDS MONEY? (WE DID)

GIVE OR TAKE a few years, I was born around the turn of the century. I won't say which century. Everyone is allowed one guess.

We had a crowded household in our Yorkville Shangri-la on New York's Upper East Side. In addition to the five brothers—Chico, Harpo, Groucho, Gummo and Zeppo, in the order of our age—there were my mother and father (in fact, they got there before we did), my mother's father and mother, an adopted sister and a steady stream of poor relations that flowed through our house night and day.

They came for laughs, they came for food and they came for advice. I don't know who paid for the food. It must have been the local markets, for we moved from one Yorkville precinct to another as often as a gypsy caravan. In those days you could move all your possessions for ten bucks, and this was much cheaper than paying the bills. At any rate, there always seemed to be enough to feed everyone.

Whatever our visitors came for, they always came to my mother—never to my father. She advised them about their love-lives, where to find jobs and how to stay out of trouble. She engineered loans when they needed money. How she did it was always a source of wonder to me, but she invariably came through. She patched up marriages that were foundering and she out-talked the landlord, the grocer, the butcher and anyone else to whom we owed money. Her manœuvres were a triumph of skill, chicanery and imagination.

MY POP was a tailor, and sometimes he made as much as eighteen dollars a week. But he was no ordinary tailor. His record as the most inept tailor that Yorkville ever produced has never been approached. This could even include parts of Brooklyn and the Bronx.

The notion that Pop was a tailor was an opinion that was held only by him. To his customers he was known as "Misfit Sam." He was the only tailor I ever heard of who refused to use a tape measure. A tape measure might be all right for an undertaker, he maintained, but not for a tailor who had the unerring eye of an eagle. He insisted that a tape measure was pure swank and utter nonsense, adding that if a tailor had to measure a man he couldn't be much of a tailor in the first place. Pop boasted that he could size up a man just by looking at him, and turn out a perfect fit. The results of his appraisals were about as accurate as Chamberlain's predictions about Hitler.

Our neighbourhood was full of Pop's customers. They were easily recognizable in the street, for they all walked around with one trouser leg shorter than the other, one sleeve longer than the other or coat collars undecided where to rest. The inevitable result was that my father never had the same customers twice. This meant that he had to be constantly on the prowl for new business, and as our neighbourhood became more populated with gents dressed in misfit clothing, he had to find locations where his reputation had not preceded him. He roamed far and wide—Hoboken, Passaic, Nyack and beyond. As his reputation grew, he was forced to go farther and farther from the home base to snare new victims. Many weeks his car-fare was larger than his income. And his corns and bunions, tended by one of my favourite uncles, the talented Dr. Krinkler, were bigger than both of them.

How my mother managed is a mystery beyond explaining. Alexander Hamilton may have been the greatest Secretary of the Treasury, but I would have liked to see him handle my mother's job as skilfully as she did.

It's amazing how proficient a man can be in one field and how incompetent in another. My father should have been a chef. He usually cooked dinner for all of us. Everyone has met a few people like this. He could take two eggs, some stale bread, a few assorted vegetables and a hunk of cheap meat, and convert this into something fit for the gods, assuming that there are any left.

Like most women, my mother hated cooking and would walk miles out of her way to avoid the kitchen. But my father's culinary skill enabled my mother to swing some pretty sharp deals in later years. When our vaudeville act was just getting started, one of mother's shrewdest gambits was to invite the booking agents over for one of Pop's meals. After eating his food the agents were softened up to the point where Mother could do business with them on her terms.

AN AUNT of mine had a daughter by her current husband. When he got a look at the kid, he blew to Canada and was never seen again. Actually, the girl had a pretty good shape, as we called it in those innocent days, and all the other necessary equipment to snare a man. One of my father's pinochle-playing acquaintances was a plumber named Appelbaum. He was around forty and a confirmed bachelor. He liked women, but had a violent distaste for marriage. My mother liked this girl, whose name was Sally, and realized that Sally would never get married through her own initiative or charms. A born matchmaker, my mother got busy. She had met Appelbaum one day while he was playing pinochle at our house. By an odd coincidence, Sally was also present. Appelbaum was persuaded to stay for dinner. My father had prepared quite a good meal that night, and after much lip-smacking and a few belches and grunts from Appelbaum, my mother informed him that Sally had cooked the whole dinner with her own fragile little hands.

Appelbaum came often after that, and Sally was always there, serving up my father's ragouts. This was a pretty soft set-up for a bachelor—a free meal, followed later in the evening by auction pinochle with my father and another pigeon who lived upstairs. Appelbaum not only left the house with indigestion, but frequently with a dollar or two of my father's money, which Pop could ill afford to lose. One night, when Appelbaum was in a particularly logy condition, my mother said, "Bernard" (for that was his name), "did you ever think of getting married? A bachelor doesn't live . . . he just exists. He ought to have a nice, cosy little flat. And with a girl like Sally to cook for him, life could be idyllic."

Appelbaum wasn't sure what idyllic meant, but neither was my mother. She just happened across the word one day while reading an ad. for an around-the-world cruise.

At that moment Sally came into the room, swinging her

hips and winking a little as she walked. My mother rushed over and, in a hoarse voice, whispered, "Beat it! I think I've got him!" This is the way fishermen talk about hooking a marlin. At the suggestion of marriage, the expression on Appelbaum's kisser resembled that of a hooked fish. My mother, seeing that she had him on the line, really played him. Darrow, at the Loeb-Leopold trial, couldn't have been more eloquent or convincing. Before the evening was over, she had extracted a weak promise that he would consent to marry the girl of my mother's choice.

THE WEDDING was held at Shafer's Casino in the Bronx, and a goodly crowd—mostly my relatives—showed up. They weren't much interested in the wedding, but the free feed that would follow the ceremony brought them flying.

There were about fifty in our gang. Appelbaum came alone. Apparently he was ashamed of the whole transaction and didn't want any of his friends to witness his defeat. I imagine if I saw this casino today it would look pretty shabby. But at the time it possessed all the majesty, in my eyes, of a combination of Windsor Castle and the Gardens of Versailles.

At last, the rabbi appeared and the ceremony got under way. The rabbi (a real ham, and I know this is an incongruity) went into a long, dreary Hebrew sermon. Harpo and I, bored with the rabbinical rhetoric, principally because we understood none of it, strayed to the men's room to kill time until the food arrived. For some peculiar reason which I don't recall, we both decided it would be a challenge to jump up and down together on one of the urinals. I'm not an expert on this kind of plumbing, but I'm sure these structures weren't built to withstand the weight of approximately two hundred pounds of boy jumping on them. Suddenly the whole thing sheared off as though it were made of cheese, and a miniature Niagara Falls began to spout from the pipes. Not knowing what to do, we rushed out and rejoined the throng watching the ceremony.

Somehow the owner of the casino got wind of the disaster. Only seconds later, he came storming out of his office, screaming, "Stop the wedding! Stop the wedding!" When the noise subsided, he yelled, "Someone's been in the men's room and knocked off a urinal! If I find out who it was," he added furiously, "I'll kill him!" Then he turned to my mother, who had made the deal for the hall, and said that unless someone forked over thirty-eight dollars for the urinal there would be no further ceremony. The wedding was off! It was long ago, and it may be only my imagination, but if I remember correctly this was the only time that I noticed a ray of hope in the groom's eye.

My mother, undaunted, grabbed somebody's hat and proceeded to take up a collection. Although there were fifty of us, the best our crowd could do was seventeen dollars, Appelbaum, by this time half-hooked by the ceremony, the rabbi's fee, the rent and the dinner, reluctantly put up the balance of the thirty-eight dollars. The wedding then proceeded, and Sally and Appelbaum lived happily ever after. This story is true, even including the happy ending. Only the names have been changed to protect me against one of the prettiest lawsuits since the Peaches Browning case.

ONE DAY shortly after the Appelbaum nuptials, my father came home in high spirits. He had finally persuaded a fat, rich confectioner named Stookfleisch to order a suit for Easter. My father's regular fee for one of his sartorial monstrosities was twenty dollars, but Stookfleisch weighed 350 pounds, and they finally settled on twenty-eight dollars. Because of the extra cloth required, my father realized he wouldn't make any money on this deal, but this confectioner was a social leader in the candy and ice-cream circles, and Pop knew that if the suit pleased him there was a likelihood that he could capture the trade of all the prosperous butchers, grocers, brewers and shopkeepers on the East Side. My father was so determined to clinch this lucrative business that he invested three dollars in a competent tailor to help him measure this man-mountain. Stookfleisch had a preliminary fitting, and to my father's amazement, the suit needed very little altering.

On Saturday the suit was finished and carefully packed in a cardboard box. With the promise of a free ice-cream soda, I was instructed to deliver it early Sunday morning in time

for the Easter Parade on First Avenue. With the precious box
under my arm I skipped happily toward Stookfleisch's con-
fectionery store and the creamy chocolate soda I had finally
decided upon. Halfway through the soda I heard the roar of
a wounded animal. Descending upon me was this huge, fat
giant, wearing just the upper half of the suit my father had so
carefully tailored. The bottom half was his underwear. "What
the hell did you do with my pants?" he trumpeted. Reluctantly but hastily leaving the half-finished soda, I leaped for
the front door and ran all the way home.

When I arrived, my father, beaming with anticipation, was
waiting to greet me at the front door. "Well," he asked eagerly,
"how did Stookfleisch like the suit? I'll bet he never had a
pair of pants that fit him like that!"

"Pop," I said, "you may be right, but there wasn't any
pants."

"What do you mean, there wasn't any pants? There was
pants in that box yesterday and they certainly didn't walk out
by themselves!"

My father was right. They didn't walk out by themselves.
They were lifted out. Naturally, suspicion pointed to Chico.

W HEN ANYTHING was missing around the house—the
shears my father used for cutting the suits, the silver watch
Gummo had received for his Bar Mitzvah, the silver-headed
cane my grandfather carried when he went for a walk—the
finger of suspicion immediately pointed toward Chico and a
pawnshop on Third Avenue. The missing objects invariably
meant that, financially, things were once again going badly
for Chico at the poolroom in Harlem.

Today, when foreign nations need money, they just tap the
Treasury in Washington. But for Chico there was no such
financial haven. The only way he could get quick cash was
to hock one of the pitifully few possessions that the Marx men-
age offered. Thanks to Chico's diligence, there were times when
the pawnship on Third Avenue contained more of the Marx
family's possessions than the Marx flat did.

Pop knew exactly where to go for the missing pants. Monday morning, hanging gaily in the window of the pawnshop,

were Mr. Stookfleisch's roomy trousers, and inside the shop was my father negotiating a new deal. In exchange for Stookfleisch's missing ones, he agreed to make the pawnbroker another pair of pants.

After I had described the confectioner's rage, there wasn't anyone in the house with enough courage to deliver the bottom part of the suit. To make matters worse, now that the Easter Parade was over, Stookfleisch didn't want the coat or the pants. A few days later he sent the coat back.

My father's dream of capturing the East Side trade had resulted in a financial nightmare. And who was to blame? No one but that prince of gamblers, Chico. Determined to get his hands on Chico's throat, Pop waited up for his eldest son to come home. But Chico, no fool, had sneaked in the back way, up the fire escape. My father, torn between vengeance and drowsiness, finally fell asleep in a chair by the front door. When he woke up the next morning, Chico was already off to more exciting pastures.

The huge suit hung unwanted in the closet for months. None of my father's customers could wear it. No one could wear it except Stookfleisch. One day, my father, being short of ready cash, took the suit back to the pawnshop and hocked it for ten dollars. It hung in the window for two weeks. On the third week a stout gentleman waddled into the shop and inquired about the suit. The pawnbroker, now realizing he had a dead horse on his hands, let it go for eight dollars. And the lucky owner? You guessed it. The prominent confectioner from the East Side—Stookfleisch.

Pop's income as a tailor hovered between eighteen dollars a week and nothing. I don't know whether he ever worried about this or not. If he did, he never displayed it. He was a happy man, full of the *joie de vivre* of his native Alsace in France. He loved to laugh. Frequently he laughed at a joke he didn't understand, and after we explained it to him he would laugh all over again. He loved auction pinochle with a passion most men reserve for fame, fortune or a dame. He preferred Harpo's or Chico's company to mine, for they were both excellent pinochle players, while I was hopeless. I have

never possessed any talent for playing cards. I have occasionally played poker for high stakes, but I've always emerged a
loser. After thirty minutes of forced concentration, my mind
begins to wander and I start cracking jokes or talking politics.
I soon found out, however, that playing cards was a grim
business and not the proper setting for humour.

My father was disappointed in me because card-playing
seemed to me a dull way to spend an evening. There were
so many other, more interesting things to do—girls, sitting on
the front stoop in the evening, singing quartet harmony, reading, going to the Nickelodeon. Pinochle was for older men,
and gamblers.

"Julie," my father would say, "until you learn to be a good
pinochle player you will never be a real man." At that, he
may have been right. I never did become a real man. But I
doubt if pinochle had anything to do with it.

Pop occasionally became disgusted with the tailoring business, and he would then embark upon something so grandiose
in concept that, if you knew my father, you'd know it was
doomed from the start. Some years later, after the Marx men-
age had moved to Chicago, he made a suit for a railroad
porter by the name of Alexander Jefferson, a talented individual who, by throwing a mean and shifty pair of dice, had
managed to accumulate fifty dollars. Mr. Jefferson assured my
father that shooting craps was not his regular profession, that
he was a porter by trade; but he added that if an unusually
attractive proposition presented itself he would not be averse
to sinking his entire fifty into it.

My father, always on the alert for some miraculous wind-
fall, told Mr. Jefferson that one day, while thumbing through
the new issue of *The Tailor's Guide*, he had come across an ad.
for a new type of pants-pressing machine. It was practically
automatic and could, with a minimum of human help, press
two hundred pairs of pants a day. In those days, pants were
always pressed by hand. No pants-presser, even if he were
loaded with benzedrine, could possibly press more than fifty
pairs a day. Inflamed by the porter's fifty bucks, my father
shouted hysterically, "We'll buy this machine and drive all
the independent pants-pressers out of business. Look how
simple it is. They all charge twenty-five cents a pair. We'll
press them for twenty! Let's see, two hundred pairs at twenty
cents—that's forty dollars a day, not counting Sundays. That

makes two hundred and forty dollars a week!" Floating along on his rosy dreams, Pop continued, "And, furthermore, we won't stop here. We'll open stores all over America, and after we've bottled up the American business, we'll invade Europe!"

Mr. Jefferson, possessing fifty dollars in hard cash, was naturally more cautious than my father. "Mr. Marx," he asked, "how much does this machine cost?"

"Eight hundred dollars. But what's the difference? We'll pay it off in no time. It's just a hundred dollars down and a hundred a month. After Europe, we'll tie up the Orient!"

My father didn't know it, but at that time they were still wearing kimonos in the Orient.

Despite my father's wild enthusiasm, Mr. Jefferson was still loath to part with his fifty. "Okay, Mr. Marx. If you think it's all right, I'll put up my fifty. But before I put up my money, I'd like to see your fifty."

My father didn't expect this from Mr. Jefferson and he resented it. He wouldn't have resented it, but the fact of the matter was, he didn't have fifty dollars. He had thirteen dollars in pinochle winnings, stashed safely away and carefully concealed from my mother. But thirteen dollars was a far cry from the necessary fifty. In order to become the tycoon of the pants-pressing industry, he still needed thirty-seven dollars.

Of all people, he told his problem to Chico, who of course immediately tried to borrow the thirteen dollars from my father. Failing at this, he came up with his stock reply to any problem. "There's a big crap game tonight at a poolroom on South State Street. If you let me roll for you and the dice are hot, we can take your thirteen dollars and run it up to fifty." Chico was hot, the dice were hot and my father now had the necessary fifty for Mr. Jefferson—enough for his share of the down payment on the pressing machine.

Two weeks later, the magic pants-presser was installed. Outside, on a swinging sign, the names of Marx and Jefferson proudly waved. Today, these two names represent political theories that are as far apart as the average married couple; but to this particular Marx and Jefferson it meant only fame and fortune.

This machine was everything the ad. claimed it was. It was almost human, but much faster. It could press a pair of pants in fifteen seconds, and it stood ready and eager for the avalanche of pants that was soon to descend upon it.

Automation was about to shake the pants-pressing industry to its foundations.

Only one thing had been overlooked. Customers. It developed that most people had cleaners and pressers in their own neighbourhoods and they didn't seem to want to lug their pants blocks out of their way to save a measly nickel.

I visited the shop the second week to see the machine in action. The place was as calm and peaceful as a small Mexican village during the siesta hours. Neither of the partners was present. In the back of the shop I found a little coloured boy playing with a top. "Where is Mr. Jefferson?" I asked.

"Oh, Dad?" the boy answered. "He got a job as a porter again. He said Mr. Marx should run the machine."

"And where is Mr. Marx?" I asked.

"Mr. Marx said if anyone calls for him, he's back of the cigar store, playing pinochle."

The first of the next month, the company backed up a truck and carted the magic machine away. My father went back to the tailoring business, a sadder and wiser man. No, not wiser —just sadder, for his thirteen dollars was gone for ever. He might just as well have given it to Chico.

CHAPTER THREE

HOME IS WHERE YOU HANG
YOUR HEAD

As FAR BACK as I can remember, my grandmother and grandfather lived with us in whatever Yorkville flat we happened to be occupying at the time. They had been performers in Germany—he a ventriloquist and she a harpist who yodelled while plucking the strings. His name was Lafe Schoenberg and her name was Fanny. (In those days the name Fanny still had vestiges of respectability.) When he was fifty they migrated to America.

Lafe lived to be a hundred and one, and in doing so thumbed his nose at all the rules of longevity. He smoked ten long black cigars a day; these he rolled from the leavings of a tobacco factory. Between cigars, he smoked a pipe that had all the fragrance of an old suit of heavy underwear burning in a damp cellar. Any time he wanted to be alone, all he had to do was enter a room with his pipe. One whiff of his miniature incinerator sent the occupants rushing for the open air. His pipe could give any skunk in the land a lesson in pungency. We tried hiding it, but he was always able to track it down by the odour.

Lafe drank a pint of whisky a day. This was not bonded bourbon, but a concoction made from the residue of a small distillery that was only too happy to give the stuff away. Lafe's eyesight was as good as Daniel Boone's, and until he was ninety-five he never wore a pair of glasses. He was as straight and erect as a telephone pole, and almost as tall.

Since neither my grandfather nor my grandmother spoke any English, they were unable to get any theatrical dates in America. For some curious reason there seemed to be practically no demand for a German ventriloquist and a woman harpist who yodelled in a foreign language.

Lafe, disappointed at his theatrical reception in the new country, reluctantly decided to abandon show business, and for some inexplicable reason he chose a career as far removed from the theatre as he could conceivably get. Having never repaired an umbrella, he decided, after much deliberation, to become an umbrella-mender. From the number of umbrellas he repaired, it must have been the driest season in the history of the New York Weather Bureau. During one solid year he repaired exactly seven umbrellas for a grand total of $12.50. This was hardly a great sum, certainly not enough to keep a man and his wife in luxury. Licking his wounds, Lafe decided to retire from the umbrella-mending business and embark on a new career. The new career consisted of never doing another day's work until he died, forty-nine years later.

WHEN MY grandparents first arrived in America, my grandmother used to play the harp and sing every day. As the reports of her husband's career in the umbrella-repair business drifted in, the singing gradually ceased. After a while, the little harp was stowed away in the closet, never to be heard from again —until, one day, Harpo discovered it. Some of the strings were missing and it had no pedals for the sharps and flats; but to a boy whose only musical instrument up to then had been a ten-cent tin whistle, this cheap little harp, by comparison, had all the majesty of a concert piano. In time, Harpo wangled enough money from my mother to get the missing strings replaced. Soon he could play any simple song—unless, of course, it had sharps or flats.

One day the harp disappeared. Harpo was frantic. He searched our flat a dozen times. He searched the halls, the streets, the neighbourhood. The harp had vanished as mysteriously as if it had been removed by unseen hands. The fact is, the harp *had* been removed by unseen hands, but we knew only too well from previous experience that the unseen hands belonged to Chico.

Harpo was inconsolable. Without his beloved harp the world was just an empty planet. My mother's instructions to my father were brief and direct. "Sam, go to the hock-shop on Third Avenue. Somewhere in there you will find the missing harp."

After much haggling, my father made a deal with the owner of the pawnshop. In exchange for the harp, he promised to tailor a pair of his famous, ill-fitting trousers. Later that day he triumphantly brought the instrument home and put it back in the closet. That done, he proceeded to beat the hell out of Chico. Fortunately for Chico, his hide was made of stern stuff; the occasional beltings he received never seemed to deter him from his constant and frantic search for funds. Chico actually had three homes: the pawnshop, the poolroom and our crowded flat. To the flat he came only for food and shelter.

IT HAS ALWAYS been a matter of wonder to me how one set of parents can spawn so many different kinds of children. Chico, for example, had a brain as fast and accurate as a calculating machine. He could solve mathematical problems in his head faster than I could do them with pencil, paper and an abacus. His mind worked like those of the Russian chess prodigies who, at the age of twelve, can casually stroll among a dozen chess experts and, with a few magical moves, leave them bewitched, bothered and destroyed. With his natural flair for mathematics, Chico should have followed in the footsteps of Euclid or Einstein, but as with all of us, the scholastic life never appealed to him. He always had high marks in public school, but he had no interest in it. His interests lay far afield, in the galloping nags at Belmont and Pimlico, the ten ball in the side pocket, and bridge, poker and pinochle for stakes always higher than he could afford. If there was no action around, he would play solitaire—and bet against himself.

When we were young we lived on Ninety-third Street and played all the kid games together, such as prisoner's base, stoop ball, one o'cat and the rest. Chico found out early that these same games were also being played on Ninety-fourth Street, but there they played for money. So, except for eating time and sleeping time, we saw very little of Chico. I'll never understand how he found time to practise the piano. I have a hunch that, to make it interesting, he always bet with himself whether he would hit the C or the D flat.

Harpo was the solid man in the family. He inherited all of my mother's good qualities—kindness, understanding and friendliness. I inherited what was left. At that time Harpo was an errand boy for a butcher's shop and had very little interest in the provisions he was lugging around for his boss.

His thoughts were miles away from pot roast, calf's liver and stewed rabbit. He was thinking of Beethoven, Mozart and Bach.

When Chico practised the piano, my mother used to sit alongside him with a broom handle to make sure that he fulfilled his allotted half-hour. Once this compulsory chore ended, Chico would disappear. As soon as the piano stool was vacant, Harpo would slide in and sit there, experimenting with chords and runs. Harpo should have had the lessons, but they cost twenty-five cents each, and there wasn't enough money for both of them.

ALTHOUGH WE had very little money, we went to Europe when I was five years old. My mother came from a small town in Germany, called Donum. It had a population of about three hundred. This included four cows that had accidentally strayed there from a neighbouring town.

A cousin of ours was going along with her two little daughters. They were six and eight years old. My mother would have liked to take all of us along, but she had borrowed the money from her cousin and there was only enough to take two. Not wishing to show any partiality, she called us all together and explained that only two could go. She added that the two who didn't go would each get a three-dollar express wagon. Harpo and Gummo, with their customary acumen, elected to take the express wagons. So my mother, Chico and I, and the two little girls and their mother, embarked on a tub that could be called a passenger liner only because it carried a hundred impoverished passengers.

At that time, my mother was very young and very pretty, and a young chap who was taking fifty horses to Germany (probably to be cut up into bologna) relentlessly pursued her around the ship. She was happily married and wanted no part of him or anyone else. Besides, he always smelled like horses. Hell hath no fury like a potential lover rejected, so the night before the boat docked at Bremen he came to our cabin, woke us up, gave us each a bar of chocolate and told us there was a masquerade party on the top deck, and that my mother had asked us to come up naked. We were very young and pretty sleepy, but when he waved those bars of chocolate under our noses, we didn't hesitate. We caused quite a sensation when we walked into the party.

Mother had light-blonde hair and the kind of hour-glass figure that, in those days, was taken for granted. When I was young, men (and even boys) would talk admiringly or otherwise about a girl's legs or, in more genteel circles, her "limbs." Today the leg has virtually disappeared as a sex symbol. You can still view them—in fact, better than ever—but they are no longer an object of conversation. The emphasis has shifted from below the knee to the full-blown bust. It doesn't even have to be a genuine one. Underneath the dress or blouse may be rubber or canvas or both. Apparently all that matters is that whatever substance there is behind the blouse should protrude an unreasonable distance outward. This form of female deceit may conceivably be responsible for more first-year divorces than the inability of the groom to support his wife in the manner the bride's mother feels she is entitled to, the clashing of totally different temperaments, or any of the other frictions that send young couples scurrying to the analyst's couch and the divorce courts.

As my mother advanced towards middle age, the inevitable spread appeared, accompanied by the greying of the golden hair. In those days, beauty parlours were few and far apart and were patronized only by the rich. My mother started applying peroxide to hide the tattle-tale grey, but she was so busy bringing up five boys and running a home that she had neither the time nor the patience to do it properly. The result was, she applied the peroxide quickly and haphazardly. Frequently one side of her hair would be a golden yellow and the other side a speckled grey. One day, disgusted with the whole approach to perpetual girlhood, she chucked the peroxide in the ash-can and bought a bright golden wig.

My mother, like almost all women of that period, wore corsets. When my folks were going visiting it was one of the evening's highlights to watch my father tugging at the corset strings in a desperate, and sometimes futile, attempt to encase her increasingly buxom figure in a corset that was always two sizes too small. Once the final string was tied and her blonde wig adjusted, off they would go to someone's house for an evening of two-cent poker. As soon as the game was in full swing, my mother would head for the bathroom and return a few minutes later with the corset carelessly wrapped in news-paper and the garters gaily dangling from the sides. A few hands later there would be another disappearance. This time the wig would come off. Only then was she really ready for a fling at Lady Luck.

I once asked, "Mom, why do you wear that tight corset and that silly wig? They're uncomfortable and, besides, every-body knows they're phony."

"Julie," she would answer, "you don't understand. When a lady goes out for the evening she likes to look nice."

"I know, Mom, but as soon as you get to someone's house you remove the wig and corset."

"Naturally," she replied. "I take them off because they're uncomfortable. But look how nice I look when I arrive!"

I couldn't follow this logic, but to her it made sense.

CHAPTER FOUR

OUT ON A LIMB OF MY FAMILY TREE

I'M SURE IT'S no great secret, nor is it terribly important, but for posterity and the ages my real name is Julius Henry Marx. The original reason I was tagged with this name was pretty logical, but like most things that happened in our family it didn't turn out the way it was planned.

Most parents who name their children Julius do so because of their admiration for that renowned Roman statesman, general and all-round lover. Some name their children Julius because they happen to have a record at home of Julius La Rosa singing "Love Me Tonight." As John Ruskin once said, of the two reasons the second one is certainly the more sensible. It is better to name a kid after a live singer than a dead general.

I was named Julius for a more practical reason. Late in the nineteenth century there was an Uncle Julius in our family. He was five feet one in his socks, holes and all. He had a brown spade beard, thick glasses and a head topped off with a bald spot about the size of a buckwheat cake. My mother somehow got the notion that Uncle Julius was wealthy, and she told my father that it would be a brilliant piece of strategy were they to make him my godfather.

At the moment I was being born, Uncle Julius was in the back room of a cigar store on Third Avenue, dealing them off the bottom. When word reached him that he had been made my godfather, he dropped everything, including two aces he had up his sleeve, and quickly rushed over to our flat.

In a speech so moist with emotion that he was blinded by his own eyeglasses, he said that he was overwhelmed by this sentimental gesture on our part and hinted that my future—a rosy one—was irrevocably linked with his. At the conclusion of his speech, still unable to see through his misty lenses, he kissed my father, handed my mother a cigar and ran back to the pinochle game.

Two weeks later he moved in, paper suitcase and all. As

time went by, my mother discovered that Uncle Julius not only seemed to be without funds but, what was even worse, that he owed my father thirty-four dollars.

My father offered to throw him out, but my mother thought that would be a mistake. She said she had read of many cases where rich men led miserly lives and then left tremendous fortunes to their heirs when they died.

Well, he remained with us until I got married. By this time he had the best room in the house and owed my father eighty-four dollars. Shortly after my wedding, my mother finally admitted that Uncle Julius had been a hideous mistake and ordered my father to give him the bum's rush. But Uncle Julius solved everything by kicking off and making me his sole heir. His estate, when probated, consisted of a nine ball that he had stolen from a poolroom, a box of liver pills and a celluloid dickey.

MY MIDDLE name is Henry because of a sentimental attachment my mother formed towards a five-dollar bill, loaned to her by my Uncle Henry. After a while Uncle Henry realized that getting blood out of a turnip was going to be child's play compared to the effort that would be required to get back his fiver. Many years passed. One day, when my birth seemed inevitable, he said, "Minnie, if you have another boy, name him after me and I'll call off the five-dollar debt. I realize I'll never get it, anyway."

Some day there will have to be some new rules established about name-calling. I don't mean the routine cursing that goes on between husband and wife, but the naming of defenceless, unsuspecting babies.

Even horses and dogs are named with more logic. I know this dates me, but I would rather have been called Man o' War Marx than the monicker that was foisted upon me. Just compare that illustrious name with Julius Henry Marx. A more pedestrian name would be hard to find. If you, dear reader, had any intelligence (which I doubt, otherwise you wouldn't have been fool enough to buy this book—or, worse, are you one of those literary freeloaders who borrowed this copy from some loyal friend of mine who cared enough about me to buy a copy?), I'm sure you would agree.

My favourite uncle was a character named Dr. Carl Krinkler. He was a handsome man with iron-grey hair and blue eyes. He always carried a small black bag, and if you didn't know him you might size him up as a very expensive specialist in rare diseases. Actually, he was a chiropodist. He couldn't afford an office, but he visited us at regular intervals and, after cadging a meal, he would open his little black bag and neatly carve away the corns and bunions that my father accumulated while pounding the pavement in search of new customers. The doctor's fee was small. Twenty-five cents for both feet. And to my father's aching dogs, it was worth every penny.

Late in the autumn when the leaves began to fall and the nights grew long and cold, Uncle Carl's visits would cease and we wouldn't see him again until spring. One spring, however, he failed to appear. Five years elapsed before we heard from him again. It was a postcard from a medium-sized jail in upper New York State, and all it said was, "I'll be out soon!"

When next we saw him, he told us the whole story. It seems he had been in the employ of a gang of pyro-maniacs. His job was to apply the torch to any resort hotel that wasn't doing too well financially. For practical reasons, this could only be done in the winter when the hotels were vacant. He was quite proud of his achievements and boasted that, over the years, he had laid waste a substantial portion of the Catskills. He had no regrets about his career, adding that it was unfortunate he had been caught because he had about decided to break away from the gang and go into business for himself. His plan was to leave the Catskills flat and move to the Adirondacks, where the hotels were larger and where the financial rewards would naturally be greater.

I didn't see him again for many years. This time he was a cashier in a Broadway lunch-room. Maybe he had reformed. Maybe he was just biding his time. I don't know. But knowing his past record, the last place I expected to see him was guarding someone else's cash register. When I paid my check, I guess he surmised what was going through my mind. As I started for the door, he called me back and whispered, "You know, Julius, if the cops hadn't caught me, by this time I could have burned down a good part of the Adirondacks!"

Well, that's life. Sherman did precisely the same thing when he marched through Georgia and today, in many sections of the North, he's acclaimed as a hero. Carl Krinkler emulated Sherman and spent five years in the cooler.

I HAVE NOW told you about three uncles who were all nice fellows, but miserable failures in their respective careers. I might as well confess all and tell you that I also had an uncle who was a great success. He was my mother's brother. His name was Shean and, with a partner named Gallagher, he sang a song that, today, is as much a part of America as baseball. If you don't remember the famous catch-line, "Absolutely, Mr. Gallagher; positively, Mr. Shean," send me ten dollars in stamps. I won't send you anything in return. Just send me ten dollars in stamps.

Al Shean had been a pants-presser in a sweat-shop in downtown New York. He loved to sing and he sang well. But in the pants factory he sang too often. He had organized a quartet, and every time they met in the shop they would go into close harmony. There is nothing a pants-presser likes less than pressing pants, so when Al's quartet warbled their lush harmonies, all pressing would cease. As a result, so did my uncle's job. The proprietor, who hated Al and music (in that order), finally threw him out, advising him to go on the stage if he wanted to sing.

This is certainly a roundabout way of telling you how I got into show business. Originally, I wanted to be a doctor. But my Uncle Al's success convinced my mother that the theatre was a soft and lucrative racket, and that I had better forget about the world of medicine and the Hippocratic oath, for the simple reason that she had never heard of Hippocrates. The only oaths that were heard in my family were uttered by my father. Pop cursed fluently in his native French, but his American oaths were run of the mill.

My Uncle Al was a handsome dog, and when he came to visit us things started moving. We were all rushed to different stores to buy the foods he liked. I was usually commissioned to go and buy kümmel cheese. Harpo would rush for the huckleberry cake. Chico, being the oldest, would go for the beer. It meant two or three trips for him, but each time he entered the swinging doors he stole enough free lunch to make it worth while. At the end of the meal, each of the boys got a buck from Uncle Al. Since my allowance was only a nickel a week, this gift of a dollar meant luxury for many weeks.

Today, actors don't look any different from the rest of mankind, but in those days they were a group apart. For example, when my uncle came to visit us he had long hair down his neck, pre-Presley sideburns, a frock coat, a gold-headed cane and a silk hat.

By the time Uncle Al left the house, there would be quite a crowd hanging around the front stoop. On leaving, he would toss a handful of nickels in the air and watch the kids scramble for them.

Here was glamour! Why should anyone want to be a doctor, listening to the complaints of invalids and hypochondriacs, when by embracing the theatre he could have a silk hat and enough money to spare to throw nickels to the rabble?

So goodbye, Hippocrates, with your little black bag, stethoscope and Latin prescriptions. The show business virus was coursing through my veins, bringing visions of silk hats, frock coats and nickels. What more could any lad want?

CHAPTER FIVE

MY YOUTH—AND YOU CAN HAVE IT

MONEY DIDN'T COME easy to me in those boyhood days. My allowance was five cents a week, and I spent those five pennies carefully. I had one good gimmick going for me. Bread was a nickel a loaf, but day-old bread could be bought for four cents, so I always tried to get the job of going for the bread. I would buy the four-cent loaf and pocket the extra penny. Many years later my mother told me she had never been fooled by the semi-stale bread I brought home, but she didn't want to curtail my income or stifle my initiative, so she never said anything about it. For years my family ate stale bread, and I was getting away with as much as a nickel a week. I didn't realize it at the time, but I was doing the family a favour, for today doctors tell us that the promiscuous eating of fresh bread can be very harmful.

All-day jaw-breakers were four for a penny. I'm not sure what they were made of, but one ball could be sucked for two hours before it finally disappeared. From the way it resolutely refused to dissolve, my guess is that they were made of paint, sugar and one of the poorer grades of concrete. They were about the size of a golf ball, and no mouth, with the possible exception of Joe E. Brown's, was large enough to accommodate more than one at a time.

One cold, snowy day I had purchased four jaw-breakers, stuck one in my mouth and carefully cached the other three in my cap. I know this must seem like a strange place to hide candy, but there were practical reasons for this strategy. For example, if a boy came along and asked you for a jaw-breaker you would say, "Sorry, I ain't got any more." If he was still suspicious, you would then allow him to search your pockets. No one ever thought of looking under your cap.

That day a large, tough kid from a rougher neighbourhood came along and, seeing the jaw-breaker bulging out my cheek, said, "Hey, you, give me a jaw-breaker." As usual, I replied, "Sorry, I ain't got any more."

"You're a liar," he said. Since he was much larger than I was, I chose to ignore his vulgarity.

"Okay," I replied, "if you don't believe me, search me."

As he went through my pockets, I said triumphantly, "See? I told you I ain't got any more."

Angry and frustrated, as a final gesture he grabbed my cap and flung it on the ground. To my horror the three precious jaw-breakers rolled out into the snow. He quickly grabbed them, stuck one in his mouth and stuck the other two in his pocket. He then hauled off and hit me a fearful blow on the chin. For some time I slept peacefully in the snow, as cold as an iced fish. When I came to, the boy was gone and my chin ached.

This unexpected blow on the button taught me a valuable lesson. Thereafter, whenever I bought jaw-breakers, I kept one in my mouth and the other three I hid in my bedroom under the mattress until I needed them.

I HAD ONE other opportunity for scrounging some fast change in those days. There was a teacher in our school who was an outstanding snob. Most of the teachers brought their lunch and seemed resigned to eating their meagre grub out of a paper sack or shoe box in the school yard. But not Wilbur Bream. He would have none of this box-lunch stuff. Each year a lucky boy would be honoured with the task of scouring the neighbourhood for tidbits for Bream. In addition to the normal distaste most pupils have for their teachers, this one was hated for his arrogance and snooty attitude towards everything in and around the school. He dressed much better than all the other teachers, including the principal. How he did it I don't know, but now that I am older and more worldly I have a hunch he had some elderly dame keeping him.

At any rate, I was the lucky boy who was finally selected for the dubious distinction of gathering his lunch five days a week. There was no mention of salary or gratuity. This was an honour he had conferred upon me, and my job was to look properly grateful and happy.

Wilbur's taste in food ran to the unusual and exotic. I had only an hour for lunch, and in that time I had to gulp down my egg sandwich and an apple, or bologna sandwich and half an orange, so that I would have sufficient time to scramble to those far-flung places where he daily sent me—German restaurants, Greek, Spanish, kosher, Turkish. Every day, rain or shine, I would have to lug back these strange dishes. Sometimes the plates were hot and bulky, but I never heard a word of thanks from this pasty-faced gourmet.

At the end of the semester, thin and anaemic from bolting my food and then racing for his lunch, I was reluctantly handed a dollar by Bream. I had dreamed of twenty, but knowing his reputation, expected ten. When he called me into his room, he pushed a dollar bill into my hand and gave me a fast shove towards the door. I had had big things planned for the ten I didn't get. I was going to buy a suit for nine dollars, and with the remaining buck I was going to buy my mother something we desperately needed—a coffee-pot. We had a coffee-pot, but it was so old that its bottom leaked from three sides. If someone wasn't in the kitchen to watch it carefully, it would frequently snuff out the gas flame. I can recall three occasions when members of my family, overcome by the gas fumes, had to be dragged out of the kitchen in a semi-conscious condition. Anyway, I didn't get the nine-dollar suit, but I did buy my mother a brand-new dollar coffee-pot. And from that day to the day I went into show business I can proudly say that no member of my family was ever again asphyxiated in our kitchen.

My PRECARIOUS financial status had, up to the age of twelve, been the single uncomplicated problem of my life. But a new dimension was about to be added—and boy, oh boy, was I ready for it!

Love is a many-splendoured thing. I don't quite know what this means, but song-writers have to make a living, too. I suppose it means that love is all-important. It's a word that is difficult to contain in any specific mould. Today the word "love" is flung around so carelessly that it's almost meaningless. One man will say, "I love Cheddar cheese"; a girl will say, "I love Paris in the spring"; a boy will say, "I love the way Mickey Mantle swings from both sides of the plate"; and someone will sing, "I love to see the evening sun go down." This character is probably a burglar. The word "love" should be confined to just one subject—the relationship between a male and a female, a man and a woman, a boy and a girl.

Anyway, love hit me when I was twelve. I was still in short pants, but tiny hairs were beginning to sprout from my upper lip. A young girl lived in the flat above ours and she, too, was twelve. She had "a good shape." In addition to her shape, she had a number of light-brown curls that fell pleasantly around the back of her neck, and teeth as even as the kernels on a good ear of corn. By some careful manœuvring on my part, she invariably encountered me in the hallway as she climbed the stairs to her flat.

I had been saving my pennies and nickels for some time, and I finally had accumulated enough of a bank-roll to invite her to go to Hammerstein's Victoria vaudeville theatre. I had never been there, but I had heard about it. I had seventy cents saved up and I had it all measured out. Two tickets in the second balcony, fifty cents . . . car-fare both ways, twenty cents . . . total: seventy cents.

We could have walked, but we lived on East Ninety-third Street and the theatre was on West Forty-second. It was January, the days were short and the weather was giving a pretty good imitation of Lapland.

Lucy looked charming, and I looked handsome, as we disembarked from the street-car in Times Square. But there was a fly in the ointment. The fly was a push-cart vendor. He was parked in front of the theatre, hawking coconut candy at a nickel a bag. True to her sex, Lucy spied the push-cart and murmured that coconut candy was her favourite confection— what did I intend to do about it? I did what every sucker has done all his life when beauty demands something. What this beauty didn't know was that her casual request for candy had knocked my carefully budgeted bank-roll sky high and ruined the afternoon before it had begun.

We sat in the second balcony, far, far above the stage. The performers all looked like midgets and the sounds they emitted were barely audible from our perch. Louder than the actors' voices, however, was the steady crunch of the coconut candy as each piece slid gracefully down the fair Lucy's gullet. Perhaps she was too wrapped up in the show to offer to share the candy, or perhaps she assumed that I had diabetes and, being madly in love with me, didn't want to endanger my health. Whatever the reason, she ate every bit of it, crumbs and all.

I was rather upset at Lucy's greediness, but I had a problem that made me forget even the candy I didn't get. As I searched my pockets hopefully, I still found only one lonely nickel nestling there. Living was cheap in those days, but it wasn't so cheap that two passengers could ride home on a street-car for one nickel.

The performance was finally over. We left the theatre in silence. As we walked out into the street we encountered both darkness and a raging snowstorm. Today I feel terrible about this, but remember, I was only twelve, it was bitter cold, and Lucy had gobbled up every piece of the candy. Furthermore, if she hadn't forced me into buying the candy, there would have been ten cents left—enough for both of us to ride home on the street-car.

In spite of all these convincing arguments I still had some honour. I turned to her and said, "Lucy, when we started out for Hammerstein's Theatre I had seventy cents, enough for the theatre tickets and car-fare. I hadn't planned on candy. I didn't want candy. *You* wanted candy. If I had known you were going to want candy, I would have held off inviting you for a few more weeks. As it is, I have only one nickel left. Remember, Lucy, *you* had the candy, and you know I have every right to ride home and leave you to walk. But you know I'm mad about you and I just can't do that without giving you a fair chance. Now listen carefully. I'm going to toss this nickel in the air. You call 'Heads.' If it falls heads you get to ride home. If it's tails I ride home."

The gods were with me. It was tails.

The female of the species has always baffled me, and I have always regarded them as a race apart. For some curious reason, Lucy never spoke to me again. The next time she saw me, she cut me dead. Had she been carrying a knife, she would have used that, too.

Well, this was the end of my first romance, and, incidentally, my seventy cents. However, I believe it had one distinction. It was probably the only love affair in history that perished for the lack of a nickel.

WHEN CHICO was thirteen, he was Bar Mitzvah. This is a very solemn occasion in the Jewish family, for it's the time when a boy ceases to be a boy and becomes, even if only theoretically, a man. At the synagogue, the boy makes a speech thanking his parents for being born. He then goes on to tell how they have watched over him and cared for him. Since no one in the family had enough education to write the speech, my mother bought one from some minor dignitary in the temple for two bits. This speech was used at two-year intervals by Chico, Harpo and me.

I remember very little about my Bar Mitzvah ceremony. I spoke some mystical words in Hebrew, none of which I understood, after which I gave the two-bit speech thanking my parents for being born. Pretty soon it was all over and I was back home, where a party was being given in my honour. There weren't many presents. All I remember was a box of gum-drops, three pairs of long black stockings and a fountain-pen, which leaked just enough to make some very interesting designs on my shirt.

I loved this fountain-pen. It was the first thing of value I had ever owned.

Now that I had become a man (with a leaky fountain-pen to prove it), I was ready to take on the world. One day, I said to my mother, "Mom, if I get a job, could I quit school?"

"Don't you want an education?" she asked.

"Not if I have to go to school for it," I boldly replied. Before she could think of an answer to that, I plunged ahead. "I've been reading a book called *Julius, the Street Boy*. It was written by Horatio Alger, and it told all about how a poor young boy with nothing but grit and determination worked his way from nothing to the presidency of a bank. I've got the same name he has, so why can't I get a job and help support the family?"

"Well," said Mom slowly, "it's your life. If you'd rather be a bank president than get an education, go get a job."

The want ads. were full of "Office Boys Wanted," and I soon got a job in a real estate office on Pine Street. My boss was named William Thomas. He was kind of chunky and walked with a rolling gait. I don't know if he was half-drunk or just unable to balance himself. He said he would pay me three dollars and fifty cents a week and the hours would be from nine to five. He added significantly that he had fired the last office boy because he was always late.

"What am I supposed to do in the office?" I asked.

"When I arrive in the morning," he replied, "hand me my mail and always be ready to answer the phone."

The mail wasn't much of a problem because all he ever got were advertising circulars and a throw-away newspaper called *The Pine Street News*.

"Now about the phone," he said, "as soon as it rings, pick up the receiver and carefully write down who called, what time, and be sure to get the correct phone number."

The first three weeks I was there, there were only two phone calls. One was from a woman, inquiring if this was the office of J. Pierpont Morgan. The other call was from my boss, asking if anyone had called.

At the beginning, I arrived promptly at nine and stayed till five. The boss would lurch in around ten and leave around four. This included two hours for lunch. I ate my lunch in the office, a fried egg sandwich and a large bag of grapes which I bought from a push-cart pedlar on Park Row. Time hung heavy on my hands. Having nothing better to do, I spent most of the mornings eating grapes and spitting seeds on the carpet. The afternoons I spent picking up the seeds.

There is nothing like steady work to keep a boy out of mischief. Now that Mr. Thomas was getting in around eleven, I started getting in around ten. When he began leaving at three, I began leaving at four. After the first few weeks he began to skip lunch entirely and rolled in around two, grilling me about the phone. Was I sure no one had called? I said, "The phone rang once today." His eyes brightened. I continued, "But it was the telephone linemen. They were checking the wires."

Now that he was getting in at two, I began to come in at one. After a while, I had it timed so perfectly that I would just be getting in as his footsteps were heard clattering down the hall.

It certainly was quiet in that office. It was a little like living in a mausoleum with a carpet. One afternoon, the Giants were playing at the Polo Grounds. By this time, Mr. Thomas didn't come into the office at all. He would arrive around one, stick his head in the door and ask if anyone had phoned. When I said "No," he would turn around and leave. A few minutes after his one o'clock appearance on that fateful afternoon, I was walking down Park Row on my way to the ball-park. It was a beautiful, windy day. Suddenly I saw a man's hat fly off in the breeze, and having been brought up in the tradition of Horatio Alger, I promptly ran after it and retrieved it. As I handed the hat back to the owner, I looked up into the face of my boss. "Julius!" he demanded. "Why aren't you in the office answering the phone? You know you can never tell when the phone will ring. I put you on the job so that there would always be someone there when the phone rang." As he took his hat, he said, "Thanks for returning my hat. And, by the way, Julius, you're fired."

I was sorry to go. It was a nice office and it was at the height of the grape season. And to make matters worse, my mother insisted I return to school.

CHAPTER SIX

HAVE NOTHING, WILL TRAVEL

I WAS READY and eager for show business. School was an unspeakable bore, and the only thing that interested me was the teacher, a tall, shapely, blue-eyed Irish girl, named O'Reagan who, recited *Evangeline* in a deep, dramatic voice. I never heard anything like it again until I heard Barrymore recite the soliloquy from *Hamlet.* Her vibrant baritone, along with her other charms, thrilled me . . . until one day I discovered she liked girls, and that was the end of Longfellow and Miss O'Reagan.

The rest of my studies seemed pretty useless. Algebra and geometry were tools of the devil, devised to make life miserable for small, stupid boys.

One day when I was playing hooky, luck came my way. I read an ad. in the morning *World*: BOY SINGER WANTED FOR STAR VAUDEVILLE ACT. ROOM AND BOARD AND FOUR DOLLARS A WEEK.

To a boy whose allowance was five cents every seven days, four bucks seemed like a passkey to the mint. Also the end of school. So, putting on my best suit—which was also my worst suit and the only one I had—I hailed a street-car and in less than an hour I was walking up five flights of stairs and knocking at the door of one of the dingiest tenements I had ever smelled.

The door opened and a hook-nosed, middle-aged man in a blue kimono, wearing just a touch of lipstick on his thin lips, ushered me into an apartment even dingier than the one in which I lived. I announced that I had read the ad. and that I was a boy singer. "Go up to the roof," he said. "I'll be right up." When I got there I found that about thirty other gamins had arrived ahead of me. Some wore dancing wooden clogs (or taps, as they are now called), and since it was a tin roof, the combined racket sounded like field artillery in full blast.

Robin Larong (for that was the name of the gent in the weather-beaten kimono) finally appeared. In a voice consider-

ably higher than that of the average man, he announced that
he had signed up for a distinguished vaudeville tour and
needed a good boy singer and a boy who could dance. Luckily,
there were only three singers in the crowd. The rest were
hoofers of varying ability. From the dancers he finally picked
a tough East Side kid named Johnny Morton. After I sang
"Love Me and the World is Mine," he smiled towards me,
and pointing an imperious finger at the rest, he shrilled,
"Get out!"

I was fifteen at the time, and knew as much about the world
as the average retarded eight-year-old. I asked, "Where are we
going, Mr. Larong? And when do we start?" He replied that
we would open in Grand Rapids and then go on to Denver.
He didn't mention any other cities, and I didn't question him.
He had said he had a distinguished vaudeville tour lined up
and, as far as I was aware, two weeks constituted a tour. All
I knew was, I was in show business! The theatre was calling
me, and I was ready to listen.

I was a little nervous as to how the announcement of my
departure would be received at home. I had visualized a
family group, bent with sorrow, or if not quite bent, at least
saddened by the thought of my leaving them. Not only was
there no sorrow or recriminations, but my announcement
seemed to galvanize them into a state of joy that I wasn't to
witness again until some years later on Armistice Day. Had
they been in the street, I'm sure there would have been dancing and hat-throwing. A gay carnival spirit seemed to come
over the whole family, and all they wanted to know was how
soon I was clearing out. Furthermore, they implied that if I
didn't come back, that was all right, too.

We rehearsed about two weeks. Since the boss, Larong, lived
in one room of this tenement, we did our rehearsing on the
roof. In the August sun, the tin roof under our feet felt like
a red-hot stove, but we were young, enthusiastic and hungry
and, for the theatre, ready to endure anything. The act was
finally all set, and we were ready for Thespis.

When I said goodbye, my mother cried a little, but the rest
of my family seemed able to contain themselves without too
much effort. As a parting gesture, just as I was leaving, the
dog bit me.

My luggage consisted of a paper suitcase and a shoe-box
filled with pumpernickel, bananas and hard-boiled egg. Eggs

must have been cheap that year, for I never saw so many in one box. Though I was only going as far as Grand Rapids, I had enough eggs to carry me all the way to 'Frisco.

As for Chico and Harpo, they were older than I, and too busy to notice anything as trivial as my departure. Harpo had quit school right after graduating from kindergarten and was now knocking down three bucks a week, delivering meat and vegetables to the richer families in the neighbourhood.

Chico, the only Marx brother to graduate from public school, was making good use of his education. He was now employed as a pool hustler in a fashionable billiard parlour on Ninety-ninth Street in the slums of Harlem.

At any rate, I was in show business, even if it was for only two weeks. Our act was named The Larong Trio. To make sure the public would know us, Larong had outfitted us for the street in bellboy suits and matching hats, which were round pill-boxes with the words LARONG TRIO emblazoned on them in gold letters. When I asked why, he said it would be a tremendous ad. for the act, since we also wore these peculiar outfits on the stage. I didn't care. He could have dressed me in a bearskin and I would have been happy. Anything I wore was an improvement over my usual street clothes. Besides, it made people stare at me. And I discovered that I liked that. I felt that for the first time in my life I wasn't a nonentity. I was part of the Larong Trio. I was an actor. My dream had come true.

I didn't know what kind of train Larong had booked us on, and never having been on a train, I didn't know what to expect. If there was a Pullman car on the train, we never knew it. And that goes for the dining-car, as well. But I was fifteen and could have slept on a flagpole. It took us three sooty days to reach Grand Rapids, but I still had six eggs left in my shoe-box.

Now I had better describe the act that the unsuspecting citizens of Grand Rapids were about to have foisted upon them. We opened with the three of us dressed in short skirts, silk stockings, high-heeled shoes and large, floppy Merry Widow hats. This sort of thing was fairly common in vaudeville in those days. The three of us sang a song entitled, "I Wonder What's the Matter with the Mail." The lyric began:

I wonder what's the matter with the mail;
It never was so late before;
I've been up since seven bells,
And nothing's slipped under my door.

I don't remember the rest of this classic, but the point of the song was that this fellow was being supported by a woman named Liza, and for some reason his weekly cheque hadn't arrived. I don't know how Liza earned her money, but from the lyric I would judge that business in the house where she lived was none too good. It was fairly evident that her house was not a home. There is a name for a man who is supported by this species of female, but I won't go into that now. Anyway, that was the lyric. It might have made sense had this been sung by a man, but I'm sure the audience must have been baffled by three men dressed in women's clothing, wailing the sad tale of Liza and her bankrupt lover.

The song, like all songs, finally ended, and I quickly slipped out of the skirt, high heels and floppy hat. Then, donning an altar boy's outfit, I reappeared and sang "Jerusalem, Lift up Your Gates and Sing" to a houseful of silence. The only one who applauded was a religious fanatic who, under the impression that this song had some sacred significance, stood up on his seat and shouted, "Hallelujah!" Finally the manager, obviously an atheist, came down the aisle and threw him out.

Johnny then pranced on and did his tap-dance. Unfortunately, while executing a fancy wing step, his shoe flew off and hit a woman in the audience. At the end of our engagement, the manager deducted ten dollars from our salary, explaining that he had had to give it to the woman, who had threatened to sue for damages.

After this mishap, Larong glided on stage wearing a low-cut evening gown, complete with train, and sang Victor Herbert's "Kiss Me Again," while the spotlight played upon a bald-headed man in the audience. Larong closed the act dressed as the Statue of Liberty and holding a torch in his hand. Morton and I were decked out as Continental soldiers, guarding Miss Liberty from her unseen enemies. The unseen enemies turned out to be the audience, and only the fact that the theatre was almost empty by this time saved us from being stoned.

On the train to Grand Rapids, Larong had told us that our tour at the moment consisted only of Grand Rapids and a split week—three days in Victor and three days in Cripple Creek, Colorado—but he confidently predicted that once the news of our act reached the booking office in New York, we would be deluged with offers. Apparently the news *had* reached the booking office, for our tour still consisted of two weeks.

WE PLAYED Victor and Cripple Creek without getting killed. After the last performance in Cripple Creek I returned to our boarding-house to question Larong about our future plans, only to discover that the master showman had hastily packed his blue kimono, his evening gown and his mascara and taken it on the lam, never to be seen or heard from again.

I then looked for that wizard of the buck and wing, Johnny Morton, but he too had disappeared. As a final gesture of goodwill, he had taken with him my two weeks' salary, consisting of eight dollars, which I had cleverly stashed away under the mattress. He also took my other pair of socks.

I don't know where dire straits is, but I certainly was now in that neighbourhood. No money, no job, a minimum of talent and far, far from home. It was no use writing my mother and father for money. They didn't have any, either.

When I returned to the rooming house, I found the landlady, a kindly old witch, laying for me. She immediately nailed me with, "Where is my rent money?" I sadly recounted my tale of desertion by my ex-employer and explained how Johnny Morton had scrammed, leaving me alone and destitute. "Boy," she said, fixing me with her one good eye, "I'll give you forty-eight hours to come up with a dollar and a half—four days' rent—or out you go on your ear!" She concluded by snorting, "I never met an actor yet who wasn't a crook!"

If she thought this was an insult, she was wasting her breath. This was the first time anyone had ever called me an actor, and I could only gather from this that she hadn't been to the theatre to see our act. The fact that she also called me a crook didn't matter. "A crooked actor." It sounded dashing and romantic, and except for a lamentable lack of talent, I now considered myself the equal of Mansfield, Warfield, Hitchcock and, yes, even the Barrymores.

Larong, in fleeing, had forgotten to take my bell-boy costume. Luck was with me. While wandering aimlessly around, wondering what to do, I found a small hotel on Main Street, called the Mansion House, where I spotted a real bell-boy seated in the lobby. After much haggling, he bought the outfit for three dollars. I wanted four dollars, but he pointed out it would cost at least a buck to have the name "Larong Trio" removed from the hat and have it replaced with "Mansion House." Anyway, I now had three dollars, enough to ward off the landlady and a bit left for food. All I needed now was a job.

I regretted having had to part with the bell-boy costume. Dressed in it, with the name "Larong Trio" on the hat, I was walking proof that I was in show business. In my regular clothes, I was just a young, nondescript fellow out of work.

THE NEXT DAY I saw a sign "Experienced boy wanted to drive grocery wagon between Cripple Creek and Victor. Must know how to handle horses." Having been born and raised on Manhattan Island, the only horses I had ever had any contact with were those on the merry-go-round at Coney Island. With this doubtful background, only the thought of my dwindling bank-roll gave me the courage to go in and apply for the job.

The proprietor of the grocery store, a tall, cadaverous-looking thief, was busy short-changing a customer and barely noticed my entrance. He finally turned to me and inquired dourly, "You come for the job?"

I nodded vigorously.

"Know anything about horses? Ever handled any?"

"Oh, yes," I lied. "I've been around horses all my life. I was brought up on a ranch in Montana." He still appeared a bit doubtful, so I hastily added, "I won first prize in the Junior Rodeo in Cheyenne!"

That must have convinced him. Motioning with his thumb, he grunted, "Go out back. You'll find two horses. Hitch 'em to the wagon out there and take these potatoes to Victor. I'll pay you five dollars a week—and if I catch you stealing any food out of the store, I'll deduct it from your wages and beat hell outa ya, besides!"

Later in life, when I began reading, I recognized this character in many of Dickens' stories.

If you're not used to them, even a tame horse can look pretty fierce. Back of the store I found two of the largest animals I had ever seen. At first I thought they were elephants. They were pawing the ground, shaking their manes, baring their teeth and wearing the most malevolent expressions this side of Fu Manchu. I'm sure it was my imagination, but one of them looked enough like my landlady to be a blood relative. As I timidly approached, my landlady's relative reared up on his hind legs and whinnied loudly. In show business, when you're not doing too well on stage, the saying is that you have "flop sweat." For me, the stage was a thing of the past, at least momentarily, but the sweat was a clammy reality. I could feel it oozing from every pore and dripping down my shuddering spine.

In addition to being afraid of the horses, I hadn't the faintest idea of how to harness one. I finally got near enough to throw the reins over one of the horses, but he reared up and shook it off. I was still frightened, but I was also getting desperate. It was either harness these horses or starve to death in the back yard of a grocery store. Finally the proprietor came out.

"What are you doing here?" he demanded. "I thought I sent you to Victor. Why are you playing around instead of harnessing the horses?"

"*You* harness the horses," I replied. "I don't know how."

"Didn't you tell me you were brought up on a ranch in Montana?" he roared.

"Yes," I admitted shakily, "but we only had saddle horses."

At that, he stalked over and quickly harnessed the beasts, booted me up into the front seat, slapped one of the horses on the rump and yelled, "Get going!"

The horses charged forward and away I went. The road to Victor led through the two streets of Cripple Creek, which were fortunately deserted at the time. I tried to slow my steeds down, but it was hopeless. We then hit a narrow mountain road, with the horses galloping wildly around the curves. I kept looking straight ahead. I had already taken a quick, nervous look over the side with the idea of jumping, but all I could see was a sheer drop of four thousand feet. I desperately tried to slow the animals to a walk, but apparently they hadn't been out for days and were full of hell.

I guess I was just lucky. As we careened into the main street of Victor, one of the horses neighed loudly, staggered for a moment—either from fatigue or over-exertion—and conveniently dropped dead. I hopped off the wagon, took a quick look at the disaster and ran halfway back to Cripple Creek. I finally arrived at the boarding-house and hid there until my mother sent me enough money to come home. I don't know where my mother got the money, but I have a hunch she hocked one of my brothers.

AFTER MY my return from Cripple Creek, I regarded myself as a full-fledged actor. It's true, I was out of work, but this was a badge of honour in show business. My mother, crazed by my success, now turned the housework over to my father and started peddling me from agency to agency. This was no easy task. Occasionally I got a job singing illustrated songs in a beer-garden. Luckily for me, I went on late in the evening. By this time most of the patrons were in a stupor from the beer and they didn't pay too much attention to my singing. I remember the title of one of the songs I sang. It was " 'Neath the Old Chestnut Tree, Sweet Estelle." Although I didn't realize it at the time, this was a foretaste of the kind of jokes I was to tell later in life.

At a theatrical agency one day, my mother met a very beautiful Englishwoman named Lillian Foster. She said she was a famous actress from London and that she had an act so spectacular that in England people spent most of their time toasting her in vintage champagne. She needed a young boy singer, she added. Someone who could entertain the audience while she changed her costumes. She had seven weeks booked on the Interstate Circuit and offered to pay me fifteen dollars a week. This was quite a raise in salary from my first job, and when I saw her I jumped at the offer. I would have jumped at her, too, but I was fifteen and she was twenty-three, and I realized that we could never be happy together on my salary.

The Interstate Circuit comprised most of the large cities in Texas and Arkansas. After rehearsing two weeks with the glamorous and sexy Lillian, it was fairly evident that she had even less talent than I had.

After the customary family farewells, which they all seemed to take in stride, I was soon back on one of those dusty, semi-freight trains that, in those days, rattled reluctantly between New York and Texas. Our destination was Hot Springs. As before, I was armed with the inevitable shoe-box filled with hard-boiled eggs and pumpernickel. This time my mother, realizing I was no longer an amateur, omitted the bananas and stuck in three oranges.

In those days, the acts played the entire circuit as a unit. Like most vaudeville bills, this one had its customary quota of comedians, acrobats, singers and dancers. The headliner was a tall, swarthy Neapolitan named Professor Renaldo. He had greasy hair, a waxed moustache and an animal act. He also had a wife whom he took great care to conceal. I didn't blame the professor. She was four feet eleven, tipped the scales at two hundred and had a moustache almost as large as the lions'. She spent most of her time backstage in the darkness, cooing baby talk at the big cats. She told me one day that she wasn't allowed to say she was Renaldo's wife. If anyone asked, she was to say she was his sister. He told her if they knew he was married it would lessen his romantic appeal.

Renaldo's specialty consisted of strolling nonchalantly into a cage full of snarling African lions, equipped only with a pistol, a whip and a chair. After a tremendous amount of whip-cracking and snapping, the lions would then wearily go through their few feeble tricks. The minute Lillian Foster saw him, I realized that my affair with her, which was still in the hopeful stage, had come to a dead stop. She went for him as though he were the last lion-tamer on earth. Our act was called *The Coachman and the Lady*. I'll give you one guess who the Coachman was. It was me, dressed in a purple jacket with brass buttons, white trousers tucked into purple boots, and a yellow high silk hat with a cockade on one side.

The opening night was uneventful. The second night, just as Miss Foster and I were warbling our big duet, two of the lions broke loose while being transferred from the large stage cage to their individual cages. One of the loose lions, un-daunted by our singing, walked from the wings to the centre of the stage and roared angrily at the audience. The theatre was emptied in thirty seconds. Miss Foster and I, panicky with fear, ran for the nearest refuge. This turned out to be the men's room. I was scared and embarrassed, but happy, for this was the first time since we had met that I had her all to myself. Sad to say, we never got this close again.

The professor eventually coaxed the loose lions back into their cages. We had a much tougher time coaxing the audience back into the theatre. Not because of the lions, but because of the fear that Miss Foster and I would resume our singing.

BY THIS TIME I was more careful about money. As the weeks rolled by, each pay day I tucked away most of my salary against the day when the tour would end. I kept my money in a "grouch-bag." This was a small chamois bag that actors used to wear around their necks to keep other hungry actors from pinching their dough. Naturally, you're going to think that's where I got my name. But it's not so. Grouch-bags were worn on manly chests long before there was a Groucho.

Things went along uneventfully until we reached Waco, Texas, the end of the tour. The last night there, Miss Foster gave me my return ticket to New York and ran away with the lion-tamer, leaving behind his wife and the lions.

I was sorry to see Miss Foster go, but it was comforting to know that, this time, I was returning home with a sizable bank-roll. On the train I felt secure and happy. I patted my grouch-bag constantly and lovingly. The second day I decided I would open it and take a peek at my nest egg. Instead of the sixty-five dollars I thought I was bringing home, all I found was some folded, old newspaper. Being a Gentleman of the Old School (P.S. 86 . . . Lexington Avenue and 96 Street), I won't say that Miss Foster copped my savings. But I will say that she was the only one who knew where I kept the money.

I now had an empty grouch-bag and an even emptier stomach. Luckily for me, there were a number of little old ladies on the train, with lovely little lunch-boxes filled with lovely bananas and hard-boiled eggs. I suppose that, at that age, I must have been even more hypnotic and fascinating than I am today, for when I arrived in New York I was eight pounds heavier than when I left.

I now had had two flings at show business and had nothing to show for it except my unrequited love for Miss Foster and a distended stomach from the many yards of bananas I had consumed.

One day my father said to me, "How long are you going to keep hanging around the house? Your brothers are working. Why not you? Harpo is working in a butcher shop and Chico is playing piano in a Nickelodeon. Why don't you get some kind of a regular job—or are you going to be a bum all your life?"

One night, when my mother came home from her daily round of haunting the theatrical agencies, she informed me that Heppner was looking for a boy.

"Is it a job in show business?" I asked eagerly.

"Yes, in a way," she replied. "Heppner is the biggest wig-maker in New York. He makes wigs for most of the big stars on Broadway. If you work there I'm sure that, in time, you are bound to make some good theatrical connections."

"How much will he pay me?" I inquired.

"Three dollars a week," she said.

"Mom, this is less than I got with the Larong Trio!"

My mother said, "Grab it! It's a golden opportunity to meet the stars."

I went to see Heppner and he gave me the job. Five minutes later he stuck two large five-gallon tin cans in my hands and said, "Go over to Tenth Avenue and get these filled with kerosene. When you come back, take them out in the back yard, pour some kerosene in a pail and wash these wigs."

"Mr. Heppner," I said, "I am an actor."

"Nonsense," he replied, "you're too small to be an actor."

Apparently he had never seen Singer's Midgets, Mickey Rooney or Tiny Tim. I persisted. "I tell you, I am an actor. I have just finished a tour with that famous English actress, Lillian Foster."

"Never heard of her," he said. "If she was any good, she would be having her wigs cleaned here."

"She doesn't wear a wig," I replied hotly. "She is a young, beautiful woman and she has her own hair!"

Heppner dismissed the conversation with a shrug. "If she

doesn't wear a wig she can't be much of an actress. Go get the kerosene." As I dejectedly turned away he said, "Don't worry. Here you'll meet all the stars."

After four weeks the only stars I saw were the ones that came out at night while I was out in the bitter-cold backyard, washing grease-paint out of the wigs.

One day Mr. Heppner excitedly called me into the shop. This was the first time I had been allowed to enter those hallowed grounds. He steered me over to a booth and pointed to an elderly gentleman sitting in a chair. He was wearing a white wig that was being dressed by one of the attendants. In a voice filled with respect, Heppner whispered, "That's Jacob Adler, the famous Jewish actor from the East Side." He then patted me on the head. "My boy," he said, "stay with me, work hard and learn the trade and some day maybe you will be dressing his wigs."

As soon as I got paid that Saturday, I quit. I had been there a total of seven weeks, and all I ever saw was a dirty backyard, some dirtier wigs and a fleeting glimpse of Jacob Adler.

CHAPTER SEVEN

THE FIRST ACT IS THE HARDEST

My THEATRICAL CAREER had slowed to a crawl. Chico and Harpo were prospering in their respective professions. I was getting nowhere.

Chico, thanks to my mother's persistence, could now rattle off a fairly recognizable piece on the piano. His repertoire, although not nearly as extensive as that of Horowitz or Rubinstein, made up in fortissimo what it lacked in accuracy. Luckily, the average untrained ear found it difficult to distinguish between the melodies originally conceived by the composer and the clinkers that emanated from the instrument when Chico was in the driver's seat.

That summer he had been engaged to play the piano at a moth-eaten hotel is Asbury Park, New Jersey. If the job had depended entirely on his piano-playing, I'm sure they would have thrown him out. But this job required two talents. During the day he was to patrol the beach as a lifeguard. At night he was to sit in the musty dining-room, and by the sheer wizardry of his piano-playing, distract the guests from the slumgullion that was being dished out to them.

By this time you are probably aware of the fact that the brothers were congenital liars. You mustn't be too hard on us, because we had discovered early in life that steady and consistent lying was the only road to survival. Therefore, when the proprietor asked Chico if he swam well enough to be a lifeguard, Chico looked him squarely in the eye and proudly replied that only a year before he had been captain of the Y.M.H.A. swimming team in Yorkville. This was true. What he neglected to add was that although he had been the 100-yard sprint champion, he was a total loss beyond 100 yards.

Chico got the job and patrolled the beach faithfully, ready to rescue any swimmer in distress—within a radius of one hundred yards. One guest, more foolhardy than the rest and unaware of Chico's limitations, got into trouble about two hundred yards from the shore. He naturally called for help. Chico, no coward—but also no fool—pretended to be busy building a sand tunnel for a small boy on the beach. The yells grew progressively fainter. Chico continued to dig.

Finally, the owner of the hotel, hearing the commotion, rushed out and practically booted his lifeguard into the surf. Finding himself between the proprietor and the deep blue sea, Chico bravely swam out to the waterlogged victim and grabbed him carefully by the throat—in true life-saving fashion. Whereupon they both began to drown. Had there not been an alert lifeguard with a fast boat at the adjoining beach, that would have been the end of Chico. As it turned out, it was the end of Chico's job. That night there was a new piano-player in the dining-room, and the following morning a new lifeguard on the beach.

At about this time, Harpo's dream of becoming a wealthy butcher came to a sudden and abrupt end. It had been his custom, while delivering frankfurters, to nibble off an occasional dog. Not because of hunger, particularly, but mainly because of boredom with the job. One day, more despondent than usual about his career and the utter hopelessness of ever becoming a master butcher, he suddenly blacked out while delivering a dozen frankfurters to a Mrs. Fuchtwanger, and in a frenzy of futility and despair ate all twelve of Mrs. Fuchtwanger's wieners.

I don't know what the Fuchtwangers had for dinner that night, but the following morning Mr. Fuchtwanger burst into Mr. Schwein's butcher's shop, demanding to know what had happened to his sausages. Unfortunately for Harpo, it was just at that moment that he sauntered into the shop, ready to begin his daily grind. Schwein apologetically handed Fuchtwanger a dozen new frankfurters and turned upon Harpo, who was still blissfully unaware of the gathering storm. Shaking an accusing finger under his nose, Schwein backed Harpo into a corner. "You crook, you! Where are the frankfurters I gave you to deliver to Mrs. Fuchtwanger yesterday?"

"Mr. Schwein," Harpo answered bravely, "I cannot tell a lie. I ate them."

Mr. Schwein handed Harpo two dollars and eleven cents and informed him that the balance of his three-dollar salary had been deducted for the dozen sausages. Shaking his head sadly, he said, "I always knew you stole a little—but when you eat the whole order, it just means you can't be trusted." He then put a sign in the window, ERRAND BOY WANTED, after which he booted Harpo out of the shop.

Harpo had no trouble getting another job. The next day he spotted an ad. in the papers, BOY WANTED, and a few hours later he was a bell-hop at a very fashionable hotel in the Murray Hill section. The manager told Harpo his salary would be two dollars a week, which was a dollar less than the butcher had paid him. But, he added, if Harpo was on his toes and kept his eyes open, he could collect a lot of fat tips. For example, Cecilia Langhorne, the famous English tragedienne, was living at the hotel. Whoever walked her pet around the block in the morning always received a twenty-five cent tip. Harpo had never heard of Cecilia Langhorne, but this seemed like a ridiculously easy way to make money.

BEFORE I proceed with this narrative, and I know the suspense is such that you can hardly forgive me, I would like to say a few words about an American institution that is rapidly going the way of the street-car, the ice-wagon and draught beer. I am referring to the old-fashioned bell-boy. Dressed like a drum-major, he sat jauntily on a bench in a hotel lobby, ever alert to the clang of the bell on the room clerk's desk and the cry of "Front!"

In the good old days, if a travelling salesman was unlucky enough to be stuck in one of those dreary, god-forsaken towns and the hotel that invariably matched it, after unpacking his few belongings he would sit and dejectedly survey the cell to which he had been assigned. This usually contained an iron bed, a steel dresser (painted to look like wood), a pitcher and a bowl. Over the latter hung two threadbare face towels. There was also a cake of soap and, from the amount of lather it yielded, it must have been made of pure granite.

The unfortunate traveller now had two choices. He could either haul in the emergency fire-rope that dangled outside the window and hang himself, or he could send for the bell-boy. A push on the room buzzer and, like a magic genie, the bell-boy would appear. He was yours to command . . . more towels, ice-water, and if you happened to find yourself in dry territory, perhaps a bottle of booze. He also warned you not to eat in the hotel—unless you had no particular desire ever to see your family again.

Oh, by the way, he knew a girl—"No, sir. She isn't a pro. The truth is, she's a friend of my sister's and comes from a very good family—and be sure you don't offer her any money. She gets awful angry if anyone offers her money. But if you give me a ten-dollar bill, I'll see that she gets it. That way she won't be embarrassed. . . . No, no, I don't want anything out of it. I just want you to have a good time."

My point is, the world isn't always going forward. It's true, you can now enter a hotel elevator, press a button and arrive at your room smoothly, silently and spookily. If you want ice-water, all you have to do is push a button over the sink and out flows a cold, clear, sparkling stream. Towels are provided in abundance, and they even beg you to take the soap home as a souvenir. But despite all these improvements, the modern hotel is a cold, soulless, mechanical combination of steel, wood and indifference. Furthermore, if that's what's on your mind, a subway train during the rush hour will give you far more personal contact.

WELL, BACK to Harpo and the lobby of the hotel. The second day, the hotel clerk's bell clanged and Harpo was ordered to take Miss Langhorne's pet for an airing. The clerk said, "Be sure to take it out the back way. We don't want to alarm the guests in the lobby." Harpo was a little puzzled by this. How could a pet dog frighten anyone, he mused. Miss Langhorne, however, being of the theatre, didn't travel with anything as mundane as a pet dog. What she was carting around the world was a baby leopard.

This was quite a change from Harpo's previous job. He now had something in tow that, unlike the frankfurters, he couldn't eat. It was even possible that the whole procedure could be reversed, with the leopard eating Harpo. But "Dodo," the playful little pet, was on a leash, and for the moment Harpo felt moderately secure. To turn back meant losing the two-bit tip waiting for him, so there wasn't much choice.

Halfway around the block, the leopard spotted a dog, jerked himself away from the leash and quickly killed the hound. Harpo, panicky, ran back to the hotel and handed Miss Langhorne the empty chain, along with the information that Dodo had been shot by a customer just emerging from Abercrombie & Fitch. Miss Langhorne was put under forty-eight-hour sedation and immediately thereafter left for India. Presumably to pick up another pet. The management gave Harpo the old heave-ho, and an hour later he was back home again, reading the HELP WANTED columns.

CHICO MEANWHILE had happily given up his budding career as a combination lifeguard-pianist in New Jersey for the social life of the pool hall in Harlem. Circumstances beyond his control now forced him to turn over a new leaf and get a job. He went to work for a wholesale paper house that specialized in blotters. Chico's job consisted of wrapping the blotters in cardboard packing cases, a thousand blotters to the case. His salary: four dollars a week.

In spite of his passion for gambling, Chico was a good boy and he promised his mother that, now that he was gainfully employed, he would never again stray from the straight and narrow. He added that the repeated whippings administered by my father had helped to cool his ardour for the pool cue and the galloping dominoes. He solemnly promised that each Saturday night he would dutifully deposit his salary in my mother's lap as his contribution to the family exchequer.

During the first two weeks he lived up to his promise. My father was so happy at Chico's apparent reformation that he said, "Chico, you do that for a few more weeks and I'll make you a new suit."

Chico was so shaken by this threat that he was almost ready to turn crooked again. "Please, Pop," he answered, "never mind making me a suit. Just give me ten dollars and I'll buy one off the rack at Bloomingdale's Department Store."

Packing the blotters required no skill and very little physical effort, but after the exciting apprenticeship he had served in the pool-room, monotony soon began to seep in. His fever rising again, Chico went looking for action. He found it the third week in the cellar of the blotter establishment. A flourishing three-handed crap game was in full swing, and in the time it takes for a boy to go from a standing position to a kneeling one, the game had four players instead of three.

Unfortunately, this was Saturday—pay-day—and Chico's four-dollar salary was quickly transferred from his pocket to that of one of the more expert dice-handlers. He realized it would be suicidal for him to return home without his wages. He cringed at the thought of another walloping. What could he tell Mom and Pop? What kind of plausible excuse could he concoct? Suddenly he was struck with an inspiration so brilliant that he stood in awe for five minutes, marvelling at his own cleverness.

Some few hours later he arrived at our flat, lugging a large cardboard package. As he opened the front door, my father stood there to greet him with a smile. "Well, Chico, did you work hard today? Give Mom your salary."

"Pop, I haven't got my salary."

My father's smile disappeared. "You haven't got your salary? Where is it?"

Chico pointed to the box at his feet. "Well, I'll tell you, Pop. Today the factory had a sale on blotters, but only for the employees of the company. I was lucky enough to be an employee of the company, so I took my four dollars and bought you and Mom four thousand blotters." As he said this, he started backing away.

There wasn't anything Chico could have brought home of less use to us than blotters. If he had brought home plain garbage, we might have sold it to a farmer for fertilizer. If he had brought mice, we might have sold them to a passing cat. But blotters! Four thousand of them! Enough to keep the New York Post Office in good supply for a year. We weren't a literary group, and the little writing that was done in our household was done with a lead pencil. One blotter would have lasted our family a lifetime.

My mother pulled my father away from Chico just as Pop was about to strangle him. Then Mom began to cry. Chico, a fast thinker, handed her a blotter and said, "See how useful these things are, Mom? Whenever you feel like crying, just take one of these blotters. They're better than handkerchiefs, and it will cut the laundry bills in half."

With this parting advice he nimbly ducked away from my father and beat it down the back fire escape, with Pop in hot but hopeless pursuit.

THE SCORE was now as follows: Chico was back on Ninety-ninth Street, shooting pool for the house. Harpo's career as a bell-boy had just met an untimely death. I was an actor "between bookings," and Gummo was still trying to convince his schoolteacher that Harrisburg was the capital of Montana. I don't mean to imply that Gummo was dumb. It was only that his interests, like Chico's, lay elsewhere. He wanted to get out of school and become an inventor.

My mother finally came to the conclusion that the best way to break into show business was not to launch one boy at a time, but to do it wholesale. This idea crystallized one day when she came home and found that Gummo, following in the footsteps of his idol, Thomas Edison, had taken most of Chico's piano apart and was attempting to convert it into a xylophone. This naturally delighted Chico, who was standing by, full of advice and moral support, but it made my mother furious. Gummo, she realized, had the soul and instincts of an inventor, and she had better get him out of the flat before he converted everything in it into something else. At the moment he was eyeing my father.

Then and there Mom made the decision that was to change our entire lives. She announced that Gummo was to become an actor. Gummo, of all people! He had about as much equipment for the stage as the average Zulu has for psychiatry.

"I am going to build an act that will be a sensation," she declared. "We'll get a girl singer. That will give it some sex. And Gummo and you," she said, pointing to me, "will be yachtsmen. Sailors and sex. It can't miss!"

A bit startled, I queried, "Mom, why yachtsmen?"

"I'll tell you why," she replied. "I happened to be passing Bloomingdale's Department Store this morning, and they had white duck suits on sale for $9.98. We'll get some straw hats cheap—they're on sale now because summer is almost over— and some white shoes. They're on sale, too, because they're odd sizes. I already made a dress for the girl in the act."

"Mom," I interrupted again, weakly, "how do you know the dress will fit the girl we get?"

"Don't be foolish," she shrugged. "There are hundreds of girl singers around. All we have to do is find one that fits this dress!"

It wasn't long before we were rehearsing in the front parlour, decked out in white suits, white straw hats, white shoes, bow ties that clipped on, celluloid collars and paper roses in our lapels. I don't remember exactly what the girl was wearing. All I remember is that it didn't fit.

We still had no name for the act, but after my mother heard us sing a ditty entitled "How'd You Like to be My Little Sweetheart?" she said, "I've got the perfect name for the act. We'll call it The Three Nightingales!"

"But why nightingales?" I asked.

"Because," she replied, "everybody knows nightingales spend all their time singing."

There are three logical reasons why she could have called us The Three Nightingales. One, she had never heard a nightingale. Two, she was tone deaf. Three, she had a great sense of humour.

Actually, the only one who could sing was the girl. The other two Nightingales' voices were in the process of changing, and from day to day no one could tell what sounds would emerge from their gifted throats.

Through my mother's wizardry and charm and my father's cooking, we managed to latch on to a few weeks' bookings. We would have played longer, but the girl singer, although she sang beautifully, had one unfortunate characteristic. This was her total inability to remain on key. For a solo number she sang "Love Me and the World is Mine." This song has a wonderful crescendo at the finale, winding up with a D above high C. In all the weeks she sang with us, she never was able to hit high D. She would sing higher than that, sometimes lower, but apparently she had a basic distaste for this particular note and was able to avoid it consistently over a period of many months.

So The Three Nightingales flew away into Never-Never Land, never to be seen or heard from again.

If you think this discouraged my mother, it's only because you never knew her. She now had an even more brilliant idea. She would throw out the unreliable soprano and get a good, steady boy singer in her stead—preferably one who could remain on key. Then she played her trump card. She would take Harpo, who had no vocal talent whatsoever (but also no job), and make him the bass singer. This didn't strike Harpo as much of a future. But before he could protest, my mother, vibrant with enthusiasm, rattled on. "I have a great idea," she said. "Instead of calling the act The Three Nightingales, we'll call it The Four Nightingales! It's a great name! I'll go over to Bloomingdale's this afternoon and get two more white outfits. And you, Harpo," she added, "while I'm gone, you practise singing—bass."

"Mom," he pleaded, "you know I can't sing."

"Keep your mouth open and no one will know the difference!" she replied.

Harpo now veered to a new tack. "Okay, but if we have white suits, why can't we call ourselves The Four Yachtsman?"

"We can't," she replied. "There already is an act called The Four Yachtsmen."

Harpo insisted. "Well, do they dress as yachtsmen?"

"No," she answered. "Not altogether. They just have the hats."

"Then why do they call themselves The Four Yachtsmen?"

My mother's answer was one of the most mysterious I had ever heard. She said, "They call themselves yachtsmen because every Sunday they hire a small boat and go fishing in Jamaica Bay!"

This must sound pretty nutty to the reader, but you must remember that I'm writing about early vaudeville, and in those days it was even screwier than it is today.

FOUR YEARS PASSED. The Four Nightingales were now playing at Atlantic Pier in Atlantic City. At the end of this pier was a fish-net that reached far out into the ocean, and twice a day they hauled in enough fish to feed the entire state of New Jersey. For two dollars and a half, a boarding-house could buy a week's supply of fish, and in Atlantic City only the very rich had meat on their tables.

My mother negotiated the contract, and we were very happy when she came home and told us what a wonderful deal she had made—forty dollars a week and free room and board.

We were pretty good trenchermen in those days and could hardly wait to get started at the boarding-house. Breakfast was served at eight. We were ready at seven-thirty.

"What would you boys like to eat?" asked the waiter. We each ordered a steak. "No, I guess you didn't understand me," he said. "I meant, what kind of fish would you like for breakfast?"

"We don't want fish," we answered. "We want steak."

"Okay," he said. "How about some nice halibut steak?"

"Look," I said, "we're actors and we're hungry and we want *meat*!"

"Well," he shrugged, "if you want meat, you'll have to go some place else. Here you either eat fish or you don't eat."

We ate fish for breakfast. We ate fish for lunch. And that night, just to vary the monotony, we had crabs. We had bluefish on Tuesday, whitefish on Wednesday, and on Thursday we had red snapper for lunch and fried eels for dinner. By this time, two of the Nightingales were growing fins. Friday morning, while we were having our fish for breakfast, to while away the time we told each other our dreams of the previous night. Curiously enough, all our dreams seemed to be about the same subject. We all dreamed about steak, pork chops, veal cutlets and fried chicken.

On the broadwalk, right next to the theatre, there was a man selling roast beef sandwiches. He had a little stand and on this stand there was a slab of roast beef about the size of a suitcase. We were doing four shows a day, and in order to get into and out of the theatre it was necessary to pass this roast beef shrine eight times—four times on the way in and four times on the way out.

By Friday, we were so desperate for meat that we were even eyeing one another. We went to the manager and asked him to advance us some money on our salary. "Not a nickel," he replied. "The last act I advanced money to was The Three Flying Simpsons. Two of them got drunk and the one who flew landed on top of a woman in the fifth row!" So there we were, four hungry Nightingales, with almost as much fish in us as there was in the local aquarium.

The tantalizing odour of the roast beef was driving us mad, and the thought of another meal of fish was more than we could bear. There seemed to be only one solution. In order to get some meat, we had to sell something of value. There was only one object among the four of us that could possibly be converted into roast beef sandwiches. That was my fountain-pen. I had treasured and guarded this Bar Mitzvah present for four years. I don't know what it was worth, but sentiment-ally it meant a great deal to me. The thought of parting with it saddened me beyond words. But the smell of that juicy meat, coupled with the pleading and threats of my brothers, finally broke me down, and after some haggling I let the pen go for eight roast beef sandwiches.

We didn't work the following week, so we stayed over in Atlantic City. Together, we spent on roast beef sandwiches almost twenty dollars of the forty we received. After getting paid, I tried to buy the pen back, but the meat-pedlar told me he had lost it. He said he had gone to the end of the pier one morning to watch them haul in the net. While he was leaning over, the pen had slipped into the water and disap-peared into the depths. I only hope some squid found my pen, because they could be very happy together. As for me, I was seventeen when I lost it. The next time I ate fish, I was forty.

It DIDN'T ALWAYS hold true, but a good many of the small-time vaudeville acts' salaries were based on the number of people there were in the act. We had been The Four Nightingales for four years, and we were now earning two hundred dollars. Four people, two hundred dollars. Six people, three hundred dollars, and so on. This gave my mother a brilliant idea. My mother was fifty at the time and she had a sister who was fifty-five. She decided that if they joined our act, we could raise our salary from two hundred dollars to three hundred dollars. The fact that neither my mother nor her sister had the slightest talent didn't bother my mother in the least. She said she knew many people in show business who didn't have any talent. At the moment she was looking at me. Mom was travelling with us at the time and she told me she didn't know if her sister Hannah was available, but that she would communicate with her immediately and per-haps she could persuade her to come on. Apparently it didn't require much urging, for Hannah arrived the next morning with a paper suitcase, a beat-up guitar and a white organdie dress which she had worn at her daughter's wedding.

"Mom," I said, "if you'll forgive my curiosity, what do you and Aunt Hannah plan to do in the act?"

"Well," she answered, "the first thing we'll do is change the name of the act from The Four Nightingales to The Six Mascots. That will add a hundred dollars to our salary."

"But what are you going to do in the act to justify the increase?" I asked.

"We'll have two guitars," she said, "and Hannah and I will sing 'Two Little Girls in Blue' as a duet. We'll pretend we're schoolgirls. We'll dress real young, in blue dresses, and the audience will think we're two little girls. I'm sure they'll love it."

Schoolgirls! I didn't want to remind my mother that she was fifty and her sister was fifty-five. "Mom," I said, "about the guitar. I didn't know you could play the guitar."

"Oh, yes," she replied. "The last time you were on the road Harpo showed me and Hannah the three basic chords."

That day we nervously discarded the name The Four Nightingales and burst anew upon the theatrical horizon as The Six Mascots. There was no change in the act except, at one point, two little girls would appear from opposite sides of the stage, each armed with a guitar, drape themselves on adjoining chairs in the centre of the stage and render "Two Little Girls in Blue."

The opening matinée we four boys stood in the wings, curious and slightly apprehensive as to what the audience's reaction might be. We didn't want to shake the girls' confidence by bluntly telling them that their specialty was hopeless. We just prayed they could sneak on and off without the audience noticing them.

Before going on, Mom and Hannah decided not to wear their glasses. They told each other that, *sans* glasses, they would not only look like schoolgirls, but might even be mistaken for tiny tots.

As they arrived at centre stage, whether because of the normal nervousness that all theatrical novices experience, or of the fact that they could barely see without their glasses, they gracefully proceeded to sit down in the same chair. The fragile gilt chair, not having been designed for the combined weight of two buxom middle-aged women, did what any other chair would have done in similar circumstances. It collapsed.

Mom and Hannah fell to the floor with a thud and the guitars flew out of their hands. The bored piano-player, apparently accustomed to such minor catastrophes, quickly broke into "The Star-Spangled Banner" as Mom and Hannah, in a panic, groped their way to the wings.

The following morning, Mom announced that their maiden performance the night before had also been their farewell performance. They then kissed us all goodbye and took the train back to New York.

The Two Mascots having flown, we again became The Four Nightingales, and the extra hundred dollars a week we had hoped to get was just another dream.

CHAPTER EIGHT

A WAND'RING MINSTREL, I

I AM NOT SURE how I got to be a comedian or a comic. Perhaps I'm not a comic. It's not worth arguing about. At any rate, I have been making a good living for many years, masquerading as one. As a lad, I don't remember knocking anyone over with my wit. I'm a pretty wary fellow, and I have neither the desire nor the equipment to analyse what makes one man funny to another man. I have read many books by alleged experts, explaining the basis of humour and attempting to describe what is funny and what isn't. I doubt if any comedian can honestly say why he is funny and why his next-door neighbour is not.

I believe all comedians arrive by trial and error. This was certainly true in the old days of vaudeville, and I'm sure it's true today. The average team would consist of a straight man and a comic. The straight man would sing, dance or possibly do both. And the comedian would steal a few jokes from other acts and find a few in the newspapers and comic magazines. They would then proceed to play small-time vaudeville theatres, burlesque shows, night-clubs and beer-gardens. If the comic was inventive, he would gradually discard the stolen jokes and the ones that died and try out some of his own. In time, if he was any good, he would emerge from the routine character he had started with and evolve into a distinct personality of his own. This has been my experience and also that of my brothers, and I believe this has been true of most of the other comedians.

My guess is that there aren't a hundred top-flight professional comedians, male and female, in the whole world. They are a much rarer and far more valuable commodity than all the gold and precious stones in the world. But because we are laughed at, I don't think people really understand how essential we are to their sanity. If it weren't for the brief respite we give the world with our foolishness, the world would see mass suicide in numbers that compare favourably with the death-rate of the lemmings.

I'm sure most of you have heard the story of the man who, desperately ill, goes to an analyst and tells the doctor that he has lost his desire to live and that he is seriously considering suicide. The doctor listens to this tale of melancholia and then tells the patient that what he needs is a good belly laugh. He advises the unhappy man to go to the circus that night and spend the evening laughing at Grock, the world's funniest clown. The doctor sums it up, "After you have seen Grock, I am sure you will be much happier." The patient rises to his feet, looks sadly at the doctor, turns and ambles towards the door. As he starts to leave the doctor says, "By the way, what is your name?" The man turns and regards the analyst with sorrowful eyes. "I am Grock."

WHEN FUNNY MEN play a serious role it always gives me a lingering pain to see the critics hysterically throw their hats in the air, dance in the streets and overwhelm the comic with assorted kudos. Why this should evoke such astonishment and enthusiasm in the eyes of the critics has always baffled me. There is hardly a comedian alive who isn't capable of doing a first-rate job in a dramatic role. But there are mighty few dramatic actors who could essay a comic role with any distinction. David Warfield, Ed Wynn, Walter Houston, Red Buttons, Danny Kaye, Danny Thomas, Jackie Gleason, Jack Benny, Louis Manny, Charles Chaplin, Buster Keaton, Red Skelton and Eddie Cantor are all comedians who have played dramatic roles, and they are almost unanimous in saying that, compared to being funny, dramatic acting is like a two-week vacation in the country.

To convince you that this isn't just a notion exclusively my own, here are the words of S. N. Behrman, one of our better playwrights:

"Any playwright who has been up against the agony of casting plays will tell you that the actor who can play comedy is the fellow to shoot for. The comic intuition gets to the heart of a human situation with a precision and a velocity unattainable in any other way. A great comic actor will do it for you with an inflection of voice as adroit as the flick of the wrist of a virtuoso fencer."

Nevertheless, the critics are always surprised.

WHEN WE originally started in show business we all had good voices . . . for vaudeville, at any rate. In the process of growing up, though, Harpo's and Gummo's voices disappeared. The only good one left was mine and now that, too, was beginning to crack. We soon realized that if we were to survive, both theatrically and physically, our act required another dimension. I got a blond wig. It was an old one that my mother had discarded. With this, plus a market basket with some fake frankfurters hanging over the side, I pretended I was a German comedian. All comedians using German accents were called Dutch comics. The accent came easily to me. We lived in Yorkville, a German neighbourhood, my uncle, Al Shean, was a Dutch comic, and we were surrounded by breweries, all swarming with Germans. It was a character the audience recognized and liked.

The act wasn't built around much of an idea. The plot consisted of me, as a butcher-boy delivering wieners, asking Harpo and Gummo (who were dressed as yachtsmen) how to get to Mrs. Schmidt's house. While Gummo pointed me in one direction, Harpo stole the wieners. I'll admit this isn't much of a story line. I'll even concede that it isn't in the same league with *Front Page* or even *My Fair Lady*, but at least it was a beginning. What was even more important, this brief, home-made dialogue gave the audience a chance to forget the fact that we had just sung.

AT THAT TIME, the actor's position in society was somewhere between that of a gypsy fortune teller and a pickpocket. When a minstrel show arrived in a small town, families would lock up their young daughters, put up the shutters and hide the silverware. To give you an idea of the actor's social status, a Southern planter in Shreveport, Louisiana, once told one of my brothers that he would kill him if he ever spoke to his daughter again. Only the fact that the planter was busy attending a lynching that afternoon prevented him from shooting my brother.

The so-called glamour of the stage didn't reach as far as the theatres and towns we played. To gain access to the dressing-rooms of the average vaudeville theatre, you first looked for the dirtiest alley in town. Somewhere down this alley would be the stage door. You would then grope your way down a flight of grimy stairs and enter a dimly lit, damp and frequently rat-infested cellar, where the dressing-rooms were located.

I must admit that there was some justification for the actor's unsavoury social reputation. Most of us stole a little—harmless little things like hotel towels and small rugs. There were a few actors who would swipe anything they could stuff in a trunk. One actor was caught trying to get away with a midget who was part of another act. Nothing was safe. Most actors could tell you where they had played all season just by looking at the names on the hotel towels. Fortunately for the hotels, most of them were too expensive for us. We generally lived in boarding-houses. Room and board, seven dollars single per week. Two in a room, six dollars each. Three in a room, five-fifty apiece. One act I knew never patronized either a hotel or a boarding-house. They slept on army cots in their dressing-room and cooked all their meals on a Sterno stove.

Though we were poorly dressed, we were actors from New York and I guess we looked pretty glamorous to the town girls in the sticks. Naturally, the town boys hated us, and for years we never left a theatre at night without blackjacks tucked away in our back pockets.

I think I was in show business ten years before I had a room with a bath. The boarding-houses usually had a bathroom at the far end of a drafty hall, and in the morning as you sneaked down the corridor, you were apt to glimpse four or five heads of varying sexes peeking around half-open doors, waiting for the bathroom door to open. When it finally did, the race down the hall would reveal some fairly startling sections of anatomy.

The bedrooms in these boarding-houses generally contained an iron bed, a lumpy mattress, a thin rug and a bowl and pitcher. Draped over the pitcher would be two sleazy face towels and two threadbare bath towels. These were yours for the entire week. By the end of the week the towels would be so dirty you would usually by-pass them and fan yourself dry. If you were lucky enough to land in a boarding-house where the landlady was a widow or had a few daughters, things were sometimes a bit easier.

WE WERE playing for Gus Sun in Cincinnati and living in a flea-bag hotel that I hope, for the sake of Cincinnati's fair name, has disappeared by this time.

The Gus Sun circuit consisted of a string of little vaudeville theatres throughout Ohio and a few neighbouring states. The shows consisted of five acts, appearing at two, four, six, eight and ten. The rest of the day was yours, unless business was exceptionally good. In that case the manager would slip in an extra performance or two for which you didn't get paid.

The burlesque theatre down the street was housing a show called "Cook's Runaway Girls." I don't know what they were running away from, but it could have been the show they were in. The entire company lived in one hotel, and at night after our five performances we used to go over to their hotel and gaze longingly at the girls, the way a poor, underprivileged kid gazes in the window of a candy store.

Theatrically, we were at the bottom of the social ladder. Five performances a day in a ten-cent vaudeville theatre was about as low as you could get. The only things below us were the carnival shows, one-ring circuses and the crooked medicine hustlers, selling fake nostrums on street corners to gullible yahoos.

The burlesque company opened one day before we did, so we had an opportunity to see their show. It was awful. The leading lady was forty-five and weighed about 150 pounds. Her costume consisted of white silk tights and an American flag draped around her ample middle. The flag puzzled me. At first I thought she wore it because she was proud to be an American, but after viewing her performance I decided it was worn purely as a protective measure.

The manager of the show had a wife and a number of children in Brooklyn, but despite these matrimonial barnacles he was hopelessly in love with his leading lady. As hopelessly in love as a sixty-year-old man can be with a forty-five-year-old, flabby soubrette.

Each night, after our five shows, we headed for their hotel

and hung around the lobby, hoping to make some headway with the chorus-girls. One night the show's manager noticed us. "You boys actors?" he inquired.

"Yes," we answered in unison. "We're playing the Gus Sun theatre down the street."

He didn't seem much impressed with this. Perhaps he had seen our act. Anyway, he continued, "Tomorrow is my girl's birthday, and since you boys are in the show game you are all invited over to a free dinner after the show."

What luck! Not only a free meal, but also a chance to make some headway with those twenty-four wonderful burlesque cuties.

Freddy, a boy who was in our act at the time, was a real fresh kid. He told us when we signed him up that he always told the truth and never pulled any punches. If there was one thing he couldn't stand, it was a hypocrite. "Whenever I have anything to say," he boasted, "I come right out and say it!" That night he did himself proud.

At the banquet table, the party was running smoothly. Each of the brothers was seated next to an enchanting chorus-girl, and we all felt that love was not only in the air, but that before the night was over, love (or a reasonable facsimile) had a pretty good chance of being consummated.

When the birthday cake was wheeled in we all sang "Happy Birthday," and then the leading lady's boy-friend, the manager (slightly crocked), swayed to his feet and began a romantic eulogy about his fat-hipped lady love. The words and the emotion would have done credit to Patrick Henry. At one point in his public declaration of love he said, "It is hard to believe that this little lady has achieved all this success at the tender age of thirty."

Freddy, who like us was only there because of the speaker's generosity and kindness, stood up and in a loud, clear voice announced, "Oh yeah? I'd hate to hang for every year she's over forty!"

For a moment there was a dead silence. Then a rumble of angry voices in a rising crescendo, the sound of chairs being pushed back and the grabbing of anything that might serve as a weapon. The speaker, flourishing a large knife, advanced slowly and murderously towards honest Freddy.

Cries of "Kill the little bastard!" echoed through the banquet hall. Harpo, Gummo and I, taking our cue from Freddy's hasty departure, reluctantly began to edge away from the girls at the table and headed towards the exit. By this time the entire burlesque company, fully armed with crockery and silverware, had decided not only to kill Freddy, but also to do away with his three companions. A chase began around the dining table, down the hall, into the hotel lobby and out into the main street. To the citizens of Cincinnati it must have seemed strange to see fifty assorted semi-drunken males and females chasing four boys down the main street of the city. Only some pretty fancy sprinting on our part enabled us to escape without mortal wounds. Later that night we took care of Freddy and proved to him that honesty is not always the best policy.

TODAY, WITH actors, musicians and all the affiliated crafts unionized, it is hard to conceive the relationship that existed in those days between the actor and the theatre manager. What Henry the Eighth was to English history and Torquemada was to the Spanish Inquisition, the theatre manager was to vaudeville. His powers were absolute. If you incurred his displeasure he could fine you or he could cancel you—"cancel" being a euphemism for throwing you bodily out of the theatre. There was no appeal. He was judge, jury and prosecuting attorney. A bad report from him to the booking office could mean the cancellation of your entire route. Even if you were lucky enough to have a written contract, it meant nothing. He could tear it up and throw it in your face.

I won't mention the name of the theatre or the manager, even though it happened a long time ago, but at the time this story took place we were doing a musical tabloid with nine boys, nine girls and a special set of scenery. We had risen a little higher than the Gus Sun circuit, and now Chico, too, was in the act. I was the earliest riser of the brothers, so I was given the chore of rehearsing the music each week. As I entered the theatre that particular Monday morning, I was a pretty natty sight. Wearing a checked cap, Norfolk jacket with belt, a cane, patent leather shoes, and puffing urbanely on a long, cheap cigar, I was a fairly representative figure of the poorly dressed, small-time actor.

As I stood there, happily puffing away at my stogie, the manager, a large gorilla who at one time had achieved considerable success in the prize-ring, loomed above me. "Smoking, eh?" he boomed. "Smoking backstage is a violation of the theatre rules. You're fined five dollars!" With that he ripped the ten-center from between my teeth, threw it on the floor and ground it out.

This bully's reputation had preceded him. He was known and feared around the circuit. He had once fought Tommy Burns, the World Heavyweight Champion, to a draw. Though I was no coward, I was also no fool.

Backing carefully away, I stuttered, "Hey . . . What's the idea of ruining my cigar? You can't fine me . . ."

"I can't, huh?" he interrupted. "Don't you see that NO SMOKING sign over there?"

"No, I don't," I replied defiantly.

"Well, just come over here and I'll show it to you." Grabbing me by the scruff of the neck, he dragged me to a tiny sign on the back wall. It read ANYBODY CAUGHT SMOKING WILL BE FINED $5.00.

Later that morning, when Harpo, Gummo and Chico decided they had had enough sleep for one night, the three of them condescended to come to the theatre. Upon entering our cellar dressing-room they spied a dejected and badly frightened actor. I sadly recounted the morning's events, the loss of my cigar and the five dollars that was going to be extracted from our salary at the end of the engagement.

At the time, we were getting nine hundred dollars a week. That sounds like a lot of money, but there were eighteen people in the act and, what with baggage, railroad fares, and agent's commission, it averaged down to about thirty-five dollars a head. A five-dollar fine wouldn't have bankrupted us, but we were rebels; after a brief council of war we notified the manager (not personally, but by messenger) that unless he rescinded the fine, we wouldn't go on. It wasn't that we were so brave, but there were four of us and we decided that he couldn't lick all of us simultaneously. Actually, we weren't champing at the bit to put this theory to the test, but we all carried blackjacks, fairly lethal weapons when properly administered, and if we had to, we would use them. We knew one thing—if we didn't go on, the manager had no show. He quickly came backstage and down to our dressing-rooms. We

1. Me, Groucho, age fifteen. The Beau Brummell of the early twentieth century, complete with celluloid collar, clip-on tie, paper boutonnière and phoney jewelled stick-pin.

2. My mother at seventeen. A great beauty, *sans* any artificial adornment.

3. My father, dressed to kill. You will note that he's sitting down. This is because the seat of his trousers had a patch.

4. My grandparents on their Golden Wedding Day. You can see they still loved each other, even though he wouldn't go to work.

5. *Reading from left to right:* me, Harpo and a dog we stole from the fire-house.

6A. Here are all the brothers and our parents, happy after a triumphant matinée. *Left to right:* Harpo, Chico, Father, Zeppo, Mother, Gummo and me.

6B. Victor, Colorado, where I was stranded after my first fling at show business. Some places become ghost towns over the years. This was *always* a ghost town.

7. Me at seventeen, a hot sport in New Orleans. Notice the ten-cent cheroot. Cigar and me both burning furiously, on the prowl for the not-so-elusive female.

8A. Harpo, Gummo, Chico and me at the Palace. The collars were ideal for concealing Adam's apples.

8B. Here I am in Great Neck, Long Island. The suburban squire, with rumble seat, plus fours and the face of a saint.

were making no effort to unpack our trunks or get ready for the first performance.

"Hey, you guys, the first show starts in half an hour and you better start getting ready!" he threatened.

"There's not going to be any show," we said. "Take back that five-dollar fine and we go on. If you don't, we go back to the hotel and leave you here with the audience. You do the show!"

Here was an attitude this bruiser had never encountered before. If one little act rebelled, he could throw it out and still have a show. But *we* were the show. If we didn't appear, his theatre would be dark. He bristled, he threatened, he cajoled. We just sat, stony-faced and adamant, idly swinging our blackjacks to and fro.

Underneath our feigned nonchalance, however, we too were nervous. As nervous about losing our nine-hundred-dollar salary as he was about having a closed theatre on his hands. We all needed the money. It was just a week before Christmas, and the Salvation Army lassies were busily collecting coins for their street-corner pots. We did not want to partake of their pot luck.

Chico, the Disraeli of his time, always the conciliator, finally piped up. "I'll tell you what we'll do. We'll pay the five if you'll add five dollars of your own to it. Then we'll give the ten to the Salvation Army."

At first I doubted that the manager would agree to this compromise, but it was now fifteen minutes past show time, the theatre was full and the natives were getting restless. The thud of stamping feet was growing louder and he finally threw up his hands in a gesture of defeat. "Okay," he said. "It's a deal! Now you guys get ready for the show." We had no further trouble with him. He didn't come backstage and we didn't go out front.

Saturday was pay-day. Our last show was over at eleven and we had to catch a train at eleven forty-five to reach the next scheduled town. This left very little time to change clothes, remove our make-up, pack the scenery and get to the railway station.

At ten minutes after eleven, four ushers arrived backstage, lugging heavy canvas bags. As they dumped them at our feet, one of them said, "There's your salary . . . eight hundred and ninety-five dollars in pennies!" We opened one bag and started counting. By the time we reached the bottom it was twenty minutes after eleven. Having no choice, we hastily threw the other unopened bags on the truck carrying our trunks and scenery and managed to get to the station and swing aboard the train just as it was pulling out.

The four of us stood on the back platform, watching the town recede in the distance. As it disappeared from view, one of my brothers, in words much stronger than the following, said, "What a dirty trick! I hope his damned theatre burns to the ground!"

He got his wish. The next morning the local paper reported that a huge conflagration had destroyed the theatre in the town we had just played. It isn't often that one is lucky enough to call down a curse on someone and then see it fulfilled within twenty-four hours.

CHAPTER NINE

A SLIGHT CASE OF AUTO-EROTICISM

WHEN I WAS IN my late teens our family moved to Chicago. Pop had exhausted the possibilities of his misfit tailoring on the Eastern seaboard, and was all set to conquer new and unsuspecting worlds on the shores of Lake Michigan.

Chicago was a big vaudeville centre, and Mom lost no time in storming the offices of the luckless booking agents there. So, when we boys were not on the road, we were living on the South Side of Chicago in an old house that my mother bought for eight thousand dollars. She had paid a thousand dollars down, and the landlord was under the delusion that he eventually would get the balance.

The summer months usually found the entire Marx family in residence here for the simple reason that in the summer we were out of work. Many things that we take for granted now didn't exist in those days. For example, air-conditioning. When it got hot in the summer it got *hot*. And *stayed* hot.

As a result, when June thirtieth rolled around, all the theatres closed until Labour Day. If, after a long winter of theatre-going, you were still hungry for the sight of a small-time vaude-ville actor, you could put on your blazer and straw hat and hop a trolley car to one of the amusement parks that sur-rounded the city.

These amusement parks didn't pay much for entertainers, but there was usually a lake with row-boats, a merry-go-round and ferris wheel. If you were working there you were allowed to ride free on all the concessions. One day I rode a horse on the merry-go-round for six hours. I never did that again. I was saddle-sore for a week.

Unfortunately, there weren't enough of these places to go around, and except for the few stars whose salaries were high, the small-timers faced the hot summer months and their accompanying lay-offs with anxiety and apprehension. The trick was to save enough during the season to tide yourself over until the theatres reopened in September. Ex-cept for Chico, we were all pretty frugal. Gummo and I had each salted away three hundred dollars for our hibernation.

It was unusually hot that first summer in Chicago. When the wind blew in off the prairie it not only seared your skin, but on the way to our house it picked up the fetid smell of the stockyards and the slaughter-houses. There was only one escape from this semi-tropical stench, and that was to get over to the North Side and inhale the cooling breezes of Lake Michigan.

In addition to the comparatively cool, clear air of Chicago's North Side, Gummo and I knew a pair of girls over there who were well worth visiting. The elevated train ran out towards their apartment, but it was a tedious journey and it took an hour to get there and another hour to get back. The round trip cut deeply into our evenings and left very little time for romance. There seemed to be only one solution—an automobile.

Gummo and I had always dreamed of owning an automobile, but in those days cars were as rare as parking space is today. A new car was out of the question. Our funds were extremely limited. Whatever the other requirements, anything we bought had to be cheap. Our top was two hundred dollars.

DRIVEN TO desperation by the girls' charms and the long, dreary nightly ride on the clattering El train, we each put up a hundred dollars of our summer money and bought an old Chalmers. It was a beauty—low-slung and fiery red, with wire wheels. Thanks to its racy lines, it looked about three feet longer than the average truck. It had huge brass lamps, a brass front and a gear-shift on the outside. Because of the beat-up cushions, the seats were so low you needed a periscope to see over the top. It was like flying blind. It was a convertible two-seater, and when the canvas top was raised it revealed a hole almost large enough to stick your head through. Except for the patches, the tyres were worn smooth, and they stood about as high as the average fifteen-year-old boy.

These were its assets. Its liabilities were infinite. To begin with, it had no power. It was just a hollow shell, like a large, muscular giant with a bum ticker. At top speed it could hit twenty-five. It was a good thing it couldn't do thirty-five, because, on our first ride, we discovered that the brakes had no lining. The brake drums were still there, but the lining was just a memory. We lived on Forty-fifth Street, and if I wanted to stop the car there, I had to start pushing down on the brake pedal around Fortieth Street. If I didn't start pressing the pedal until Forty-second Street, the car would glide past our house and come to rest around Forty-eighth Street. This was a problem, because I didn't know anybody around Forty-eighth Street.

The car was at least fifteen years old, and in that time must have travelled a hundred thousand miles or more over the roughest roads in America. It grunted and groaned and heaved like a professional wrestler. Luckily, gasoline was cheap. If the car was driven carefully, nursed along and petted occasionally, it would go almost five miles on a gallon.

One would have to travel a long way to find two people less equipped to handle this monster than Gummo and I. Mechanically, we knew as much about the innards of an automobile as the average Hottentot knows about nuclear fission. But we didn't care. We were young, we were happy and we had two girls who were almost as flashy as the red auto. It was a wonderful machine.

WHAT WE didn't know about a car, Zeppo knew. I suppose there are any number of mechanically minded geniuses around the country who are born with an instinctive flair for machinery. Zeppo was one of these freaks. He could take an engine apart, grind the valves, adjust the timing and clean out the carbon with no more fuss or effort than I would use in sharpening a pencil.

The first night we made it to the girls' apartment in fifty minutes. This wasn't much faster than the El train, but it was an exciting gamble to sit at the wheel of a car without brakes and sneer at the lowly pedestrians as they scrambled for safety. I suppose the car was weary from its ten-mile journey to the other side of town, for the second night it flatly refused to move. This could be catastrophic. We had made quite some headway with these babes the night before and, when we bade them good night, they had implied that, the following night, they might not be averse to the notion that Gummo and I deliver the *coup de grâce*.

Having no garage, we always parked the car in front of our house. Gummo and I had one white flannel suit between us, and inasmuch as we were the same size we took turns wearing it. This happened to be my night. I didn't want to get it dirty, so I said, "Gummo, get under the car and find out why it won't go. And while you're under there fixing it, I'll kick it a few times. Maybe that will get it started."

A half-hour later, Gummo crawled out from under the car and conceded defeat. Things looked pretty dark for us. Gummo looked even darker. What to do? At best, our relationship with those two charmers on the North Side was none too secure. Like most pretty girls, they were thoroughly unreliable, and we knew if we were late for the date they would be out with two other Lotharios.

As we stood there, nervous, dirty and depressed, Zeppo wandered out of the house. "What's the matter, boys?" he asked casually. "Having a little trouble with Old Ironsides?"

"We can't get it to go," we whimpered in unison.

"Well," replied Zeppo, feigning concern, "let's see if I can fix it. Suppose we take a look at the engine, shall we?"

We should have suspected from this phony politeness that something was up. "Let's look at the engine," he had said. We weren't even sure where it was—or that there was one. Look at the engine? This had never occurred to us. We were deeply impressed. These were the words of an expert. By using our combined strength, the three of us finally were able to lift the hood. Zeppo peered long and studiously at the huge, dark, rusty power plant. He then walked around it a few times as though it were some wild beast, tapped it thoughtfully with a wrench and then gave the two palpitating lovers his considered diagnosis.

"Well, I'll tell you, boys," he began, "I'm afraid you got stuck with this job. Your transmission isn't pumping properly against your magneto, and like it or not you're going to have to take that carburettor off and time it against your universal joint."

Gummo and I looked at each other with glazed eyes, and at Zeppo with deep admiration. Here was a man who obviously knew engines. Of course, we didn't have the faintest idea what he was talking about, and we cared even less, but his highly technical analysis of our broken-down chariot raised our hopes sky high. All we wanted to do was get over to the North

Side and head off those two dames before it was too late.

"Well," I said, "how long will it take you to fix it? Can you do it right away? If not, we'll leave the car here and take the train."

Zeppo shook his head. "Nope, it'll take at least a couple of days of steady work. My advice to you fellows is to leave the car here with me and take the train."

At the word "train," we sprinted towards the El station and those two lovelies. As soon as we were out of sight, as we discovered later, Zeppo pulled a small part of the ignition out of his back pocket, inserted it in its proper place, cranked the machine and drove off to meet his girl friend.

Dumb as we were, we caught on during the third week. We discovered the car ran fairly well except on the nights Zeppo had a date. Since this was about five nights a week, we were getting very little use out of our spavined chariot. Yet, for some curious reason, we were paying out a fortune for gasoline. We finally surrendered and sold it to our youngest brother for one hundred dollars. We each lost fifty dollars on the deal. But what was even more tragic, we also lost the two girls to two lucky fellows on the North Side who each owned a Harley-Davidson motor-cycle.

Having irrevocably lost the two girls, Gummo and I decided to dissolve our disastrous automobile partnership and go our separate ways romantically. Thereafter, whenever either one of us had a girl who insisted on riding in a car, Zeppo permitted us to rent our old Chalmers for two dollars a night. It was more than we could really afford. But I must say, with a deep bow to Zeppo, that our chronic invalid, the sick Chalmers, had a miraculous recovery. The squeaks and groans disappeared, the brakes responded to the slightest touch of pressure, the headlights glowed as brightly as a lighthouse, and the Chalmers became a joy to drive—all thanks to the sheer mechanical genius of Zeppo, that low-down, no-good auto thief!

THE AUTOMOBILE has played an important part in my life. The following year I was a year older and, oddly enough, all the girls I knew had also aged a year. I realized that, romantically, it was going to be a barren summer unless I could get a car. After weeks of prowling the used-car lots, pretending I wasn't a potential buyer, I finally exchanged a hundred and fifty dollars for a Scripps-Booth. Very few of these cars, if any, are still around. Like an old roué, the Scripps-Booth had had its fling, but it finally kicked the bucket and went the way of the Maxwell, the Essex, the Auburn, the Kissel and all the other ghosts that now sleep peacefully in those tin graveyards that blight the countryside.

The Scripps was a tiny car. It had two seats and an auxiliary seat that swung out from under the dashboard. The gimmick that sold me on this auto was a button on the top of the right-hand door which was, in some mysterious way, connected with the battery. It was like something out of the Arabian Nights. Press the button and the door flew open. It was sheer magic! I was so intrigued by this electronic device that I neglected to examine the motor, and before I knew it the salesman had my money and I had his car.

A few miles away from the car lot I heard a clanging and a gnashing of metal. I thought perhaps the former owner, a music-lover, had stuck a cheap xylophone under the hood. I quickly pulled over to the kerb, leaped out, lifted the hood and discovered that the car had suffered a mortal wound. Five of the push-rods were missing. At the time I didn't know that they were called push-rods; I knew they were made of steel, that they were about the size of a lead pencil—and that they were missing.

With my head bent down, I slowly walked back four blocks in the middle of Michigan Boulevard's traffic and miraculously found all five of the missing rods. Not only didn't I get run over, but I had the car towed back to the used-car crook with me sitting in it, murder in my heart. The thief who had bilked me out of my hundred and fifty dollars was standing in front of the lot, busily looking for another sucker, as I was dragged in. Baring a large expanse of yellow teeth, he said, "Don't tell me! Don't tell me! You lost your doggone push-rods, didn't you? It's a funny thing, but that's the only weakness the Scripps-Booth has. We've had this trouble with every doggone one of 'em!"

"Why didn't you tell me that before I bought this lemon?" I demanded, advancing towards him threateningly. (Lemon was pretty hot slang in those days.)

"Look, fellah," he answered, "do you think we'd let that little beauty go for a hundred and fifty dollars if the push-rods were any good? Now I'll tell you what I'm gonna do. For fifty dollars more we'll put in a whole new set of push-rods—and we'll guarantee 'em!"

My three hundred dollars for the summer was going fast. One hundred and fifty for the car and now an additional fifty for push-rods.

"Why didn't you guarantee them when I bought the car?" I insisted.

"We never guarantee a second-hand Scripps when we sell it," he answered. "That's our policy. Their push-rods stink. But when we put Buick push-rods in a Scripps, we never have any more trouble."

I was so dazed trying to follow this logic that I handed him the fifty dollars and slunk away.

THERE WAS a girl in our neighbourhood who was a beauty. I met her by accident one night in a movie theatre. She was munching popcorn, and part of it, either by accident or design, was falling into my coat pocket. I'm not going to describe her looks in detail, but she was so beautiful that I even returned the lost popcorn. She seemed quite impressed with my gallantry, and soon we were gaily sharing the popcorn.

She was nineteen and, as far as I knew, since she was sitting down, she had everything a young girl is supposed to have at the age of nineteen. Suffice it to say (this is how a lawyer friend of mine starts every statement), I wanted my arms around her . . . and anything else I could possibly get.

In talking to her, I discovered she was an automobile nut. She said there was nothing she disliked more than walking. She pointedly told me that even if she was madly in love with a man, she never dated him unless he had a car. I hadn't told her that I had an auto. I also didn't tell her that the auto I had was lying upside down in a garage, having its vital organs repaired. I was biding my time. The day my Scripps-Booth came back from its major operation, I called her up and asked if she would care to go for a spin.

Today my appearance is compared favourably with that of

William Holden, Tony Curtis and even Clark Gable, but I must say that in those days my profile was nothing to brag about. I was five feet eight, with a set of irregular teeth, a sallow complexion, a hang-dog look and a mass of unruly hair that slanted in whatever direction the wind happened to be blowing.

It had been raining all day and the streets were still full of water. But the night was clear and the moon was shining. And for the first time in weeks, so were my shoes. When I arrived at my beautiful one's house, I happily blew the rubber horn. After thirty nervous minutes the front door opened, and descending the stairs was one of the prettiest sights since Maud Muller on a summer's day raked the meadows sweet with hay. She was wearing a white dress, a large white picture hat and white shoes. I met her halfway, greeted her with all my well-tempered elegance, and quickly rushed back to open the car door for her. The door stuck a little and in my eagerness to get it open before she arrived, I slipped a foot or two under the car. I brushed off the mud, moved in beside her and away we drove towards the lake. I was delirious with joy. My heart was making more noise than the engine, and when she smiled at me I knew that, at last, I had found the girl of my dreams.

The car wasn't too well balanced, and even at slow speeds it lurched around corners like a rolling drunk. As we went around one corner, she tried to steady herself by placing her hand on the door. What she didn't know was that this was the door with the electric button. To my horror, the door flew open and the glamorous creature slid gracefully out of the car into a large, muddy puddle. I was so panicky that I started to drive away, but I had just seen a movie with Francis X. Bushman and I realized that, in such a situation, Francis X. would not have taken it on the lam. I quickly backed up, almost running over her in my excitement, hopped out of the car and helped her to her feet. Though she was wet and muddy, I recognized her immediately. I tried to explain and apologize, but all she said was, "Take me home, you bastard!"

We rode back in silence. The only sound to be heard was the rattling of the motor and my teeth. When we arrived at her house, she flung open the car door and ran screaming up the stairs. The next day I got a registered letter from her father. He wrote that his daughter's dress, hat and white shoes had been ruined, that it would cost sixty-five dollars to replace them, and unless the money arrived in forty-eight hours he would arrive at my house with a large horsewhip and flog the hell out of me. At first I thought of accepting the flogging and saving the sixty-five dollars, but after a sleepless night I reluctantly sent the money.

This was really the summer of my discontent: one hundred and fifty dollars for the car, fifty for the new push-rods, and now sixty-five to refurbish this girl's wardrobe. A total of two hundred and sixty-five dollars—and I never even got the girl as far as the lake! This was the last time I ever aped Francis X. Bushman.

MOST SHOW PEOPLE, when they finally write their autobiographies (and don't think they don't), invariably relate in glowing terms a steady succession of triumphs. The smart ones sometimes throw in an occasional flop, for they know there is nothing more disheartening to the average reader, who is usually a failure in life, than to read about some lucky ham who, through a series of accidents (and a minimum of talent), has achieved fame, fortune and a steady procession of wives.

Before I get through with this chronicle, I too plan on boring you with a few of my triumphs, but you will have to be patient. At the moment, like Picasso, I am still in my automobile period.

After the Chalmers and Scripps-Booth incidents had shattered my love life, there came a long line of tin cans: a Nash, an Essex, an Elgin whose rear axles kept shearing off, a Ford sedan as high as an elephant's eye and so out of balance that a strong wind would send it careening, and a Cord whose emergency brake handle kept coming off in my hand every time there was an emergency.

Most everyone has some goal or ambition in life that they ultimately hope to attain . . . President of the United States, manager of a major league ball club, superintendent of janitors. My only goal in life, in addition to not starving to death, was to own a shiny new automobile—a steering wheel untouched by human hands, seats unretouched by food stains, unblemished tyres and a speedometer that read 00000.

We were playing in Philadelphia, at the Walnut Street

Theatre, in a show called, for some reason that I never understood and still don't, *I'll Say She Is*. We played there all summer, and since it was the only show playing in Philadelphia at the time, it was a huge success. I was getting two hundred dollars a week.

After a few weeks of careful shopping along automobile row, I finally settled on a Studebaker sedan with wire wheels. I bought the car on a Wednesday morning and was panting to drive it away, but the salesman said it would take a few hours to tune it up and that he would deliver it that afternoon.

I said, "I have a matinée this afternoon."

He said, "Brother, I'll deliver it to the theatre."

My big scene in the show was in the second act, where I played Napoleon Bonaparte. Needless to say, I was superb. My costume consisted of a French general's uniform, a sword, boots, a three-cornered hat and a large, oversized painted black moustache on my upper lip. I must admit I didn't look much like the original Napoleon, but you must remember I was going for laughs, and who knows, maybe the original wouldn't have had such an unhappy ending had he done the same.

The Napoleon scene came on shortly after the fifteen-minute intermission, and the salesman delivered the car just as the intermission began. I was now in full Napoleonic regalia. The salesman said, "Here are the keys, and God bless you." I found out later that he had never been a religious man, but this had been one of those years when the auto business had turned sour and he had been going to church to see if steady prayer and religious phrases would help him find some new customers. As he handed me the keys he said, "Ride it around the block, my good friend. You'll think you're in a Pierce-Arrow." As he left, he added, "Peace be with you, brother."

The car was black and shiny and it looked wonderful. Since the intermission had just begun, I knew I had time to drive it around the block. It would only take two or three minutes.

PHILADELPHIA IS one of the old Colonial cities of America. It has the Liberty Bell, the *Saturday Evening Post* (which they still claim was founded by Benjamin Franklin), and around where the Walnut Street Theatre stands are some of the narrowest streets this side of Bombay. Two street-cars rumbling along in opposite directions will just miss knocking each other off the tracks as they pass.

As I drove around the corner, I found myself blocked by a street-car, and in front of this street-car there was a long row of street-cars. And now in back of me was another street-car and in back of that they stretched out endlessly. Alongside the street-cars were trucks, cars and wagons—a huge blockade of miscellaneous vehicles extending as far as the eye could see. Not a wheel was turning. The only things that were moving were the hands on the car clock, telling me that it was time to play Napoleon. What to do? I had no licence plates. If I left the car there, someone would undoubtedly steal it. If I stayed with the car, I'd miss the Napoleon scene.

A policeman spied me exiting from the Studebaker. He probably thought, "Here's a new way to steal a car . . . disguise yourself in some daffy outfit so the police will think you're advertising something." We both started running, but he had me at a disadvantage. I had on large, sloppy boots, and halfway down the block one of them flew off. It must have been an unusual sight—a Philadelphia policeman chasing Napoleon down Walnut Street.

He finally nailed me. "Don't you know it's against the law to leave an auto in the middle of the street?" he shouted. "And what the hell are you doing in that screwy outfit?"

I explained who I was and what had happened. The cop was a typical Philadelphia policeman and he quickly apologized and retrieved the flying boot for me. He then ran with me to the theatre. I arrived just in time to make my entrance.

I played the scene that afternoon, but as lovely as Josephine was, I didn't care whether she was true to me or not. All I could think of was my brand-new Studebaker with no licence plates, no driver and, worst of all, no insurance.

By the time I came off the stage and explained what had happened, the blockade had disappeared and so had my car. Four weeks later the police found it in Lancaster, Pennsylvania, and brought it back to me. Surprisingly enough, it was none the worse for having been stolen, but I didn't get the new car I had always dreamed of owning. The speedometer now read 3,027 miles and the seats were full of ink-stains.

Despite its being untrue to me for 3,027 miles, I loved that

Studebaker as though it were something alive. I treated it tenderly and never drove it more than twenty miles a day. I was afraid it would strain its insides and, besides, there was no reason for driving more than that. By this time I was married, and amorous expeditions were unnecessary.

My routine with the car was as follows: Fairmount Park was ten miles from my furnished room. After breakfast I would drive out to Fairmont Park, find a shady spot and Simonize the car until my back ached. I would then dust the insides and polish the windows. That done, I would drive the car back to the garage and go for a walk.

On rainy days I kept the car in the garage. I ran up very little mileage on the Studebaker, but my friends were unanimous in saying I had the cleanest and shiniest car in all of Pennsylvania.

CHAPTER TEN

TANK TOWNS, PTOMAINE AND TOMFOOLERY

WELL, BACK TO show business. Today it's a different profession. If you're on the right television show at the right time, you can become famous overnight. In twenty-four hours you can zoom from obscurity to fame. One click and you can wake up in the morning and find a good section of Madison Avenue frantically shoving contracts under your hotel room door.

Recognition didn't come overnight in the old days. We bounced around for many years before we made it. We played towns I would refuse to be buried in today, even if the funeral were free and they tossed in a tombstone for lagniappe. Every so often, while journeying to some place I'm headed for, I find myself again in some dusty hamlet we once played in the old days. Having lost part of my mind over the years, I forget what these places looked like. When I see them now, I'm appalled. The six nationally known chain stores, the threadbare hotel, and the restaurants that dish out grub so far removed from food that it's a wonder we're still alive. I once ate cream of tomato soup in some beehive in Saginaw and it made me so sick that I didn't touch a tomato again for twenty years.

ON ONE OF our Orpheum Circuit tours there was an act called "Come On, Red." It was written by John B. Hymer and was a wonderfully funny sketch. I don't remember the entire plot, but there was one chap who played the heavy ("heavy" means the villain), and in this playlet his name was Tiger Smith. I never did know his real name. We all called him Tiger. He was a huge man and was built as though he had once played professional football.

I'm sure you all know what a miser Jack Benny is supposed

to be. Actually, he's one of the most generous men I know, not only with his money, but with his time and talent. He is the antithesis of the character he portrays on his television show. However, Tiger Smith was, in real life, what Benny purports to be.

His salary was two hundred dollars a week, and from the way he lived, he must have socked away a hundred and eighty-five of it. Taxes were negligible then, and I doubt if he ever paid any. He had a deep-seated aversion to parting with money. If the manager of the theatre didn't object, he would sling up a hammock and sleep in his dressing-room.

Most of the performers on the bill were comparatively friendly—unless, of course, one of the acts was too big a hit. After the matinée, we would usually go to dinner together. All except Tiger Smith. I once asked him why he didn't join us.

"Groucho," he answered, "you think I'm nuts? If you think I'm going to pay a buck just to eat dinner, you got another think coming!" He added, "Food is food, and I'm certainly not going to throw my money away on anything as silly as that."

"Well, where do you eat?" I inquired. "Do you grow your own mushrooms in the dressing-room?"

"Nope." He shook his head. "I eat in the cheapest lunch wagon I can find, and my meals never cost me over two bits."

"But, Tiger, aren't you apt to get sick from that kind of grub?"

"Are you kidding? I've been eating in those places for years!" Then, patting himself on the stomach, he boasted, "I've never had a sick day in my life!"

"Well, how do you manage?" I asked. "Do you have some kind of secret formula?"

"Yeah," he admitted. "I guess you could call it a secret formula. I'll tell you what it is, but you gotta keep it under your hat."

"Okay," I agreed, "but do you mind if I keep it under my cap? I haven't got a hat."

He wisely ignored this pitiful attempt at jocularity. "Ready?" he asked.

"Ready," I nodded.

"Well, as soon as I finish eating," he confided, "no matter how sick I feel, I take two tablespoonfuls of bicarbonate of soda. Once that's down, I'm as good as new!"

There's not much more to this story. After our tour was

over I lost track of him. A few years later I read his obituary in *Variety*. It said that Tiger Smith had died of kidney stones caused by eating too much bicarbonate of soda. He left an estate of two hundred thousand dollars. I don't know who got the money, but I hope his beneficiary had enough sense to frequent the better restaurants. You can eat real good for many years in those places for two hundred thousand dollars.

Actors on the road are like armies—they travel on their stomachs, too. So food—or the lack of it—was an important issue.

We were living in a boarding-house in Elizabeth, New Jersey. This wasn't the customary frowzy theatrical boarding-house where we were usually stabled. It was so refined that it was uncomfortable. The landlady wore a silver comb in her hair, and the tablecloths were changed twice a week. The clientele consisted mostly of fairly well-to-do, dowdy widows and widowers. Only when one or more of her boarders moved or died did the landlady consent to take in actors.

Apparently there had been a number of deaths that Christmas week, for she had room for the four of us. After considerable haggling about the rates, which were higher than we usually paid, we were assigned to two rooms on the third floor back. Compared with the places we usually lived in, this was a pretty fancy inn. The next day was Christmas, and we could hardly wait to get our teeth into that large juicy turkey that all boarding-houses served on Christmas Day. Life was wonderful. It was snowing outside, we had warm, cosy rooms and, most important, we were working.

This was an old house, and the dining-room was on the ground floor. The room contained three tables, each seating eight people, and it had one table in a far corner to which we were relegated. Apparently our hostess didn't approve of mixing actors with normal people. But we didn't care. Our motto was, "Bring on the turkey and to hell with segregation."

That night her husband, a beaten-looking nonentity, had his fast moment of triumph as he carried in the Christmas turkey. I don't know who cooked it, but it looked brown, crisp and succulent. The permanent boarders all took a hack at the bird as it was passed around. The better parts were going fast. After the regulars had been served, the platter, instead of moving towards our table, was carted back to the kitchen. Our plates were still as bare as the president of a nudist colony.

We began to fidget, but Chico said, "Take it easy, boys. Be patient. That turkey was almost gone. In a minute they'll bring in a fresh one for us."

A few minutes later another drudge appeared from the kitchen and headed towards Devil's Island. That was us. She was carrying a large covered vessel, and when she unveiled it at our table, there lay a large, grey mackerel.

We rose in a rage and marched out of the dining-room, the fish untouched. You know that "the show must go on" routine. We went to the theatre. Our act that evening consisted entirely of a series of variations on one theme—a dead mackerel. The audience was mystified. They didn't laugh, but we were in hysterics. Probably from hunger.

Later that night while the boarding-house slept, we crept into the kitchen and raided the ice-box. To our surprise, we found half a cold turkey. We quickly finished it, bones and all. We also discovered the rejected mackerel, which the landlady was undoubtedly saving to serve us again the following day. Quickly transferring the fish to the now empty turkey platter, we inserted a note in its mouth. It read simply, "Guess who?"

The following morning we checked out and moved into a dingier but more hospitable boarding-house.

As an appropriate way of topping off these sumptuous repasts, I began smoking Pittsburg stogies. These were long, thin and black as stove polish (the resemblance didn't end there). They were three for a nickel, and for your nickel you got about four hours' steady smoking. I must have had an unusually strong stomach, for they only made me sick about once a day. I know I should have quit, but I enjoyed smoking cigars. It wasn't the taste that intrigued me, but I thought they made me look manly. With one of those in your mouth there was no chance of your being mistaken for a girl. Eventually, however, I concluded that Pittsburgh stogies were stronger than I was, which left me two choices—either abandon them or pass on to another world.

At the ripe old age of fifteen, I graduated from Pittsburgh stogies to the nickel cigar; and as I grew more affluent, I progressed to the ten-cent sheroot. At that time there was a popular cigar called La Preferencia. Their ads. were plastered all over the countryside: "Smoke La Preferencia. Thirty Minutes in Havana for Only Fifteen Cents." This advertisement fascinated me. It sounded so tropical. Imagine, thirty minutes in Havana for fifteen cents! I had never before spent that much for a cigar—but I had also never been in Havana.

The ad. finally got me. I walked into a cigar store, slapped fifteen cents on the counter and said, "La Preferencia, please." As the clerk handed it to me I said, "Now then, your ad. says thirty minutes in Havana. Is that true?" He smiled and nodded affirmatively.

That night, after our last performance, I went back to the boarding-house, put on my nightgown and set the alarm clock. Reclining on the bed, I started puffing away. The cigar had a nice taste. The aroma was mild and fragrant, far removed from the carbonized stink of the Pittsburgh stogies. I won't say that I was transported to Havana, or even as far south as Florida, but I must say its aroma was much better than anything I had ever puffed before. At the end of twenty minutes the cigar was so short that it could only be held by sticking a toothpick into the stub. At the end of twenty-two minutes it had ceased to be a cigar and was just half an inch of wet tobacco. I was pretty angry. Fifteen cents gone up in smoke!

Early the next morning, I went back to the cigar store with the soggy evidence in a small paper bag. The clerk greeted me with a smile. I up-ended the bag and the damp cigar butt slithered across the counter top. "Thirty minutes in Havana, eh?" I snarled. "I smoked it as slowly as I could, and the best I could get out of it was twenty-two minutes! I want my fifteen cents back!"

Like all clerks, I'm sure he encountered many strange people. "Look," he said, "I have nothing to do with La Preferencia cigars or their advertising. I'm just a clerk here."

"Well," I shouted, "they advertised thirty minutes in Havana, didn't they? I only got twenty-two minutes. That's crooked!"

He was a nice man, and he realized that before him stood a shining example of a boy idiot. "Look, son," he said, "I only work here and I haven't the authority to refund any money."

"That's none of my business," I replied hotly. "I bought

that cigar here and I want my money back! I hold you personally responsible."

By this time two customers had backed out of the store and
the clerk was getting nervous. "I'll tell you what I'll do," he
said placatingly. "You keep quiet and I'll give you another
La Preferencia free."

That night I again set the alarm to ring in thirty minutes.
I lit up and leaned back against the pillow. Maybe this time
I smoked faster. I don't know. At any rate, on the second try,
the thirty minutes in Havana only lasted eighteen minutes!

The next morning I went back to the cigar store and again
slapped the wet butt on the counter. "Well," I demanded,
"how about it? Last night I was only in Havana eighteen
minutes!"

"Now see here, son," the clerk said. "I told you I only work
here. Don't bother me if you don't like our merchandise. Write
to the company and tell them your troubles." He handed me
a slip of paper bearing the name and address of the factory.
I went back to the boarding-house and wrote to the President
of the company, explaining in detail how I had been gypped.

I guess they were a pretty nice crowd, despite their crooked
advertising claims, for two weeks later I received a certified
cheque for fifteen cents. Because of their generosity I continued
to smoke La Preferencias for many years. But I still maintain
they were crooked, for no matter how slowly I puffed, I never
was able to spend more than twenty-two minutes in Havana.

I DID MANAGE to spend a fair share of time in Indiana,
though. "*Oh, the moonlight's fair tonight along the Wabash.*" Indiana
was always a wonderful state for girls. Elkhart, Hammond,
Lafayette, Muncie. Ah, Muncie!

Attired in my new suit with the Norfolk jacket, checked cap,
cane and spats, I was strolling along the main drag of Muncie,
Indiana, looking 'em over. We had just finished the matinée,
and as was the custom as soon as the show was over, we all
quickly got dressed and rushed out to the lobby to case the
stuff that was coming out of the theatre. This was called "three-
sheeting." Sometimes the results were very satisfactory, but
nothing much emerged that day.

Throwing a fake yawn at my brothers, I told them I didn't feel too well and that I was going back to the boarding-house to take a nap. Ducking down a side street to avoid them, I again hit the main drag for whatever fate had in store for me.

I hadn't walked more than ten minutes when I spied a beautiful girl, pushing a baby carriage. We were both about the same age. I now employed one of the stalest devices known to mankind. I stood in front of the carriage and started talking baby talk. Not to the girl, but to the baby. "What a beautiful child!" I exclaimed. "And what a remarkable resemblance. She's very lucky to have you for a mother." (I could see from the pink ribbons that it was a girl.)

"Thank you," the chick replied, "but I'm not her mother. This is my sister's baby. I'm just taking care of her while she's shopping."

This was pretty good, so far. If it wasn't her child, there was a fairly good chance that the pusher of the baby carriage was single. "Are you married?" I asked.

"Of course not," she dimpled. "I'm only nineteen."

Well, that made sense. I, too, was nineteen and I wasn't married. "Where are you headed for, kid?" I asked.

"I'm taking the baby home to my house until my sister calls for her," she replied.

"Well," I said, throwing her one of my more ingratiating smiles, "don't you need someone to help push the carriage?"

"You're welcome to come along if you want to," she simpered.

Her invitation excited me so that I almost jumped over the baby carriage in a frenzy of joy. Welcome to come along! It looked as if I had struck a bonanza! As we strolled along, I gave her the customary routine about loneliness and what a gasser she was—unquestionably the prettiest girl I had ever seen. (This may be stale stuff, but don't kid yourself—it works!)

We finally arrived at her house, a typical Midwestern architectural monstrosity. It was a two-story, yellow frame, two-family dwelling, and it was peeling as though it had a bad case of sunburn. My friend lived on the second floor. The two of us lifted the kid out of the carriage, carried it upstairs and quickly put it to bed.

Strategic as ever, I immediately planted myself on the couch, and to make sure she would be impressed by my cosmopolitan ways, I pulled a large cheap cigar out of my pocket and began fouling up the room.

She sat down beside me and before she could say "Jack Robinson," or even "Joe Delaney," I had one arm securely around her and the other one ready to go. She had a lovely waist. Just the right size. Maybe it was my imagination, but it seemed to yield to my slightest pressure. What bliss! Except for the kid, I was all alone, sitting on the couch with a knock-out. And considering that I had only known her for twenty minutes, I was moving along pretty well.

"How is it a beautiful girl like you isn't married?" I asked.

"My sister is married," she replied, "and from what she tells me, it's not as much fun as it looks."

"Well," I asked shyly, "do you like me?"

"I'll say!" she answered. "I think you're real nice. In fact, I'd say you were real cute."

This kid was quite a conversationalist. From her repartee you knew instantly that here was no Dorothy Parker or Cornelia Otis Skinner. On the other hand, I must say in her defence that she had two very pretty legs.

"The boys in Muncie ain't got anything on you," she continued.

Having been in Muncie for only two days, I had no idea what the boys in Muncie had, but apparently she preferred what I had. All this time she had been sitting three inches from me, and now she moved even closer. Love was all around me. Ecstasy was around the corner. I was floating in mid-air.

Still floating, I heard a sharp, decisive masculine knock on the door. She hollered, "Oh, my God! My husband!"

"I thought you weren't married!" I yelped as I leaped from the couch.

"Oh, I was just teasing."

Teasing, she said! Here I was, halfway to the morgue, and she called it teasing!

In the meantime the knocking had grown louder and more insistent. A heavy voice from outside the door shouted, "Gladys, open the door! Open up, Gladys, before I kick it down!"

From the sound of his voice, I surmised he was about six feet six and an ex-All-American guard. I was getting pretty panicky. "Gladys," I whispered, "what'll I do?"

"Hop in the closet," she said calmly, "and don't worry. I'll get you out of this."

From her cool, deliberate instructions, I began to suspect that this was not an unusual incident in Gladys' life. I quickly dashed into the closet and closed the door behind me. It was filled with overcoats, blue jeans, suits and rubber boots. I crouched behind them, grateful for the camouflage. I couldn't see what was going on, but I could hear her unlocking the front door.

He didn't say "Hello" or "How are you?" Nothing as formal as that. Apparently he, too, was accustomed to this little episode, for his opening line was, "Where the hell is he?"

"He?" Gladys asked innocently, with a piece of acting that would have put Helen Hayes to shame. "There's no one here, honey."

"You're a liar!" he roared. "I heard a man's voice!"

"Ralph," she said soothingly, "you must be tired. Let me fix you a bite to eat."

"Don't fix me anything! If I find the louse who's hiding in here, I'll fix him—but good! Where is he?" he yelled. "I'll strangle him with my bare hands!"

In the closet I thought to myself, "If he was a gentleman he would at least wear gloves."

I was getting a little faint from the lack of air in the closet, and I now began shaking, so that all the clothes in the closet began shaking along with me.

"Don't tell me there's no one here!" he bellowed. "I smell smoke!"

"Don't be silly, darling," said Gladys. "That was me. I was smoking a cigarette."

"You're a liar! You don't smoke cigarettes!"

"I just started this morning," she replied.

Pointing to my checked cap on the chair, he said, "I suppose you've also started wearing caps?"

He then stomped over to the closet where I was cowering and quivering. I held my breath. Luckily, I had done a pretty good job of draping the clothes around me and he didn't spot me. He started to turn away. Then a thought struck him. He wheeled around and began feeling through the clothes with the largest pair of hands since Primo Carnera. I could feel his fingers all over me. They were long fingers, too. It was like getting a massage from an octopus.

Satisfied that no one was in there, he finally closed the closet door and began searching the rest of the layout.

As soon as he left the room, Gladys rushed over, threw open the closet door, hauled me out, handed me my cigar and cap, opened a window and said, "Jump!"

I looked down. It was a good fifteen feet to the ground. But, unfortunately, I had no choice in the matter. It was risk either a broken leg or eternal rest in the local cemetery.

I guess the god of love was with me, for I landed in a clump of bushes. Except for a few major scars, I arrived back at the boarding-house all in one piece. I then collapsed on the bed, nursing my aching bumps and bruises.

A short while later I heard my brothers coming up the stairs. Not in the mood for lengthy explanations, I dropped back against the pillow and feigned sleep.

As the door opened, I heard one of them say, "See? I told you he'd be here. I guess the poor guy really wasn't feeling well."

Little did they know.

CHAPTER ELEVEN

A HOMEY ESSAY ON HOUSEMANSHIP

I RETURNED FROM a visit to London last September. I was there eleven days, and if you know London you know it rained eleven days. I was stopping at the Dorchester Hotel. It is a very expensive hotel, and in the immediate vicinity there are five or six others, equally luxurious. In the summer these hotels have a fairly substantial, rich tourist clientele, and because of this the street corners around there are thickly populated with prostitutes. It's a sad sight on any night, but on rainy nights it's doubly sad to see these women huddled in doorways, hoping someone will pick them up. The police rarely bother them. These girls have what is known as "tacit approval." Apparently the British regard them as a necessary evil and don't bother to do much about it.

How much more honest the British attitude is than ours. We're smug and say that this sort of thing doesn't exist in the States. Unfortunately, it does exist, but instead of being confined to a specific district as it was in the old days, it is now practised everywhere. Yet we close our eyes and loftily declare in highly moral tones that we do not approve of prostitution.

I believe that, today, hundreds of thousands of boys rush into matrimony poorly prepared for the many responsibilities that are a normal part of marriage. They delude themselves into thinking that they are marrying for love. A good percentage of them discover, to their sorrow, that it wasn't love at all, but just a desire to satisfy the normal sexual urge.

Before I am thrown into the pokey for defending legalized vice, I want to hasten to my defence and point out that I am not in favour of prostitution; nor do I approve of it. But no one can deny that this problem exists, and I believe that we had a healthier approach to sex a few decades ago. I truly believe we'd be much better off today if we had legalized prostitution, with houses and madams and the precautionary medical examinations that were obligatory in the days I am about to describe.

The average vaudeville actor led a lonely life. The towns-people regarded him with suspicion and contempt. Because of this, when the actor was on the road (and in most cases away from his family), he was obliged to create his own social life. The boarding-house or the dreary hotel was usually dowdy and shabby, and completely devoid of anything that could make him forget his lot. This left the pool-room and the sporting house. It would be difficult today to convince anyone under forty how important and glamorous the sporting house was to these lonely pariahs. I suppose these places existed all over the United States, but, for some curious reason, my memories of them are mostly in the South . . . Baltimore, Memphis, Nashville, Birmingham, Montgomery, New Orleans, Dallas, Houston.

The opening matinée at the local Orpheum or Majestic Theatre was a pretty fancy social event. Each box would have its madam and her group of girls, and if they liked your act you would receive a card backstage reading, "Will you join us after the show tonight?" This didn't necessarily mean that you were invited to go to bed with one of the girls, although I must confess there were times when it did happen. You must remember, we were all in our early twenties and, to put it euphemistically, "wild for life."

In addition to the girls, the house had many other attractions. If they liked you, there was free food, free liquor and miscellaneous fun. I don't mean to brag, but we had the perfect act for these places. Many times we were more successful in these houses than we were in the theatres. What more could any madam or her girls want? We were young and good-looking, with pompadours six inches high; Harpo and Chico both played the piano and Gummo and I sang. It wasn't just a house of assignation to us; it was a club. And I might add, it was much more fun than the Elks, the Eagles or even the Shriners.

Don't get the idea that the sporting houses were the only places in town where we had social entrée. We were also cordially received in the pool-halls. For an actor on the road, these distinguished salons were more inviting than the average dump he lived in. And besides, if he was handy with a cue, there was always the likelihood of picking up a few bucks. We used to pick up quite a bit of change backing Chico against the local pool sharks.

The Pantages Circuit was composed of a string of semi-medieval theatres stretching from Chicago to the Coast and back again. We were on our way from Duluth to Calgary and had a three-hour layover in Winnipeg. We stashed our hand luggage in the depot and all the boys, except me, automatically headed for the nearest pool-room. In recent weeks I hadn't been too hot with the cue, and I decided that I needed a brief sabbatical from the green cloth. I left the boys and the depot (in that order), and walked up the main street. A half-block away from a frowzy-looking theatre I heard roars of laughter. I decided I had better go in and see who could possibly be that funny. On the stage were eight or ten assorted characters in an act called "A Night at the Club." One of these actors wore a very small moustache and very large shoes, and while a big, buxom soprano was singing one of Schubert's *lieder*, he was alternately spitting a fountain of dry cracker crumbs in the air and beaning her with overripe oranges. By the end of the act the stage was a shambles.

Leaving the theatre, I went back to the depot to meet my brothers. I told them I had just seen a great comic. I described him . . . a slight man with a tiny moustache, a cane, a derby and a large pair of shoes. I then penguin-walked around the depot, imitating him as best I could. By the time I finished raving about his antics my brothers could hardly wait to see him.

The Sullivan-Considine Circuit and the Pantages Circuit ran parallel to the coast, and we finally caught up with him in Vancouver. I had talked him up so much that my brothers were all a little sceptical. Then he appeared, and in less than five minutes they were willing to concede that he was everything I said, and more.

After the show we went backstage and introduced ourselves. We found him in a dingy dressing-room which he was sharing with three other eccentric comics. After the preliminary introductions, we told him how wonderful he was. During the ensuing conversation he told us he was getting fifty dollars a week and, although he had been promised a raise to sixty, it had never come through.

He had already created considerable excitement in the movie

industry. In fact, he told us that some movie mogul had offered him five hundred dollars a week to work for him. We congratulated him. "When do you start?" I asked.

"I'm not going to take it," he answered.

"Why not?" I asked, astonished. "You're only getting fifty a week now. Don't you like money?"

"Of course I do," he replied (and, boy, did he prove this later in life!). "But look, boys, I can make good for fifty dollars a week, but *no* comedian is worth five hundred a week. If I sign up with them and don't make good, they'll fire me. Then where will I be? I'll *tell* you where I'll be. Flat on my back!"

He was a strange little man—this Charlie Chaplin. The first time I met him he was wearing what had formerly been a white collar and a black bow tie. I can't quite explain his appearance, but he looked a little like a pale priest who had been excommunicated, but was reluctant to relinquish his vestments.

We became real chummy in the ensuing weeks. He was terribly shy, and I particularly remember a night when we all went to a sporting house in Salt Lake City just for laughs. The madam took a shine to Charlie, but he would have none of her, nor did he want any of the younger girls. Instead, he spent the entire evening lying on the floor, playing with the madam's English bulldog.

As we left there that night we spotted three ash-cans sitting in front of the house. We lined them up at the regulation distance and then spent most of the night playing leapfrog over the cans for nickels and dimes.

I ran into Charlie again while we were playing the Orpheum Theatre in Los Angeles some years later. He still affected the peculiar collar and tie combination. The only difference was that this time they were spotless. Oh, yes—there was another slight change. He was now the most famous comedian in the whole world.

He came back to see us after the show and invited us all to dinner at his house. There were twelve of us at the table. The plates were solid gold, or close to it, and I think the furniture was made of the same metal. There were six uniformed man-servants. This was quite a jump from the first time I saw him in that ten-cent theatre in Winnipeg, spitting crackers and throwing oranges at the soprano.

Charlie lives in Switzerland now, but it doesn't make any

difference where he lives. He's still the greatest comic figure that the movies, or any other medium, ever spawned.

After Chaplin's success, the movie moguls began to realize that there were some pretty good comics in vaudeville and on Broadway. At one time or another most of them were brought out and given a fling at the movies, but most of the great comedians of the stage never were too successful on the screen. We were one of the luckier groups.

Ed Wynn, Bea Lillie, Willie Howard, Bobby Clark, Frank Fay and many, many others were never able to duplicate their tremendous Broadway triumphs. The real big comic movie smashes were Buster Keaton, Charlie Chaplin, Harold Lloyd and Laurel and Hardy, most of whom had very little stage success.

Don't laugh, but I think the logical successor to Chaplin is Skelton. Red, to my mind, is the most unacclaimed clown in show business. I've seen most of the great, legendary clowns of the circus, but I must confess I've rarely seen one who could amuse me for more than a minute. True, they all wear funny clothes and funny hats and paint their faces, but it takes much more than that to be a great comic.

The last time I watched Skelton perform in a theatre, he came onstage in an outfit that could conceivably have been worn by the head of the National Association of Manufacturers at a board meeting. With one prop, a soft battered hat, he successfully converted himself into an idiot boy, a peevish old lady, a teetering-tottering drunk, an overstuffed clubwoman, a tramp and any other character that seemed to suit his fancy. No grotesque make-up, no funny clothes, just Red. There is no one around who can take a comic fall as completely and as magnificently as he can. He also sings, dances, delivers a deceptively simple comic monologue and plays a dramatic scene about as effectively as any of the dramatic actors, Method or otherwise.

Some day I'm afraid the eggheads will take him up and start reading social significance into his antics. Let's hope they don't, because this has ruined many a good performer. And we need all the pure comedians like Red we can get.

CHAPTER TWELVE

SOME CLOWNING THAT WASN'T IN THE ACT

WE WERE PLAYING a mangy vaudeville theatre on the West Side of New York. A real old joint that must have been built shortly after the Civil War, or perhaps during it, this place was rococo at its gaudiest. It was a mass of creaking plush chairs and worn-out carpeting; it had upper and lower boxes on both sides of the stage. Actually, it should have been preserved as a shining example of bad taste, but progress came along and razed the theatre. (In its place, of course, an even uglier office building was erected.)

We always flirted with the girls in the audience, no matter what scene we were playing. And I must say, with a minimum of modesty, that they almost invariably flirted back. This particular night, there were two very attractive girls sitting in the upper box. They didn't seem to be particularly interested in the events taking place on the stage, and at the moment, neither were we. They were quite a distraction. They were trying to tell us, by frantic signalling, that they were not only desirous of meeting Harpo and me, but were also trying to indicate to us where to meet them. Whether it was because we weren't very clever at reading signs, or because they were inept at sending them out, we weren't making the contact that was necessary to consummate the rendezvous. Luckily, Harpo is a master of pantomime, and he finally got through to them. By some fancy finger-waving, he instructed them to write their names and addresses on a piece of paper. As is customary at the end of the act, the curtain came down and we then gave those hammy smiles that all actors assume when bowing and scraping to the audience.

As the curtain went up again, Harpo, to our surprise, went up with it. As the curtain reached the upper box, he perilously hung on with one hand and with the other hand reached towards the box. One of the girls quickly handed him a piece of paper, containing all the necessary information.

Harpo and I quickly removed most of our make-up (we

always left some of it on so that people would know we were actors), donned our street clothes and soon were on our way along Eighth Avenue. It was now almost midnight. As we walked along, we came upon a lone push-cart pedlar who was just about to close up for the night. In desperation, he had stuck a sign on the wagon which read, SELLING OUT! TAKE THESE 4 DOZEN ORANGES HOME FOR 40 CENTS!

I guess we were sorry for the pedlar, or perhaps it was one of our more lunatic moments—or maybe it was just that we couldn't resist a bargain—but we were now on our way to a romantic rendezvous, not with candy, flowers, perfume or any of the normal gifts that girls expect from their gentlemen callers, but with forty-eight oranges.

When we arrived at their apartment, the girls emitted little squeals of delight on spying the four bulky bags. I don't know what they thought we had brought in them. Certainly they didn't expect jewels or expensive clothing to be packed in brown-paper bags. Reluctant to keep them in suspense any longer, we quickly opened the sacks and displayed with pride our four dozen oranges.

The room was fairly large, with a bed on each side of it. I separated twenty-four oranges from their mates and bowled them to one end of the room. Harpo then proceeded to bowl his share to the other end of the room. I don't know who started it, Harpo or his girl, but as I turned away, an orange clipped me on the back of my head. I quickly retreated behind one of the beds, picked up one of my oranges and caught Harpo's girl square in the small of her back.

Harpo, bristling with chivalry, picked one up and scored a bull's-eye on my girl. By that time he and his girl friend were barricaded behind the bed on their side of the room and it now became open warfare. The girls quickly got into the spirit of things, and demonstrated a deadly marksmanship of their own.

For some curious reason, love had flown out the window. It had now become a question of survival. It was trench warfare all over again. It was the Maginot Line with oranges. The fruit was flying thick and fast, and in thirty minutes the room was a shambles. Furniture had been overturned, a layer of orange peel covered the carpet and now the neighbours were pounding on the walls and shouting, "Cut out the racket or we'll send for the police!"

As the oranges became mushier they became more difficult

to handle, and the firing gradually ceased. At that moment the front door opened and the landlord entered. He didn't say much, but we quickly surmised that we had worn out our welcome. Grabbing our hats, without so much as a goodbye to the girls, we made a hasty exit. The landlord's foot just missed me by three inches. Harpo wasn't that lucky.

This was the end of our Orange Period. No love, no nothing —and our forty-cent investment shot to hell.

ONE OF MY closest friends was a confirmed bachelor. He, like all others lucky enough to have escaped the matrimonial net, sneered at marriage and ridiculed its alleged charms. He brayed frequently and belligerently that he was immune to the wildly heralded attractions of the other sex. "I've seen friends of mine," he told me one day, "who get hooked—and after a few years, what do they have to show for it? Deep wrinkles, kids and debts! Most of them are so hag-ridden that they're just ghosts of the men I once knew. No dame is ever going to snare me," he boasted. "Marriage is for the birds. I'm one of the smart ones. I'm a lone wolf. I'll run alone and like it!"

It wasn't too long after this that I received an announcement of his impending marriage. No one was less surprised than I was. He had been protesting too much, and I knew it was just a matter of time until some dame would make him run up the white flag.

A few days later, I received the inevitable invitation to a bachelor dinner that his many friends were giving him. To those who are not familiar with this semi-public humiliation, the chief reason for a bachelor dinner—in addition to getting loaded—is to give the victim's married friends an opportunity not only to escape from their wives for an evening, but also to spend a few hours revelling in the poor lout's imminent misery.

The invitation bore the address of a fashionable and famous chop-house in New York's middle forties. (Name deleted for legal reasons.) It had five floors and five different dining-rooms. In answering the invitation, I pointed out that the show in which we were appearing at the time wasn't over until eleven o'clock, but I promised that Harpo and I would drop in as soon afterwards as we conveniently could.

This chop-house had an automatic elevator. There was no hall or vestibule between the dining-room and the elevator on each floor. You pressed a button, the elevator rose to the floor you had indicated, the doors flew open and there you were in the dining-room.

Harpo and I hatched out a brilliant scheme. We would each bring a suitcase along, get into the elevator and take off all our clothes. We would then put the clothes in the suitcases. When the elevator arrived at the floor where the party was being held, the doors would open and we would step out wearing nothing but our birthday suits and straw hats, and carrying our suitcases. This was sure to get a big laugh. In addition to being funny, it had shock value. We could hardly wait.

As the elevator doors slid open, the two practical jokers made their grand entrance. But something had gone wrong. Instead of the hearty roar of masculine laughter that we had anticipated, three women fainted and the rest of them started screaming for the police! It seems that friends of the bride were giving her a dinner that same evening on the floor above. In our eagerness and excitement, we had pressed the wrong button in the elevator!

In a panic, we wheeled around, but it was an automatic door and it had quietly closed behind us. There we were. Trapped! We looked for the stairs, but couldn't find any. Apparently some enemy of ours had removed them. We finally spotted a large rubber plant in one corner. Cowering and shivering with embarrassment, we ran over and hid behind it.

Fortunately, the head-waiter came to our rescue. He quickly snatched up two large tablecloths and rushed over to us. We draped the cloths around us and with sickly, apologetic smiles at the outraged ladies and a pathetic attempt at dignity we were led to the stairs by a buss-boy. Bringing up the rear was the head-waiter with our suitcases. The two Mahatma Gandhis then made a hasty exit to the cellar, where they quickly dressed and went home.

Neither Harpo nor I was invited to the wedding.

I DON'T RECALL his name, but some famous, misanthropic philosopher, after a fitful night of deep thought and tossing and turning, rose one morning and (after cutting himself three times with his safety razor) announced to an indifferent world that no one was completely unhappy at the failure of his best friend. There is just enough truth in this sweeping generalization to make most of us feel guilty, and it can certainly be applied to show business. Over the years, I have observed too many examples of man's inhumanity to man to argue with the philosopher's statement. And, anyhow, the sage who made this observation croaked many years ago and, to quote the Two Black Crows, "I wouldn't want to dig him up just for that."

Having been in the theatrical profession only, I don't know how people in other walks of life react to success and failure. But I'm sure you'll find that a wide streak of envy is part of almost everyone's make-up.

Show business is a mercurial profession. The star of today is often the bum of tomorrow, and vice versa. I will probably be stoned for the following, but it's my contention that the laying of a large-sized theatrical egg on Broadway brings joy and relief to a substantial section of the entertainment world. This doesn't necessarily mean that the morning after a resounding flop, all the producers, directors and actors rush out into the streets and dance the fandango (or if they are Reds, the mazurka), but the brutal truth is, almost everyone gets uneasy when a rival producer not only gets ahead of the pack, but stays there. Permanent success in show business is unforgivable. The flop proves conclusively that the one who has just fallen on his face has no more talent than the rest of the pack, and that most of his successes were pure luck.

I have sat at dinner parties in Hollywood and noticed the ill-concealed gleams in the eyes of some of my friends as they joyously discussed the review of a new flop picture, or the trade papers' announcement that, because of low ratings, Joe Blow's TV show will be dropped by his sponsor. Except for the people involved, nobody breaks down and cries. I have seen actors (men who have been carefully watching their diets for months) suddenly break loose and devour a meal that would do credit to Henry the Eighth, just because they heard some bad news about a competitor.

I must confess, with considerable shame, that my own reaction to some of my contemporaries' failure hasn't been on as lofty a plane as, let's say, the thoughts of Dr. Schweitzer. It is very disconcerting for a comic to sit in a dressing-room and listen to another comedian kill the audience with laughter. "Bravo" is a wonderful word when shouted at you, but a most disturbing accolade when bestowed upon a competitor. If I were a sneak, I could tell you about a star who used to shut the door of his dressing-room and then turn the water on in the sink, just to make sure that no sound of applause or laughter for a rival reached his insecure ears.

In brief, no actor wants anyone else to be a bigger hit than he is. This will be hotly denied by most of my brothers and sisters in grease-paint, but don't be misled by their protestations. I have seen them, watched them and listened to them.

So far, I've been talking about the theatrical profession only, but we all live in a large and uneasy jungle. And the first law of nature is survival. The best way to survive is to hope your rival falls flat on his keester. Unfortunately for the human race, I'm sure this shameful blot on man's nature can be paralleled in every other business and profession.

Certainly no one in the Chrysler organization breaks down and cries if, one year, General Motors produces a car whose frame starts disintegrating when driven over thirty miles an hour. Nor will there be any wailing at the wall of the Ford plant if Chrysler turns out a new model that rides as though it had been assembled with library paste. I only cite these crude examples to show that it's all too true—no one is completely unhappy at the failure of his best friend.

MANY YEARS AGO, when we were still in the small time (and not doing particularly well), we were playing the college town of Williamstown. Appearing on the bill with us were two young, beautiful, untalented sisters who, for the purpose of this story, we will call the Delaney twins. If I were to use their real names the more elderly of my readers would remember them, for later in their careers they became rather notorious.

Despite the fact that they possessed a notable lack of talent, they were so pretty, youthful and shapely that no one seemed to care what they did on the stage. This being a college town, the audience was composed mostly of students who, like their contemporaries all over the world, were simply mad about young, beautiful girls.

The applause at the conclusion of their act was raucous, vociferous and insistent, and to restrain the students from rushing up on the stage and attacking them publicly, the girls hastily did their entire act over again.

After the ovation subsided, we appeared. We were fairly talented at the time, and by virtue of having more people in our group than any other number on the bill, we were the headliners. Apparently the audience wasn't impressed with our billing—or our act. Or perhaps they were still thinking of those two sex-pots whose lovely shapes had transported them, even if only temporarily, into a heaven that is reserved for men under twenty-five. At any rate, to get this paragraph off the ground, we laid a large-sized egg. I have no way of knowing the precise temperature in the theatre during our performance that afternoon, but, roughly, I would say it was about the same temperature as the water that flowed around the exterior of the *Nautilus* the day it sailed under the North Pole.

By the time we had finished, removed our make-up and dressed, the twins had left the theatre. Their dressing-room door was ajar and, as we walked past, we spotted some shapeless objects dangling on a hook. They looked suspiciously like symmetricals. In case you weren't a woman thirty years ago, I'll explain what symmetricals were. Let's say your legs and thighs were too thin and you were generally on the scrawny side. You simply encased the lower part of your carcass in this "stuffing," and over it you wore opera-length stockings. Though you might look like an underfed turkey in the shower, once you donned these pads all your basic imperfections disappeared and your shape rose and fell in all the places where your Creator had originally played you a dirty trick.

It embarrasses me to tell you what happened next. A confession of this kind should never be made publicly, but should only be revealed to your personal head-shrinker. Even though it happened more than thirty years ago, I'm still ashamed of my behaviour. Posting Gummo (who was basically a peeping Tom) at the door as a look-out, I furtively stole into their dressing-room, quickly lifted the symmetricals off the hook, took them to my hotel and gently laid them away in a dresser drawer.

That evening, when we returned to the theatre, there was a tremendous commotion going on backstage. We could hear the manager shouting that dreary, inevitable cry, "The show must go on!"—mingled with the sobs of the lovely twins, hysterically insisting that it was impossible for them to appear. The manager, puzzled, kept asking why. They finally broke down and told him about the lower "falsies," conceding that without them they were just two thin girls without much talent. They had looked everywhere, they added, but the foundation of their act had mysteriously disappeared.

In the midst of the tumult, I, hypocrite that I was, sauntered into the girls' dressing-room and innocently inquired what all the shouting was about. They were too embarrassed to tell me. The manager, never one to let modesty come between him and the box-office, yelled, "Some dirty bastard sneaked in here and stole the girls' shapes! And now, with a sold-out house full of students, they flatly refuse to go on!" (Knowing what I did, I found the word "flatly" rather amusing.)

"Well," I said, rather airily, "don't worry about the students. They'll see us."

"The hell with you and your brothers!" retorted the manager. "That audience out front wants to see these girls. They're not interested in your lousy act!" He looked frantically around the room. "Now where can those damned symmetricals be?"

At the word "symmetricals," I gallantly averted my gaze. The twins blushed to the roots of their hair, which I now noticed had recently been touched up. "Hmmm," I said, in my best Sherlock Holmes manner, "can't find 'em, eh? Well, you know this is a college town, and it's my guess that a couple of love-crazed students sneaked backstage between the matinée and evening performances and, just as a boyish prank, hooked the pads." As an afterthought, I asked, "Were they insured?"

With that, the two skinny young beauties burst into a new storm of tears, and the manager threw up his hands in defeat and stalked out.

Since the twins couldn't appear that evening, and the only other number was a dog act, we were a tremendous hit. I don't know about Gummo, but I slept badly that night. I kept thinking about those two poor, helpless, shapeless girls, with a substantial part of them reposing in my dresser drawer. It was a dirty trick, and I lay in bed wallowing in my own guilt. They were nice kids, I thought, and had they been a trifle fleshier, I could have fallen in love with either one . . . or both.

By morning, my conscience had me down for the count. I

put the symmetricals in my suitcase and, before breakfast, without consulting Gummo, took them back to the theatre. After making sure no one was around, I sneaked into the dressing-room and hung their act back on the empty hook.

The girls appeared that evening. They were a huge success and, as usual, we flopped. But despite our inability to entertain the audience, I slept much better that night.

CHAPTER THIRTEEN

OUT OF OUR LITTLE MINDS AND INTO THE BIG TIME

I t's strange how life can bludgeon you into a situation you never dreamed you could handle.

For a long time we always had a stranger in the act. Our own attempts at comedy were pretty feeble and, I imagine, fairly primitive, so we always added a singer, a dancer or a comedian who we thought could give the act that additional boost it needed to play even the small time.

We were playing throughout the Midwest in what was termed "The Western Vaudeville Circuit." That, at least, is what the theatre managers called it. Since this book will, I hope, eventually be sent through the United States mails, I won't tell you what the actors called it.

We played a lot of college towns, the homes of Michigan, Purdue, Indiana, Ohio State, Illinois, North-western, Notre Dame and scores of others. Those of you who went to college will remember the towns. To those who didn't, it doesn't matter too much.

These were tough colleges. I don't mean the colleges, actually; I mean the students. We were doing a tabloid with eight young, pretty girls backing us up. Most of these universities had two or three thousand students. There were never enough town girls to go around, so you can imagine how ravenously those future executives eyed our basket of chicks.

If the boys didn't like your act, they thought nothing of throwing miscellaneous paraphernalia at you. Occasionally, part of a seat would be tossed up on the rostrum. It was quite a hazard to get the girls from the theatre to the hotel and back again. They were usually escorted by all the men in the troupe, armed with the customary blackjacks.

One night in Ann Arbor, sacred citadel of the University of Michigan, about four hundred students waited at the stage door, bent on snatching the girls from our act. They shouted, screamed and hooted, ignoring our combined entreaties to scram. The manager of the theatre nervously went out and pleaded with them to go home, but they were in no mood to be talked away. They were there to grab those eight girls—or else.

Apparently this was not a new experience for the manager. No, he didn't send for the police. There weren't enough cops in Ann Arbor to handle four hundred wild-eyed, sex-crazed kids. He gave us a far more effective escort. He sent for the Fire Department. They quickly unrolled the hoses from the wagons, hooked them up to the nearest hydrants and began dousing the students with relentless streams of high-pressure water. The crowd gradually fell back, we all hopped on to the hook-and-ladder and were safely whisked back to our diggings.

At that time we had a boy in the act named Manny Linden. He could sing a song in the Jolson manner. (In those days practically every young singer sang in the Jolson manner. It was sure-fire; it was like waving the American flag or dragging your kids out for a bow.) The audience loved him. We were each getting thirty-five dollars a week and so was Manny, but as the size of his head grew, he decided his salary should grow with it.

That week we were playing in Champaign, Illinois, to one of the tougher student audiences. About an hour before the opening matinée, Manny came to our dressing-room and announced that he wasn't happy. He added, however, that there was a simple way of assuaging his sadness. For example, if Chico, Harpo and I would each take thirty dollars a week, instead of thirty-five, the other fifteen could be added to his salary. Since we owned the act, it didn't seem quite fair to us that Manny should get fifteen dollars a week more than we. While we sat in the dressing-room looking glumly at each other, he implied (actually, he didn't imply—he bluntly *told* us) that he was practically the whole act and that we were indeed fortunate to have him in our employ. With an admirable declaration of modesty, he added, "You know I get more applause with my three songs than Harpo does with his harp specialty or Chico on the piano." He didn't even bother to mention me or my contribution. I guess he didn't think that what I added to the act was even worth discussing. At any rate, that was his ultimatum. Either he received fifty dollars a week, or he didn't appear.

Frightened as we were at the thought of his departure and the hole it would leave in our act, this was still too much for us to swallow. He paled a little when we told him, with a liberal sprinkling of four-letter invectives, to get the hell out. We added that we didn't need him or his meagre talent, and that we would manage to struggle along without him.

Since I was the only one who could sing at all, I was elected to take over the three songs that Manny had been singing. They were "Get Out and Get Under," "Won't You Be My Little Bumblebee?" and "Somebody's Coming to My House." Manny invariably murdered the audience with this last one.

After his departure, shaking with the feeling of impending doom, we went up on the bare stage of the empty theatre and evolved the following piece of business. I would sing a verse and one chorus of the song, imitating Jolson as closely as possible, Chico would accompany me on the piano, and Harpo would crouch behind it. On the second chorus, I would start to dance. In the middle of it, Chico would jump up, grab me, and we would whirl around the stage together while Harpo would hop up on the piano stool and continue the playing. Near the finish of the song, I would give Chico a hefty shove. This would knock Harpo off the piano stool. Chico would then resume playing and I would finish the song, with Harpo stretched out on the floor simulating unconsciousness.

Naturally, we were nervous, because these college kids could be awfully tough if they didn't like what they saw. But it worked. They ate it up. They screamed, yelled and stamped their feet, and we were obliged to do the whole thing over again.

I know this may not seem terribly important, but it was all-important to us. It was actually our point of departure, our coming of age, our first timid step over that mysterious line that divides the small time from the big time. For the first time in our career we realized that we could succeed as an act without any outside help. We didn't need any more extraneous singers, dancers and feeble comedians. We were now a unit. We were The Marx Brothers. At that time we never imagined that this name would ever mean anything, but we did sense that at last we possessed the confidence every actor needs. We had finally freed ourselves from always having some outsider along to put us over, and from then on we were able to steam along under our own power.

WHILE WE WERE still playing the Keith Circuit, we appeared one week at the Fifth Avenue Theatre at Twenty-ninth and Broadway. Why it was called the Fifth Avenue Theatre when it was on Broadway I never did understand, but in the theatre unanswerable things like this can always be explained with a shrug of the shoulders and, "Well, that's show business." The manager of the theatre was a fiery Irishman named Quinn, and he was a tough cookie.

Up to this time, on stage, I had always worn a hairy moustache which was stuck on with glue. It was easy to put on, but murder to tear off. It may have been just my imagination, but it seemed to me that, as time went on, my upper lip was becoming progressively thinner from the constant applying and removing of the fake moustache. I began fearing that if this gluing continued much longer I would eventually wind up as the only man in vaudeville with nothing under his nose but a chin. I had been looking for a solution to this problem for some time, and Fate finally came to my rescue. We were doing five performances a day at this theatre and we usually went out to eat around six o'clock. After I had painfully ripped off the moustache for the third time that day, we repaired to a restaurant for the sixty-five cent dinner. (Seventy-five with wine and eighty with poultry. In fact, the sixty-five-cent dinner consisted entirely of stuffed neck.)

Apparently we dawdled over the meal, for as we arrived back at the theatre we could hear our introductory music being played. Having neither the time nor the desire to glue that hairy muff on again, I hastily grabbed some black greasepaint, smeared it across my dwindling upper lip and rushed onstage to be funny. To my surprise, the audience never noticed the difference, or if they did they didn't seem to care. They laughed at the same jokes they laughed at when I wore the hairy moustache. When the act was over I happily said to myself, "Eureka!" (This is the first opportunity I've had to use "Eureka," and I think it fits here rather neatly.) At any rate, I said, "Goodbye glue and goodbye fur!"

I had no sooner arrived at my dressing-room than Quinn, the manager, rushed in steaming at the mouth. "Look, lad," he said. "You played the Palace last week, didn't you?"

Always the actor, I said, "Yes, and I must say we were a big hit. In fact, they asked us how soon we could return. Now then, what's on your mind?"

"What's on my mind!" he echoed. "I'll tell you what's on my mind! I'm paying you fellows the same salary you got at the Palace, right? Well, I want you to wear the same moustache you wore at the Palace. Okay?"

I said, "Look, you Hibernian Hun, what's the difference what kind of a moustache I wear? The audience tonight laughed just as loud as they did last week at the Palace. That's all you're entitled to. Now get out!"

I was unusually brave that unforgettable night. The reason? My three brothers were standing right behind me, casually swinging their blackjacks as a harbinger of mayhem.

My logic (and the blackjacks) had unquestionably unnerved him, but as he left he said, "You guys think you're slipping something over on me? Well, you got another think coming! First thing in the morning I'm going to report this to E. F. Albee!" He never came backstage again, and I successfully finished the week and the season with the painted moustache.

We PLAYED the big time for about ten years. We were what is known as "Palace Regulars." Vaudeville was really something in those days. To give you an idea of how many first-class vaudeville theatres there were, you could play a year around Greater New York without ever packing your trunk. (Assuming that you had one.)

Vaudeville, like everything else (well, *nearly* everything else), eventually disappeared. Movies came in and dealt vaudeville its first shattering blow. Then along came radio and, of course, the thrust mortal was television. Strange how nothing really changes. I now see the same acts on TV shows that we used to appear with in vaudeville. The only difference is, where we used to play to an audience of fifteen hundred people a performance, they now play to twenty or thirty million people on TV. A good mathematician, or even a fair one, will tell you that if you played fifty years in vaudeville, you wouldn't play to as many people as you do now in one night on television. Frightening, isn't it? Yes, and so is a good deal of TV. But more of that later.

We were a big hit in vaudeville and were getting a fairly substantial salary, but we were discontented. New worlds to conquer! That's what we were after. We were vaudeville stars, that's true, and top stars at that, but we were ambitious and we wanted to climb still higher. We wanted to fly around in that rarefied atmosphere called Broadway. You could kill 'em all your life in big-time vaudeville, but you were still a vaudeville actor. There was a definite prestige about being a Broadway star that vaudeville could never give you.

I know it doesn't sound credible, but in those days Harpo and I were shy and always underestimated out talents. Every few days, Chico would come into the dressing-room and ask, "Why don't we do a Broadway show?"

We finally told him. "Look, Chico, we're not good enough. We wouldn't be a hit on Broadway. We're vaudeville actors. A Broadway audience demands class, and that's something we haven't got."

"Class! What have they got on Broadway that we haven't got?" asked Chico, who fortunately for all of us never suffered from a lack of confidence.

"Well," I pointed out, "there's Ed Wynn, Willie Howard, Eddie Cantor, Al Jolson, Clark and McCullough, Frank Tinney, Montgomery and Stone . . . and a few other fairly well-known figures."

"Nonsense!" interrupted Chico. "They're no better than we are. Those guys are all ex-vaudevillians. If they can make the jump, why can't we?"

"But you know perfectly well," I argued, "that Broadway audiences are much tougher than vaudeville audiences."

"Look, boys," Chico replied, "they're the same audiences we've been killing for years in big-time vaudeville. The only difference is, when they go to a Broadway show they put on their best clothes and arrive late."

Maybe Chico was right. Maybe we were good enough to take a fling at Broadway. But how, we asked him, would we go about it? "This isn't like putting on a vaudeville act for three thousand smackers," I pointed out. "Once you start putting on a Broadway show you're immediately competing with Ziegfeld's *Follies*, George White's *Scandals* and all the other expensive revues."

The producers of those shows spared no expense. Even in those days, when the dollar was really a dollar instead of the semi-comic certificate to which it has been reduced, Ziegfeld, White, Dillingham and the rest of them would think nothing of gambling two hundred thousand dollars or more on a musical. It's true that in most cases very little of their own money was invested in these shows. They had backers—and also beautiful chorus-girls. I'm not implying that these glamorous dames had anything to do with raising the money, but many a rich married man would invest five or ten thousand dollars just to say he had been near these girls. Anyway, that's the way it was told to me.

RAISING MONEY for a large, expensive musical is a business all by itself. *Oklahoma*, with a score by Rodgers and Hammerstein, almost didn't open because of lack of funds. The average theatregoer has no idea of the sweat and humiliation that even the most successful producer experiences before he finally collects enough money to put a show in rehearsal. I don't remember which show it was, but the producer of one of the greatest musicals that ever hit Broadway gave seventy-five auditions (an audition meant singing the whole score and acting the book out in detail), and even then it took weeks of persuasive eloquence before the wary backers consented to put up the money.

Even though a backer does occasionally get a girl, the majority of them are not in it for that reason. Most of them are hard-headed businessmen who are just as crazy about money as the next fellow. (The next fellow happens to be me.) These men are fascinated by the theatre and get some kind of kick out of being a part of it. Besides that, the girls *are* very pretty.

There is some justification for the average backer's reluctance to invest money in a big musical. You can be a hit in Detroit and slay 'em in Boston, but New York is something else again. There are roughly (and, boy, can they be rough!) six critics in New York who count. If four out of the six reviewers indicate thumbs down you might just as well close the show the first week, sell the scenery to a passing junkman and kiss the girls goodbye. The three hundred thousand dollar investment now isn't worth one cent on the dollar, except as a tax deduction.

Even with the biggest stars it's a giant gamble. To four boys who were still in vaudeville, there just didn't seem to be any way to begin. We had the Broadway bee. All we needed now was a producer with money, someone to write the book and a team of song writers.

One day, while Chico was in his natural habitat, a card-room, he became acquainted with a man by the name of Herman Broody. He told Chico he was from Pennsylvania and that he was the largest pretzel manufacturer in Reading. He added that he had always had a yen to get into the show game, and if the proper thing came along he wouldn't be averse to investing twenty or twenty-five thousand dollars. He said that he was a happily married man with a wife and a group of children in Reading. Then, blushing just enough to make himself repulsive, he confidentially told Chico that he also had a girl friend who, up to then, had been successfully keeping Mr. Broody at a distance. She had flatly stated that she was destined for the theatre, and if he expected to get what he was after, whatever that was, he had better pull some strings and get her a job in a Broadway musical.

I don't know how she ever got the notion that an obscure manufacturer of pretzels could persuade a Broadway producer to take a girl with no theatrical experience and put her on the stage. Chico said, "Mr. Broody, you realize that a Broadway musical can't be produced for less than a hundred thousand dollars."

Broody said, "My limit is twenty-five thousand—and before I put up a quarter I want a guarantee that my girl, Ginny, will be in the show."

"You put up the twenty-five thousand," said Chico, "and we'll put Ginny in the show all right. In fact," he added, in a blaze of generosity, "we'll also find parts for your wife and kids!" Broody paled a little at the mention of his family. Chico, as an afterthought, asked, "By the way, does Ginny have any talent?"

"Talent!" exclaimed Broody. "I'll tell you how great she is. They had a waltz contest last year in Hazelton. You know where that is—it's right near Scranton. And Ginny tied for second place!"

Reassured, Chico said, "Mr. Broody, there's no question that Ginny is headed for stardom. Now then, where's the twenty-five thousand dollars?"

Mr. Broody ignored the question and babbled on rapturously. "Oh, boy! When I tell this to Ginny, she'll know I mean business." The thought of Ginny made Broody even dizzier than he had been up to then. "You know," he confided, "I've only been gone one day and I miss my little girl already. Monday the cheque will be on deposit at the Bank of the United States, and you can start drawing against it in three days."

As I mentioned earlier, a big musical will run into two or three hundred thousand dollars. However, if you know the right costumiers and the right warehouse, you can buy an awful lot of stuff for twenty-five grand. We always had fun looking at the names on the back of the scenery that we finally bought for that show. It was a sort of scenic, theatrical Who's Who. There was hardly a show that had been on Broadway in the preceding twenty years that wasn't represented in this assortment of left-overs. There were pieces of scenery from *The Girl of the Golden West*, *The Squaw Man*, *Way Down East*, *Turn to the Right*, and many others. If memory doesn't play me false (ah there, Mr. Woollcott), I'm sure we even had a piece of the river scene from *Uncle Tom's Cabin*, where Liza crosses the ice.

The scenery didn't quite fit, and the score was probably the most undistinguished one that ever bruised the ear-drums of a Broadway audience. The girls, like all chorus-girls, looked pretty good. The rest of the cast was strictly amateur night in Dixie. What we *did* have, however, was something money couldn't buy. We had fifteen years of sure-fire comedy material, tried-and-true scenes that had been certified by vaudeville audiences from coast to coast.

We decided to call the show *I'll Say She Is!* (an expression that was considered pretty hot in those days. That same expression today would be "real cool," which should give you an idea of the progress civilization has made in the last thirty years).

Unlike most of the big revues, we couldn't afford those tall show-girls dressed in a million dollars' worth of Mainbocher clothes, diamonds and furs. We didn't have that kind of money. This was a poverty-stricken revue, and we cheated all along the line. Boy, did we cut corners! We cut enough corners to build a whole new street. I don't know what they call them now, but in the 'twenties the little dancers were called "ponies." That's what we had. They were cheaper. They weren't too much on looks and they couldn't sing, but they *could* dance.

During the second week of rehearsal, the pretzel king's Ginny sauntered in, accompanied by her potential lover. He looked much happier than the last time we had seen him. From the jaunty way he walked, it was apparent he was making some progress. We quickly shooed him out front, into the empty theatre.

Ginny wasn't a bad-looking wench, and, as they say, she had a nice "built." Before her arrival we had taken the dance director into our confidence and explained to him that Ginny had to be in the show. We told him that Ginny went with the money and that a place *had* to be found for her. Before Ginny showed up she didn't seem to present much of a problem. We assumed, from what Joe Pretzel had told us, that she was a pretty fair dancer and could certainly do the normal routines that the other chorus girls did. The dance director shouted to the company, "Take ten!" (which means "Relax for ten minutes"). Being normal busybodies, the rest of the company all sat there, curious to see what Ginny was going to produce. The director turned to Ginny and said, "Okay, let's see you do a tap routine."

She knew two or three steps, but she danced as though she had borrowed her legs from her grandfather. When she finished the routine, her boy-friend out front applauded vigorously. The rest of the cast rushed to the stage door, laughing hysterically at the spectacle they had just witnessed. Now we *did* have a problem! If Ginny didn't appear, there would be no money. If Ginny did appear, there would be no show.

After her dance, Mr. Broody hopped up on the stage. Ginny gave him a careless peck on the cheek. He said, "Goodbye, darling. You were wonderful! I love you." Then, turning to us, he announced, "I'll be back on opening night."

Harpo said, "How are we going to get around this? If she appears on opening night, we're certainly going to get laughs —but in the wrong places."

I said, "How about breaking her leg?"

"What's the use?" asked Chico. "From the way she dances, I think both of her legs are already broken."

"How about kidnapping her?" I suggested hopefully. "We could hide her in the cellar and no one would know the difference."

"Broody would know the difference," countered Chico, "and if his little love package isn't up there in that line, we'll never get the balance of the money."

THE OPENING NIGHT was a huge success. Broody was out front, beaming and glowing. He had sent fifty dollars' worth of roses backstage to be presented to Ginny at the end of the show. Ginny never saw them. The stage doorman took them home to his wife. I learned later that his wife was so suspicious of this unexpected gift that three months later she divorced him, charging infidelity.

Ginny didn't appear at all. The night before, someone in the company had slipped her a Mickey Finn. (Don't blame me. I was on the stage at the time.) The second night, she danced. Although we were considered pretty good comedians, we couldn't compete with her. Her dance got more laughs than any sketch in the show. She had absolutely no sense of rhythm. She was always either one step ahead or one step behind the other girls. Actually, she wasn't a bad kid and we felt sorry for her, but every time she danced we lost ten yards.

Luckily, Broody only stayed for the first two nights. He had to get back to Reading—I guess to resume sprinkling salt on his pretzels. Whenever he wasn't there, we kept Ginny off the stage. We gave her some pretty fancy reasons why she couldn't appear. But occasionally she insisted on dancing and it was hurting the show. Columnists began writing gags about her. We were getting worried. We also had financial problems. The show had run ten thousand dollars over the twenty-five-thousand-dollar budget and we were hounding Broody for the additional money. He kept putting us off with, "Don't worry. You'll get it."

Love finally came to our aid. Two weeks after the show opened, Ginny fell for one of the chorus-boys. When Broody came backstage to see her she told him that she didn't love him . . . that she never had . . . and that she had just been using him as a stepping-stone to her career.

Broody bristled. He issued an immediate ultimatum—either we kicked Ginny out or we didn't get the additional ten thousand! We could have kissed him on both cheeks.

We explained the situation to Ginny, gave her two weeks' salary (Equity, you know), and bade her God-speed. As she said goodbye, she said, "Don't worry about me. The way I dance, there's plenty of jobs for me."

She was right. Three weeks later, she waited on me at Child's Restaurant on Forty-fifth Street. I left her a big tip—twenty-five cents—because, though she didn't realize it, Ginny was pretty much responsible for launching The Marx Brothers on Broadway.

CHAPTER FOURTEEN

RICH *IS* BETTER

THERE IS NOTHING more deadly than the typical actor's chronicle of his successes. I'm deliberately sparing you this, and only hope that some day, if you write a book, you will do as much for me.

I'll make it as brief as possible. For many years we were headliners in the big time. After we hit on Broadway in *I'll Say She Is!* naturally our lives changed. Each member of the family reacted differently.

My father acknowledged our success sartorially. He began cutting a fancy figure on the Great White Way. Someone told him we were rich, and he decided to take full advantage of it. He gave all his old clothes to my grandfather, who had been dead for seven years. His new outfit consisted of a pearl-grey derby, pearl spats, pearl vest, a cutaway coat, diamond horseshoe stickpin, pearl gloves and a cane.

Fully assembled, Pop looked like something that would have been rejected by Madame Tussaud's Wax Works. He began affecting a faint English accent and larded his conversation with fruity "pip pip's" and "what-ho's." Nobody understood him, but nobody had *ever* understood him, so it didn't make too much difference.

Chico stopped going to the pool-rooms and started to patronize the more prosperous race-tracks. After he got through with them, they were even more prosperous. He was an outstanding success. In time, his uncanny success at the track was the talk of Broadway. At the end of our first season he was thirty-seven weeks behind in his salary.

Zeppo bought a forty-foot cruiser and tore up Long Island Sound as though to the manner born.

Harpo, a shy and silent fellow, was taken up by the Algonquin crowd, at that time probably the most famous and brilliant conversational group in America. On a clear day, a good many of the following would be assembled there for lunch and mayhem: George Kaufman, Marc Connelly, Robert Benchley, Alexander Woollcott, Franklin P. Adams, Dorothy Parker,

Newman Levy, Robert Sherwood, Howard Dietz and many others. The quips flew thick, fast and deadly, and God help you if you were a dullard! The admission fee was a viper's tongue and a half-concealed stiletto. It was a sort of intellectual slaughterhouse, and I doubt if this country will ever see its like again. They also played poker and croquet for high stakes, and hardly a week went by that quiet little Harpo didn't come away from there with a large bundle of their money.

Except for becoming a father—by the way, I was married, but I don't plan to tell you about that until later (that's the kind of autobiography this is)—I didn't do much of anything. Despite the fact that I was a big hit on the stage, I was dissatisfied. I wanted to write. The fact that I hadn't graduated from grammar school scared me and held me back. Almost all the successful writers I knew had been to college. Some had even graduated, and I envied them. "What was an actor?" I thought. "Nothing! Just a mouthpiece for someone else's words. It's the writer who makes the actor good or bad."

I finally began landing little squibs in newspaper columns. Then I started writing longer articles. A few times I pinch-hit for Woollcott, Percy Hammond and others. Then I sold a few pieces to various magazines. An article I once wrote for Franklin P. Adams in the New York *World* was picked up by H. L. Mencken and reprinted in his book, *The American Language*. Nothing I ever did as an actor thrilled me more.

I liked being an actor, hearing the laughter and bowing to the applause. I still do, but my biggest kick has always been seeing something of mine in print. Now you know why I attempted this book. It wasn't only that gypsy publisher with his box of cheap cigars.

In the theatre I had a reputation as an ad-libber. Actually, this was a kind of writing, except that up there on the stage I wasn't using a pencil and paper.

THE STORY OF my mother on the opening night of *I'll Say She Is!* has been told many times. Having four sons open on Broadway in a successful show was the climax of her career. Like any other woman, she had ordered a new dress for the occasion. When I say "ordered," I don't mean she went to Bergdorf Goodman's. She sent to Brooklyn for her dressmaker. While standing on a chair, being fitted for the gown that was soon to dazzle the first-nighters, she slipped and broke her leg.

I believe a disaster of this size would have discouraged most women from going to the theatre, but not my mother. If anything, that made the opening night even more exciting. I doubt if anyone ever entered a theatre more triumphantly than she did. Smiling and waving gaily to the audience, she was carried in on a stretcher and deposited in a front row, box seat.

This was her personal victory. This was the culmination of twenty years of scheming, starving, cajoling and scrambling. And I'm sure that, to her, that night was worth every minute of it. You'll have to concede that this was a most unusual occasion. Never in the history of the theatre had four brothers appeared on Broadway as the stars of their own show, and a little thing like a broken leg was not going to rob her of that supreme moment.

In spite of the old scenery and the shabby production, *I'll Say She Is!* was a tremendous success. Critics swooned with joy. And when they came to, they raved ecstatically. A number of them wrote, "Where have these boys been hiding all these years?" The fact is, we hadn't been hiding at all. We had been playing around New York in big-time vaudeville for a long time. I guess the critics don't get much news of the outside world high up in their ivory towers.

We played *I'll Say She Is!* for three years. Then in 1926 Sam Harris, a fine producer, put us under contract. He engaged George S. Kaufman and Morrie Ryskind, probably the best two satirical writers in the business, to do the book for us. Among Kaufman's and Ryskind's many other theatrical bull's-eyes was *Of Thee I Sing*, the first musical play to win the Pulitzer Prize. To insure the success of our new show, *Cocoanuts*, Mr. Harris engaged an unknown composer named Irving Berlin, who up to that time had knocked off only three or four hundred hit songs.

The play was a big hit. It was all about the Florida boom, and at that time Florida real estate was about the hottest topic of conversation around. Though the Berlin score was a good one, there was no big hit song in it, and this gave rise to a running gag I've had with Irving over the years.

When the First World War was in full swing and Wilson

was President, it was inevitable that sooner or later we would be drawn into the conflict. But the anti-war sentiment was very powerful, particularly throughout the Midwest. Song writers always try to capture the temper of the public in their lyrics. Irving Berlin was a song-writer. So he wrote an anti-war song which I'm sure reflected the sentiments and emotions of millions of Americans. The song was called *Stay Down Here Where You Belong*. And I'm afraid it went like this:

Down below, down below, sat the Devil talking to his son
Who wanted to go up above, up above.
He cried, "It's getting too warm for me down here and so
I'm going up on earth where I can have a little fun."

The Devil simply shook his head and answered his son,
"Kings up there, they don't care for the mothers who must
Stay at home, their sorrows to bear;
Stay at home, don't you roam.

"Although it's warm down below, you'll find it's warmer up there.
If e'er you went up there, my son, I know you'd be surprised,
You'd find a lot of people who are not civilized."

Chorus:
"Stay down here where you belong
The folks who live above you don't know right from wrong.
To please their kings they've all gone out to war,
And not a one of them knows what he's fighting for.

"'Way up above they say that I'm a Devil, and I'm bad;
Kings up there are bigger Devils than your dad;
They're breaking the hearts of mothers,
Making butchers out of brothers;
You'll find more hell up there than there is down below!"*

Many years passed, and Berlin became the most famous and popular song-writer in the world. A competitor of his bitterly complained that Berlin had used up all the holidays: "I'm Dreaming of a White Christmas," "Easter Parade," and so on. Berlin also used up most of the laurels reserved for the nation's most honoured song-writers.

* © 1914 Irving Berlin. Copyright renewed 1941.

As time went on, the lyrics and philosophy of his anti-war song embarrassed Berlin, and he never wanted to hear it again. The song had always fascinated me (it would probably take an analyst to explain why), and with the possible but not probable exception of the composer, I became the only man in the United States who remembered both the words and the music. Whenever I was at a party where Berlin was present I'd arrange that at some time during the evening someone would ask me to sing this song. Berlin could never understand this. Here he was, the greatest minstrel of our time, with hundreds of song hits to his credit, and here was his friend Groucho insisting on singing that particular song. Loudly, too, and carefully enunciating each word of this deathless (and, to Berlin, loathsome) lyric.

Many years passed, and ASCAP (American Society of Composers, Authors and Publishers), the song-writers' Santa Claus, arranged a gigantic musical salute to the "master." Every composer and lyricist in Hollywood was present. All the famous Berlin songs were sung and played by practically the entire ASCAP membership. I had arranged with Harry Ruby, the well-known song writer and sometime friend of mine, to accompany me on one of Berlin's more notable efforts. You'd never guess the title. It was an anti-war song entitled "Stay Down Here Where You Belong."

Berlin isn't a large man, and as the song progressed he seemed to grow even tinier. I suppose it wasn't a very nice thing to do, and I guess it did make him unhappy, for when the party ended Irving walked over to me and said, "Groucho, why do you persist in singing that awful song?"

"Well, Irving," I replied, "it's an anti-war song, and since you wrote it we've only been involved in three different wars. One of them—I don't remember which one—was called 'the war to end all wars.' "

"Groucho," he said, "I'll make a deal with you. Whenever you feel an irresistible urge to sing this song, communicate with me immediately by phone and I will send you one hundred dollars *not* to sing it. This," he added, "can be your private ASCAP."

A few more years rolled by. It was now 1958, and in the Sunday New York *Times* magazine section appeared a wonderful tribute to Irving Berlin on the occasion of his seventieth birthday. The article quoted him as saying, "Whenever

Groucho sees me, he insists on singing 'Stay Down Here Where You Belong.' "

I wrote him a letter in which I said:

DEAR IRVING:

I was pleased to see your face in last Sunday's *Times*, and even though you were unable to produce a song hit for *Cocoanuts* I still think you're a one-man combination of Beethoven and Shelley.

Now, about that song. If you had been a failure as a song-writer, I would never sing it. I would sing "A Pretty Girl is Like a Melody," "Oh, How I Hate to Get Up in the Morning," "Alexander's Ragtime Band," "Say It with Music" or "God Bless America." But since you have become a legend in our time, I'm sure this one lyrical disaster can do you no harm.

When you are not around I always refer to you as the man who had more song hits in *Annie Get Your Gun* than the fabled Stephen Foster had in his entire lifetime.

Yours,
Groucho.

In reply, he admitted that it was true, he didn't have a song hit in *Cocoanuts*, but he defended himself by saying that it wasn't entirely his fault. It seems he had taken a song to George Kaufman; he sat down and sang and played it for him. Kaufman listened carefully and then pronounced the song worthless. The song was "Always."

"Perhaps," Berlin concluded, "this is why I didn't have a song hit in *Cocoanuts*.

IN 1928 WE were ready to bring *Animal Crackers* into New York. On top of all the problems attendant upon launching a new musical comedy on Broadway, we found ourselves in the middle of a nasty vendetta between the Shuberts and Winchell. It was quite a to-do; whom the gods would destroy, etc. Well, you know this bit. If you don't you can find it in *Bartlett's Quotations*, probably signed "Ibid."

In the middle 'twenties Walter Winchell was riding high.

His column was a must, and in addition to the column he was also reviewing the Broadway plays. Even more powerful than Winchell, however, were the Shuberts, Jake and Lee, who were damned near monarchs of all they surveyed. This was certainly true of the legitimate theatre. They succeeded Klaw and Erlanger, the previous czars. Like all producers, they loved the critics when their shows got good reviews and hated them when their shows were rapped. Winchell had thrown a few poisoned darts at some of their recent offerings and they were terribly angry. Angry enough to issue a ukase prohibiting Mr. Winchell from entering any of their theatres.

I'm not going to defend critics. The fact is, I don't know what purpose they serve. But whatever it is, they have a right to serve it in any man's theatre, however disastrous the consequences.

I have wondered about critics for years. (Here we go again.) A play is ostensibly written for an audience, but if the critics turn thumbs down, the audience never gets a chance to see it. Who originally decided it was the critics' function to "educate" the public? If the first-nighters like a play and want it, why shouldn't the rest of the theatre-going public be allowed to see it?

Somerset Maugham, in *The Summing Up*, was asked why he quit writing for the theatre. He said that it was too difficult to please both the scullery-maid sitting in the third balcony and the critic for the London *Times*. "I believe I can write for either one," he declared, "but I can't please both. Their tastes are too dissimilar."

There used to be about ninety or a hundred legitimate theatres in New York City. Now there are about twenty. Hokum and rough-house laughter have virtually disappeared from the stage. There are scores of plays about miscegenation, homosexuals, the beat generation, dypsomaniacs and hopheads, but there is very little fun left on the stage. I believe the absence of robust laughter is partially responsible for the present condition of the theatre. Most of the gaiety has been taken out of it, and it has been removed by the critics.

One prominent reviewer (there's no point in mentioning his name) recently wrote about a play called *Make a Million*, starring Sam Levene. This is what he wrote: "This is not so much a review as a confession. I spent a good part of last evening laughing at a very bad play."

There you have it. This critic laughed all evening, but finally decided it was "a very bad play." All it was supposed to do was make people laugh, and it succeeded. They didn't announce that they were bringing in *King Lear* or *Death of a Salesman*. All they promised to deliver was a funny comedy— but that wasn't good enough for this critic.

It would be interesting to know who decided that these six critical gents in New York and a dozen other assassins scattered around the country were chosen to be the official guardians of the public taste. Why don't they lay off the theatre for a few centuries and give the average playgoer a chance to see what he wants to see?

You notice they don't attack the automobile industry. You know why? Because the injured company would promptly pull out all its advertising! No one on a newspaper ever comes out in print and says, "Don't buy those shoddy sweatshirts that Delaney's Department Store is selling for $1.78." No one ever warns you not to read the current issue of the *Saturday Evening Post* because "it's not up to last week's edition."

If you ask them why they don't criticize the new autos or the electric toasters that General Electric is manufacturing, they give you that same old time-worn answer, "Well, you see, those are industrial products and we don't criticize merchandise or business. We only review art." Well, show business isn't an art. It's a business. If you think it isn't, ask some producer who's just dropped three hundred thousand dollars in a show that the audience liked but the critics didn't.

I think that if the New York critics would pack up their typewriters, move to Outer Mongolia and stay away for about ten years, the theatre would again flourish as it did in the early 1900s, despite the competition of television, movies, bowling alleys and sex.

(After this little diatribe I wouldn't dare come into New York with the best play ever written!)

AND NOW BACK to Winchell and the two little czars, Jake and Lee. It didn't seem to matter who was in the driver's seat. At that moment, it happened to be the Shuberts. Now that they were in the saddle, they started throwing their weight around just like their predecessors. They had issued the order to bar Winchell and their word was law. We were coming into one of their theatres in New York with our new play, *Animal Crackers*, and Winchell was not to be allowed to review it. Furthermore, he was not to be permitted to enter the theatre.

By this time you know that I'm no critic lover (nor, for that matter, much of any other kind). But along with Sam Harris, the producer who had also done *Cocoanuts*, we had invested our money in this show and we didn't see any reason why the Shuberts should have the right to bar anyone from watching or reviewing it. We were supplying the talent, the money and the entire production. In return, they were renting us their theatre, and for this relatively unimportant contribution they were in for a substantial piece of the gross. It was the principle of the Boston Tea Party all over again. It wasn't too important whether Winchell reviewed the play or not. What we were defending was his right to enter the theatre, or rather, our right to let him enter.

We dressed Winchel up in one of Harpo's duplicate outfits, red wig, horn and cane, and he stood in the wings and viewed the entire performance. The Shuberts' stage manager, naturally a suspicious fellow, couldn't understand why there were two Harpos backstage, but we explained that at times Harpo was subject to peculiar seizures and whenever he threw one of these fits it was necessary for his understudy to be ready to appear in his place. Well, the show went on, Winchell reviewed it and the Shuberts never found out how it was done.

THE SHUBERTS WERE not unusual. They were no more despotic than Klaw and Erlanger, or any of the other little kings that infested the amusement industry. During the reign of K. and E. a gent named General Lew Wallace completed his masterpiece, *Ben Hur*. This threatened to be not only the book of the month, but the book of the year, and the reading public took it to its heart with the same enthusiasm with which a later generation welcomed *Gone With the Wind*. Everyone was not only talking about the book, but they were buying it in carloads. The news finally seeped through to Klaw and Erlanger.

In size they resembled Weber and Fields. (Weber and Fields resembled Mutt and Jeff, and if you don't know who Mutt and Jeff resembled—well, they resembled Klaw and Erlanger.) Klaw was the tall one and Erlanger was the little one. The only difference was that Klaw, unlike Lou Fields, never stuck his fingers in Erlanger's eye to emphasize a point.

When they finished reading the book they were steaming with excitement. Quickly telephoning the General, they told him that they were eager to negotiate for the dramatic rights. If he was interested in disposing of them, Klaw added, he would immediately dispatch Erlanger to the General's lair in Louisville, where they could work out the financial details.

Erlanger was a Hebraic-looking individual who sported a faint pot-belly, an expensive stogie and a Homburg. The following morning he was ushered into the General's august presence by a butler who was exactly three years younger than Noah. By comparison, the General looked like a teen-ager, although he was around seventy at the time. It was difficult to tell how tall he was, for at the moment he was crouched low in a deeply upholstered chair.

As Mr. Erlanger entered, the expression on the General's face was one of indifference bordering on the supernatural. Apparently Mr. E. was conditioned to a lack of cordiality when negotiating a business deal and wisely ignored the General's attitude. Not one to fool around, he immediately segued into the matter at hand. "My name is Abe Erlanger, and I believe you know why I'm here. My partner and I have both read *Ben Hur* and we think it's tops in literature. We are sure it will make a great play and we're extremely interested in buying the dramatic rights. We feel it has all the elements of a smash hit, and if we can negotiate the deal we plan on doing the chariot race on a treadmill—right on the stage! As you know, we are the most successful producers of stage plays in the whole world and we have the resources to present this to the theatre-going public with all the magnificence that your great story deserves. To make it worth your while, we are willing to pay any reasonable price."

The General listened to all this with closed eyes. For a moment Erlanger thought that his eloquence had put the old man into a hypnotic trance, but eventually the General opened one eye and stared directly through Mr. E. Then the other eye gradually opened. "Mr. Erlanger," he rasped, "are you

aware of the significance of this book? I am referring, sir, to
its religious significance." His voice began to rise. "This is not
just a book to be put on the stage for financial gain. This is
the culmination of a lifetime of ecclesiastical research, written
from the deepest recesses of my soul. This book was not written
merely for monetary gain, although," he hastily added, "I am
fully aware of its financial potentialities. I must be sure that
whoever is privileged to dramatize this story is a kindred soul.
His conception of Christianity must touch a similar chord in
my heart and make the heathen and the non-believer realize
that our Saviour was God's son."

Rising from his sunken upholstery, he tottered over to little
Erlanger. Shaking a bony and withered finger under his nose, he
said, "Mr. Erlanger, do you believe in our Lord, Jesus Christ?"

Mr. E., having been in show business all his life, was rarely
at a loss for a ready answer, but this one was a little outside
of the area he was accustomed to deal in. Momentarily stunned,
he weaved back and forth like an over-confident pug who had
just been struck a lucky blow by an inferior opponent who
had agreed to take a dive.

Finally, shaking himself free from his dazed reverie, he replied in words that not only thoroughly baffled the elderly
General, but, in my opinion, should be classed as one of the
greatest verbal come-backs of all time. "General," he said,
"you ask me if I believe in Jesus Christ. Well, frankly I don't.
My partner, Klaw, does—but he's up in Boston!"

As STARS ON Broadway we had come a long way from
the days when we were kids, living in New York. We had
had wonderful times then, or at least so it seemed to us in
retrospect. We'd been poor and there were no nurses or nan-
nies around to bother us youngsters. My mother did the housework and we just went out in the street and played until we
got hungry. If one of us got run over, that was just too bad.
You couldn't expect a woman to run a house and keep an
eye on five boys at the same time.

As I told you earlier, we used to play one o' cat, stoop-ball,
prisoner's base, leapfrog and all the other games that were
played on all the other streets. I suppose this was true of every

neighbourhood, but there was a kid on our street, named Leonard Dobbin, who was better at everything than all the other kids. His superiority wasn't just confined to the physical games. He was also the best at word games and all the other minor intellectual pursuits that kids indulge in. Besides this, he was very good-looking and snared most of the girls that were worth snaring.

Leonard had always said that when he graduated from high school he would go on to college to study law. We were all convinced that with his all-round equipment it was inevitable that, one day, he would sit in one of the higher courts of the land.

I didn't see him again until we were appearing in *Cocoanuts*, twenty years later. One night, as I sat in the dressing-room removing my painted black moustache and the rest of my make-up, the stage doorman handed me a business card. It read, "Leonard Dobbin, Attorney at Law."

Leonard was ushered in. We had been kids together and all that sort of thing, and I was glad to see him. He looked like what he was, a junior lawyer.

"I was out front tonight, Julius, and watched you," Leonard said.

In show business, an opening like that is usually followed by "You were wonderful," or "I had a great time," or "You and your brothers certainly made me laugh." Even if he had said, "The show was awful and you were terrible," I wouldn't have minded too much, but he just stood there, looking at me rather pityingly.

I was hot and tired, as most actors are when the final curtain comes down, and his attitude annoyed me. I couldn't stand it any longer and finally said, "Well, Leonard, how'd you like the show?"

He clucked his tongue a few times and kept looking at me. He wasn't really looking *at* me—he was looking *through* me. Since he still didn't answer, I didn't see much point in continuing this opening gambit. I decided on another approach. "Well, how's the world been treating you?" I asked. "And what are you doing now?"

"Didn't you read my card?" he cross-examined. "I'm a lawyer." Then drawing himself up to his full height, he added, "I'm a junior partner. I'm getting a hundred dollars a week, and it's been hinted that next year I'll be getting a hundred and twenty-five!"

At that time I was making two thousand dollars a week, but I didn't tell him this. I was determined to extract some kind of opinion from him about the show. "Leonard," I pressed on, "didn't you get any laughs out of the show?"

He finally let me have it. "The fact of the matter is, Julius, I *did* get quite a number of laughs. It was rather humorous on the whole, but that's not important."

Slightly miffed, I replied, "It's important to me! That's how I make my living." I might have added, "And a damned good one, too," but I was too polite.

"Julius," he said gravely, "I'm going to speak frankly. We were kids together and I have always held you in high regard. Now I'm going to give it to you straight from the shoulder. I watched you tonight. You're thirty-five years old and you're up on that stage making a damned fool out of yourself. I saw you in vaudeville when you were in your twenties and I didn't mind it too much then. But when I see a fellow your age leaping over furniture, dancing like a maniac and making disrespectful remarks to the women in the show, it hurts me. You've got a good mind. Why don't you apply it to something useful? You're not too old. You could still become a businessman, a physician—or maybe even an attorney. Now, wouldn't that be better than making a public spectacle of yourself before thousands of strangers?"

"Leonard," I said, "I can't tell you what these words of yours have done for me. As soon as the show closes for the season, I'm going to follow your advice, quit the theatre and get a job. A hundred dollars a week would look mighty good to me!"

"Well"—he paused reflectively—"you realize you wouldn't make a hundred dollars a week to begin with. That's real money, Julius. But I think you've got a lot of talent and I hate to see you wasting it this way. Think it over."

"I'm so happy you came back here to see me tonight," I said. "This little talk we've had has been an inspiration to me." I then shook hands with the jerk and he left.

TWO YEARS elapsed before we met again. We were then appearing in *Animal Crackers*. I was getting three thousand a week, and we had just signed with Paramount to do five pictures for $1,500,000. With the picture contract and the *Animal Crackers* salary, I was getting close to six thousand a week. *Animal Crackers* was an even bigger hit than *Cocoanuts*. The tickets were more expensive and the grosses were higher. Around the fourth month of the run, our friend Mr. Dobbin showed up. The doorman again delivered his card. This time it was engraved in gold.

As he entered my dressing-room we exchanged the usual greetings and I sat there, again hoping for a few flattering remarks. I should have known better. "Well, Leonard," I began, "how'd you like the show?" (I'd decided to get the jump on him this time.)

He looked at me sorrowfully. "Julius, I'm disappointed in you. When I left you two years ago I was under the impression that you were going to follow my advice and quit show business, but I was out front tonight, watching you, and you're still doing the same silly, ridiculous things you were doing before."

"Well, wasn't it funny?" I demanded. "Didn't you hear the audience howl with laughter?"

"Yes, I did," he admitted. "And I even got a snicker or two out of the show myself. But you're thirty-seven now. Aren't you embarrassed, at your age, acting like a nut and making a public fool out of yourself?"

He was beginning to sound like a broken record. "Leonard," I said, "let's forget it." I turned to his favourite subject. "How are you doing these days?"

"I've got news for you," he beamed. "I didn't get that twenty-five-dollar raise I expected. Instead, they raised me *fifty* dollars! And," he went on, "it won't be long before I'll be making two hundred dollars a week. Imagine! At my age, getting two hundred a week!"

Being a kindly man, I didn't have the heart to mention the six thousand a week I was collecting. I just sat there and let him rave on. Except for throwing in a few even more stuffy phrases, he delivered the same lecture he had given me two years before.

When he finally ran down, I said, "Leonard, you've convinced me! This is my farewell to the theatre. Any fellow who can pull down a hundred and fifty a week at your age makes me realize the foolishness of my ways. You are a shining example of young America on the march, and *Animal Crackers* will be my swan-song in the theatre."

I didn't see Leonard again for ten years. By this time our movies were playing all over the world, I had money in three different banks and owned a vicuña coat and two Cadillacs.

It was Easter Sunday on Fifth Avenue. Leonard Dobbin was wearing a Homburg, a dark, tight-fitting suit and a cane, and was accompanied by an extremely grubby-looking wife and two unfortunate-looking moppets. We swapped greetings. Then, with his customary tact, the blow-hard began again. "I'm bitterly disappointed in you, Julius. You told me you were going to quit the stage."

I smiled politely. "I did, Leonard. I'm in the movies, now."

"Well," he replied with a shrug. "I guess you'll always be a clown. It's a real shame. You could have been respectable. You would have made a fine lawyer."

There was no point in keeping this up, so I said, "And how are you doing, Leonard?"

His face lighted up like a pinball machine. "Julius, you won't believe it, but they made me a full partner in the firm. Last year, including commissions, I earned a walloping eighteen thousand dollars!"

I didn't want to spoil his Easter stroll by telling him that, between my movie salary and my theatre salary, I was making close to eighteen thousand, too. Only I was doing it fifty-two times a year. I simply said goodbye to the overstuffed pouter pigeon, his undistinguished family and his advice, and continued my walk along the Avenue.

I'm sure that, to this day, he is convinced that my life has been an utter failure and his a great success.

CHAPTER FIFTEEN

HOW I STARRED IN THE FOLLIES
OF 1929

Soon a much hotter business than show business attracted my attention, and the attention of the country. It was a little thing called the stock market. I first became acquainted with it around 1926. It was a pleasant surprise to discover that I was a pretty shrewd trader. Or at least so it seemed, for everything I bought went up. I had no financial adviser. Who needed one? You could close your eyes, stick your finger any place on the big board and the stock you had just bought would start rising. I never took profits. It seemed absurd to sell a stock at thirty when you knew it would double or triple within a year.

My salary in *Cocoanuts* was around two thousand a week, but this was pin-money compared to the dough I was theoretically making in Wall Street. Mind you, I enjoyed doing the show, but I had very little interest in the salary. I took market tips from everybody. It's hard to believe it now, but incidents like the following were commonplace in those days.

I was riding in an elevator at the Copley Plaza Hotel in Boston. The elevator jockey recognized me and said, "You know, Mr. Marx, there were two guys in here a little while ago. Real big shots. They were wearing double-breasted suits and they had carnations in their buttonholes. They were talking about the stock market, and believe me, brother, they looked as if they knew what they were talking about. They didn't think I was listening, but when I'm riding this elevator I always keep my ears open. I ain't going to be pushin' one of these boxes all my life! Anyway," he went on, "I heard this one guy say to the other, 'Put all the money you can get your hands on in United Corporation.' "

"What was the name of that stock?" I asked.

He gave me a scornful look. "Whatsamatter, brother? Some'pin wrong wid yer ears? I *told* ya. The man said United Corporation."

I handed him five dollars and rushed to Harpo's room. I immediately informed him about this potential gold-mine I had stumbled on in the elevator. Harpo was just finishing breakfast and was still in his bathrobe.

"There's a broker's office in the lobby of this hotel," he said. "Wait'll I get my clothes on and we'll go downstairs and grab this stock before the news of it gets around."

"Harpo," I said, "are you crazy? If we wait until you get your clothes on, that stock may jump ten points!" So I in my street clothes and Harpo in his bathrobe rushed through the lobby into the broker's office and quickly snapped up one hundred and sixty thousand dollars' worth of United Corporation on a twenty-five per cent. margin.

For the lucky few who weren't ruined in '29 and have no knowledge of Wall Street, let me explain what twenty-five per cent. margin means. For example, if you bought eighty thousand dollars' worth of stock, you only had to put up twenty thousand dollars in cash. The balance you would owe to the broker. It was like stealing money.

One Wednesday afternoon on Broadway, Chico encountered a Wall Street tipster who told him in a whisper, "Chico, I just came from Wall Street and all they're talking about down the street is Anaconda Copper. It's selling at a hundred and thirty-eight dollars a share and it's rumoured that it'll go to five hundred! Grab it before it's too late! This is right out of the horse's mouth!"

Chico, a well-known horse lover, immediately rushed to the theatre with news of this bonanza. It was a matinée day and we held the curtain for thirty minutes until our broker finally assured us that we had been lucky enough to get six hundred shares. We were ecstatic! Chico, Harpo and I were each proud owners of two hundred shares of this gilt-edged security. The broker even congratulated us. He said, "It isn't often that any-one gets in on the ground floor of a company like Anaconda."

U P A N D U P the market soared. When we were on the road, Max Gordon, the theatrical producer, used to call me long-distance every morning from New York, just to give me the market quotes. He usually reversed the charges, but who cared? The news never varied. It was always "Up, up, up." Until then I had had no idea you could get rich without working.

Max called me one morning, again reversing the charges,

and told me to buy a stock called Auburn. It was an auto-mobile company, now defunct. "Marx," he said, "this is a fast rider. It will jump like a kangaroo. Get it now before it's too late." As an afterthought, he added, "Why don't you get out of *Cocoanuts* and forget about that measly two grand a week you're pulling down? That's pin-money. The way you're hand-ling your finances, you can make more money in one hour sitting in a broker's office than you can labouring through eight performances a week on Broadway."

"Max," I answered, "there's no question that your advice is sound. But after all, I have certain obligations to Kaufman, Ryskind, Irving Berlin and my producer, Sam Harris."

What I didn't know at the time was that Kaufman, Ryskind, Berlin and Harris were also buying on margin and that, eventually, they were going to get wiped out by their financial advisers. (This was certainly a good joke on them!) However, on Max's advice, I immediately called my broker and instructed him to buy me five hundred shares of Auburn Motor Company.

A few weeks later, I was strolling the fairway at the country club with Mr. Gordon. Large, expensive Havana cigars were dangling from our lips. All was right with the world and heaven was in Max's eyes. (Also a couple of dollar signs.) Just the day before, Auburn had jumped thirty-eight points. I turned to my golfing partner and said, "Max, how long has this been going on?"

Max replied, lifting a line from Al Jolson. "Brother, you ain't seen nothin' yet!"

The curious thing about the market in 1929 was that no one ever sold a stock. The public just kept buying. One day I rather timidly asked my broker in Great Neck about this speculative phenomenon. "I don't know much about Wall Street," I began apologetically, "but what makes these stocks continue to go up? Shouldn't there be some relation between a company's earnings, its dividends and the stock's selling price?"

He looked over my head at a new victim who had just entered the office, and said, "Mr. Marx, you've got a lot to learn about the stock market. What you don't know about securities would fill a book."

"Look, my good man," I replied, "I came here seeking advice. If you can't keep a civil tongue in your head, I'll arrange to con-duct my business elsewhere! Now then, what were you saying?"

Properly chastised and thoroughly cowed, he answered,

"Mr. Marx, you may not realize it, but this has ceased to be a national market. We're now in a world market. We're receiving buying orders from all the countries in Europe, South America and even the Orient. Only this morning we got an order from Hindustan to buy one thousand shares of Crane Plumbing."

Rather warily, I asked, "You think that's a good buy?"

"Nothing better," he replied. "If there's one thing we all have to use, it's plumbing." (I could think of a few other things, but I wasn't sure they were listed on the exchange.)

"That's ridiculous," I said. "I have some Indian friends in South Dakota who have no plumbing." I laughed heartily, but he didn't, so I went on. "You say they're sending in orders for Crane Plumbing all the way from Hindustan? Hmmm. If they're using plumbing in far-off Hindustan, they must know something. Put me down for two hundred shares."

As the market continued to zoom skyward, I began to get increasingly nervous. The little judgment I had told me to sell, but, like all the other suckers, I was greedy. I was loath to relinquish any stock that was sure to double in a few months.

I frequently read stories in the newspapers today about theatre-goers complaining because they paid as much as one hundred dollars for two tickets to *My Fair Lady*. (Personally, I think it's worth the hundred.) Well, I once paid thirty-eight thousand dollars to see Eddie Cantor at the Palace.

We all know that Eddie is a fine comedian. Even he is quick to concede this. He had a wonderful act. He sang "Margie," "Now's the Time to Fall in Love" and "If You Knew Susie." He killed the audience with topical jokes, and wound up singing "Whoopee." In the vernacular, he was a "smash." He had that magnetic something that sets a great star apart from the chronic small-timer.

Cantor was a neighbour of mine in Great Neck. Being an old friend of his, at the conclusion of his act I went backstage to see him. Eddie is a very persuasive talker, and before I could tell him how much I had enjoyed his performance he pulled me into the dressing-room, quickly closed the door, looked around the empty room to see if anyone was listening, and said, "Groucho, I love you!" There was nothing odd about this greeting. This is simply the way show people talk to each other. There is an unwritten law in the theatre that when two people meet (actor and actress, actress and actress, actor and actor or any of the other sex variations or deviations), they must rigidly avoid the routine greetings that normal people use. Instead, they must pelt each other with terms of endearment that, in other walks of society, are usually restricted to the bedroom.

"Sweetie," Cantor went on, "how did you like my act?"

I looked around, thinking there might be a girl behind me. Unfortunately, there wasn't, and I realized he was addressing me. "Eddie, darling," I replied with genuine enthusiasm, "you were superb!" I was about to toss a few more bouquets at him when he looked appraisingly at me with those large, glittering eyes, spread his hands on my chest and said, "Lover boy, do you own any Goldman-Sachs?"

"Sweetheart," I answered (two can play at this game), "I not only don't own any, I never even heard of it. What is Goldman-Sachs? Is it a flour-bag?"

He grabbed me by both lapels and jerked me towards him. For a moment I thought he was going to kiss me. "Don't tell me you've never heard of Goldman-Sachs?" he said incredulously. "It's only the most sensational investment and holding company on the big board!"

He then looked at his watch and said, "Hmmm. It's too late today. The market's already closed. But, baby, the first thing in the morning, grab your hat, rush down to your broker's and snap up two hundred shares of Goldman-Sachs. I think it closed today at 156 . . . and at 156 it's a *steal!*" Eddie then patted my cheek, I patted his and we parted.

Boy! Was I glad I had gone backstage to see Cantor! Just imagine, if I hadn't gone to the Palace Theatre that matinée, I never would have had this tip. The following morning, before breakfast, I sped over to the broker's office just as the market opened. I plunked down twenty-five per cent. of thirty-eight thousand dollars and became the lucky owner of two hundred shares of Goldman-Sachs, the biggest holding company in America.

I NOW BEGAN spending my mornings sitting in a broker's office staring at a big board swarming with symbols I didn't understand. Unless I got there early, I couldn't even get in. Some of the brokerage houses were playing to more people than many of the Broadway theatres.

It seemed that almost everyone I knew was in the market. Most conversations were confined to how much so and so had cleaned up last week, or about some stock that was soon going to be split three for one. The plumber, the ice-man, the butcher, the baker, all of them panting to get rich, were tossing their puny salaries—and in many cases their life's savings—into Wall Street. Occasionally the market would falter, but then it would shake itself free from the resistance of the bears and resume its steady upward climb.

Every once in a while, some financial seer would issue a glum statement warning the public that prices were out of all proportion to their actual value, and to remember that whatever goes up must come down. But hardly anyone paid any attention to these silly conservatives and their stupid words of caution. Even Barney Baruch, the Central Park Socrates and All-American financial wizard, issued a word of warning. I don't remember the exact statement, but it went something like this: "When the market becomes front-page news, it's time to scram."

I wasn't around for the Gold Rush of '49. I mean 1849. But I imagine the fever was a good deal like the one that now infected the entire country. President Hoover was fishing, and the rest of the Federal Government seemed completely unaware of what was going on. I'm not sure that anything could have been accomplished had they stuck their noses in, but anyway the market skipped gaily on towards its doom.

One special day, the market began wavering. A few of the more nervous customers got the jitters and began to unload. It happened almost thirty years ago, and I don't recall the various stages of the catastrophe that was descending upon us, but just as everyone wanted to buy at the beginning of the rise, everyone now began unloading as panic set in. At first the selling was orderly, but soon fright kicked judgment out of the way and everyone began tossing their securities into the bull-ring, which had now turned into a bear-ring, for whatever they could salvage.

Now the brokers caught the fright and began yelling for additional margin. This was a good joke on the brokers, for most traders had run out of money and the brokers began dumping securities for whatever they would bring. I was one of the dumber ones. Unfortunately, I still had money in the bank; to avoid being sold out I now feverishly began writing cheques to replace the margins that were swiftly melting away. Then, one spectacular Tuesday, Wall Street threw in the towel and collapsed. The towel was an appropriate gesture, for by this time the whole country was crying.

SOME OF THE people I knew lost millions. I was luckier. All I lost was two hundred and forty thousand dollars. (Or one hundred and twenty weeks of work at two thousand per.) I would have lost more, but that was all the money I had. The day of the final, convulsive crash, my friend, sometime financial adviser and shrewd trader, Max Gordon, phoned me from New York. In five words, he issued a statement that I think will, in time, compare favourably with any of the more memorable quotations in American history. I'm referring to such imperishable lines as "Don't give up the ship," "Don't fire until you see the whites of their eyes," "Give me liberty or give me death!" and "I have but one life to give to my country." These words sink into comparative insignificance alongside Max's notable quote. Never the frilly type of conversationalist, this time he even ignored the traditional "Hello." All he said was, "Marx, the jig is up!" Before I could answer, the phone was dead.

In all the hogwash written by market analysts, it seems to me that no one summed up the entire shambles as succinctly as my friend Mr. Gordon. In those five words he said it all. The jig was indeed up. I think the only reason I went on living was the comforting knowledge that all my friends were in the same boat. Even financial misery, like any other kind, loves company.

Had my broker sold me out when my stocks first started sliding, I would have saved a veritable fortune. But since I couldn't conceive of their going any lower, I began borrowing money from the bank to cover the rapidly disappearing margins. The Anaconda Copper stock (remember, we held the curtain thirty minutes to cinch this one?) melted away like the snows of Kilimanjaro (don't think I haven't read my Hemingway), and finally sank to $2\frac{7}{8}$. The Boston elevator boy's hot tip on United Corporation wound up at $3\frac{1}{2}$. We bought it at 60. Cantor's matinée at the Palace was magnificent and worth as much as any performance on Broadway. But Goldman-Sachs at one hundred and fifty-six dollars? Eddie, darling, how could you? At the bottom of the market it could be snapped up for one dollar a share!

CHAPTER SIXTEEN

WHITE NIGHTS, WHY ARE YOU BLUE?

BEING TAKEN TO the financial cleaners wasn't a total loss. In return for my two hundred and forty thousand dollars, I got galloping insomnia, and in my social circle sleeplessness now began to replace the stock market as the chief topic of conversation.

Up to this time I had never realized that insomnia held so much interest for so many people. At a party, if you mentioned baseball, politics or the increase in the price of pineapples, most of the women in the crowd would wiggle over to the bar and hoist a few more. If the subject turned to facials, salad dressings or the question of whether the new skirts would have one slit or two, most of the men would start pitching pennies or wrestling with the host's great Dane (or the hostess). But after the crash, when someone moaned that he or she hadn't slept a wink the night before, guests who had been half asleep for hours would shake themselves back to consciousness and with bloodshot eyes listen with both ears to the victim's detailed account of last night's harrowing hours.

I never claimed to be the top man of this weird breed, but as a professional owl since '29 I have acquired a mass of information that may be helpful to the amateurs who have only been plucking helplessly at the electric blanket for nine or ten years. So lie down and let's have a little talk about your problem, shall we? To begin with, what *is* your problem? Is it your tax bracket? Something trivial like the hydrogen bomb? Or is it something important, like a leaky faucet that, strangely enough, is silent all day and only starts dripping around three in the morning?

You must realize that not all insomniacs are afflicted with the same blights, and what cures one man is another man's poison. What about the bed you are floundering around in? Do you use a soft mattress, an orthopaedic one, or do you sleep on the springs like the Hindus? Many physicians recommend sleeping on the floor if you arrive home late at night half crocked or, in medical terms, "with a bun on." I, on the other hand, advise you to forget the doctors, and advise you to sleep on the floor when sober. It has many things to recommend it. To begin with, you eliminate the cost of a bed. The money saved here can then be used for getting drunk again. Moreover, if you sleep on the floor there is no danger of falling—unless you happen to be sleeping near an open manhole.

Sleep is an elusive minx and great care must be taken not to frighten her. If you pursue her too aggressively, she will turn tail like a fawn and scamper away.

An ex-girl friend of mine named Hornblower (who, for the sake of convenience, we will call Delaney) had a husband who hadn't slept since they were on their honeymoon. I mean their second honeymoon. He slept all through that one. She was a comparatively loyal wife and tried to help him woo sleep with hypnotism, tickling his toes and reading aloud to him out of *Fortune* magazine and a banned synopsis of *The French and Indian Wars*. None of these soporifics seemed to help, and one night, in high dudgeon, he told her to mind her own business and he would work out his problem in his own way.

One evening, while I was playing whist with his wife, I watched Delaney (*né* Hornblower) prepare for bed. This particular night he chose Formation L-2: hot noodle soup, a mustard bath, three aspirins, ear-muffs and a black sleeping mask. Early the following morning, desperate and wan from his customary sleepless night, he staggered into the living-room bent on suicide. In the meantime, his wife and I, bored with whist, had abandoned the game some hours back and were now playing a different game. Naturally, we had forgotten all about Delaney and his problem, and when he entered the room around five, still wearing the ear-muffs and the black mask, I mistakenly diagnosed a stick-up and beat a hasty and undignified retreat through the back-yard.

Some weeks later, at an off-beat *bistro*, I ran into Mrs. Delaney and, naturally, inquired about her husband and his insomnia. She told me that ever since that night he had had no further trouble getting to sleep. The cure was surprisingly simple. He had quit the bedroom and had taken to sleeping on the couch in the living-room. His wife and I never played whist again. But I still have my insomnia.

MANY PEOPLE get a good night's rest by counting sheep. If possible, it's advisable to have the sheep in the bedroom. However, if you are allergic to wool (and most of the woollen sweaters I buy seem to be), you can also court sleep by counting panthers. Of course, there is always the danger that the panthers may eat you, but if you suffer from insomnia that is really the best thing that can happen to you.

So far we have discussed only the physical or less aesthetic side of sleep. But what is your frame of mind, and how are you fixed for traumas? What thoughts are percolating through your thick skull as you prepare for nighty-night? Is your brain in a whirl? Is it shooting sparks and flying off into outer space?

If you are married, and if your breakfast companion looks like a small green guest from another planet, you unquestionably have a serious problem confronting you. Let's say Sophia Loren is your dream girl. (This is just a hypothetical statement, as mine happens to be Sophia Loren, Marilyn Monroe and Ava Gardner combined.) But for the sake of peace and quiet, let's assume it's Sophia Loren only. Now there is certainly nothing wrong with that. Millions of fine, upstanding American youths are thinking of her night and day. Now then, before you hit the sack, shake yourself loose from this folly and say, "Man," or "Julius," or whatever your name happens to be, "Look here, man (or Julius), I'm going to talk to you like a Dutch uncle. You're married to a loyal wife and a steady provider, so think clean, man, think clean!"

If this doesn't work, take a hot foot-bath, three cups of cocoa and, as soon as day breaks, hop out of bed and grab a jet plane for Vegas, Reno or Mexico City.

ANOTHER OBSTACLE to the pursuit of sleep is the habit of mulling over past mistakes. This is a fruitless hobby at best, unless you happen to be the type who goes to bed with a watermelon tucked under his arm. A minor catastrophe took place during the run of *Animal Crackers* in 1928 that enabled me to mull myself into a pretty fair stretch of insomnia.

One night I was painting on my black moustache for the evening performance when the stage doorman handed me a card and said, "There's a Mr. Evans outside. He wants to see you. Says it's important."

Being the wary type, I asked, "Is he a process-server? An insurance agent? What's it about?"

The doorman shrugged. "Search me. All I know is, he looks like ready cash. He's got an expensive suit on, and he's carrying a cane."

This didn't sound like anyone who was going to put the bee on me for a loan, so I said, "Okay, send him in."

He entered and I quickly sized him up. He was Ivy League with a dash of Rutgers thrown in for good measure. We shook hands and he went right to bat.

"Mr. Marx," he began, "you are undoubtedly one of the most renowned cigar-smokers in the whole world."

I accepted this well-deserved compliment with good grace, and he proceeded. "I am here as a representative of the advertising agency that handles the nation's biggest cigarette account. If you will endorse our cigarette, we will give you fifteen hundred dollars. I have the cheque and the contract right here with me."

Mr. Evans paused significantly and uttered the name of what was indeed the best-known cigarette made in America. By now you must have read enough of this farrago to guess the name. Yes—it was nothing less than that world-famous brand—Delaney Cigarettes!

"Mr. Evans," I said, "for fifteen hundred dollars I would find it indecent and disloyal to switch my allegiance from an industry that, time and time again, I have lifted by its boot-straps from the very depths of financial chaos. It's unquestionably true that I'm one of the most famous cigar-smokers in the world. Perhaps the most famous. And for that very reason I would deem it a betrayal of the entire Havana tobacco industry were I to endorse anything as shoddy as a cigarette."

Halfway through this pompous statement I realized I hadn't said anything that made sense. The huckster fortunately ignored this stream of bilge and continued. "Well, would you feel disloyal if, instead of fifteen hundred, we raised the ante to twenty-five hundred?"

I shook my head. I was rather angry by this time. "Mr. Evans, my integrity knows no bounds. It cannot be measured by anything as gross as money. It extends to twenty-five hundred and far, far beyond that. One of the few things a man has as he goes through life," I went on, "is his good name and his reputation for incorruptibility. I have no intention of sacrificing either of them for a paltry twenty-five hundred dollars! And now, if you please, good night."

Mr. Evans ignored this grandiose hogwash too, and proceeded as if he hadn't heard a word.

"Suppose, Mr. Marx," he craftily purred, "that instead of twenty-five hundred dollars I were to offer you a cheque for five thousand? Would you then be willing to endorse Delaneys?"

At the mention of five thousand dollars my integrity began to waver just a smidgin. Five thousand was a lot of moolah. I was tempted to yield, but after the snooty speech I had just delivered, I had no choice but to maintain my attitude.

The zealous Mr. Evans was now hot on the scent. "Five thousand dollars is quite a sum, Mr. Marx. You could buy two Cadillacs with that much money."

"Mr. Evans," I haughtily replied, "you may not be aware of it, but I *have* two Cadillacs. What would I do with four?"

"Hmmmm," he replied. "Well, you could give one to each of your brothers."

Drawing myself up to my full height, I declared, "*All* the Marx brothers have two Cadillacs."

"Okay," he surrendered, "let's forget about the cars. I must say you're a hard man to do business with. Apparently you have no interest in money." (I was about to say, "Like hell I haven't!" but caught myself in the nick of time.) "Now I am going to make you one more offer—and it's my final offer. You can take it or leave it. I'll give you seven thousand five hundred dollars if you will just put your name on this piece of paper agreeing to endorse Delaney Cigarettes."

At the mention of seventy-five hundred dollars I grew faint. My chronic low blood pressure jumped almost to normal, and the room began spinning. As greed began to replace rectitude, I quickly sidled over and locked the dressing-room door to make sure that Evans couldn't escape. I turned and looked him square in the eyes. "Now then, before I sign, are you sure this is your final offer?"

"You're damned right!" he said. "Seventy-five hundred dollars is a lot of money for doing no work at all."

"Okay. Give me the contract." I hurriedly signed it and he handed me a cheque made payable to Groucho Marx in the sum of seventy-five hundred dollars. I must confess that this puzzled me. How did he know that I was going to turn down the fifteen-hundred, twenty-five-hundred and five-thousand-dollar offers and hold out for seventy-five hundred? I quickly pocketed the cheque, we shook hands and I ushered him to the door. Just before he said goodbye, he reached into his pocket and pulled out another cheque. He showed it to me. It was made payable to Groucho Marx, and the amount was ten thousand dollars! I'll never forget his last words as he ripped it to shreds. He said, "Mr. Marx, if you had held out a little longer, you could have had the ten!"

I wasn't very funny on the stage that night.

CHAPTER SEVENTEEN

MEANWHILE, BACK AT THE RANCH HOUSE

For those readers who are not happy with an auto-biography unless the author throws in a fistful of vital statistics from time to time, this chapter is disrespectfully submitted. Besides, my meddling editor forced me. He insists he can't bill the book as an autobiography unless I tell something about myself. Frankly, I can think of much spicier subjects.

In the latter half of the 'twenties, then, to whom it may concern, my sex was male, my height was five feet eight, my hair was a grizzled black, my eyes grey, my weight 153½ stripped (which wasn't often enough), and I was living in a ten-room house in Great Neck, Long Island, with a wife and two small children. One son named Arthur and one daughter named Miriam, if you really insist on the details.

This son had appeared on the scene around the time that the Eighteenth Amendment became the law of the land. It's not much to be proud of, but during the thirteen years of pro-hibition I believe my son, Arthur, held the distinction of being the youngest bootlegger in America.

We were playing at the Orpheum Theatre in Vancouver, and in those days my family came along on tour with me. Canada, being a civilized country, was never taken in by the will-o'-the-wisp promises of prohibition. Almost every vaude-ville actor who played in Canada managed, one way or an-other, to sneak a few bottles back to the land of the free and the home of the bootlegger.

Arthur was then three months old. I don't know if this is true today, but in those days infants wore long, flowing gowns. We had bought two bottles of Canadian whisky in Vancouver. As was the custom, when you re-entered the United States, you were frisked for contraband. My wife tucked our illegal two quarts inside the folds of Arthur's gown. As the vaudeville actors trooped through Customs, the officials searched through the trunks, suitcases, scenery and other likely places of con-cealment, but we out-foxed them, for they never suspected that this picture of American motherhood and her innocent child were sneaking two bottles of fire-water into the country.

The moral of this story is, if you expect to smuggle something in from another country, be sure to provide yourself with a mother and an infant in a long, flowing gown.

PROHIBITION DID many things to me. Not only to me, but to the rest of the nation. I'm sure that many well-meaning people who voted for it, and approved of it, did so because they were convinced that it would only be a few weeks before everybody would smash their remaining booze bottles against the wall and take the pledge.

This isn't a particularly novel observation, but the world is full of people who think they can manipulate the lives of others merely by getting a law passed. There are large groups in America who, if they could swing it, would prohibit the use of everything that they didn't personally approve of—smoking, drinking, dancing, going to the movies, eating Italian salami and, if it could be regulated, even love.

Well, we now know how successful the Eighteenth Amendment was. It not only didn't stop anybody from drinking, but it helped to create the big-league hoodlum who today is almost as powerful as the Government.

We always had our normal share of pickpockets, forgers, bank-robbers, wife-beaters and assorted petty criminals. But why steal an old lady's purse or the pennies out of a blind man's tin cup when you could make millions manufacturing fake booze? Despite the Eighteenth Amendment and the gradual disappearance of real whisky, people were still thirsty and still craved a shot now and then. But the Government, with its customary wisdom, instead of allowing its citizens to drink moderately like ladies and gentlemen, now fixed it so that the bonded whisky we drank was sometimes aged in the wood for as much as two whole weeks.

Millions of people, teetotallers all their lives, who had never been in a saloon or a night club and were indifferent to the joys of a highball or a martini, suddenly developed a yen for hooch. I was one of those millions. I never had a drink before January 16, 1920. It wasn't that I disapproved of it, morally, but I just didn't like the taste of the stuff. As a matter of fact, I still don't. I drink it now and then at parties to avoid being caught sober. But with the advent of Prohibition, I came to the conclusion that if it was illegal there must be something to it that I had never discovered.

The day the big blow fell, I started to spend a good deal of my time negotiating with silk-shirted bootleggers for their watered-down booze with expensive labels. They assured me that this stuff was "right off the boat." From the way it burned my gullet on the way down, I guess it was right off the boat— just scraped off the sides and bottled.

In 1926 I was living in Great Neck, and commuting to the theatre. Talk about Sodom and Gomorrah, Fire Island or Hollywood, five years after the Volstead Act became law a good percentage of the crowd I ran with on Long Island spent most of their time getting crocked. I was still a moderate drinker, not because I was eager to obey the law, but because I was afraid that if I drank too much of the rot-gut that was being peddled, I would die before my time. I went to parties where around 2 A.M., or even earlier, the guests would be stacked up like cordwood. Oh, I know you can get just as drunk today (or even tomorrow), and if you are an earnest drinker you can wake up the next morning with a good-sized hang-over, but at least you're drinking whisky. And real whisky won't kill you unless you're a pig.

Despite the fact that the drinking of fire-water is now legal, America still seems self-conscious about it. You can't advertise it on TV, not even on the late, late shows that don't come on until after midnight. In the magazine ads., for example, no one comes right out and says, "Brother, if you want to get stinking drunk, Old Snake Bite is the booze for you." No, they warily circle around the truth like a man locked in a small room with a wounded wild cat.

If they're selling bourbon, the ad. will show an old colonel sitting on a tree stump outside a small distillery. He is fault-lessly attired and topped off with a cream-coloured Stetson. In his right hand he is holding a glass of ten-year-old red-eye and exhorting you in pure, homestead Kentuckian, in the following fashion, "Lissen, friend, we're jes a li'l ol' distillery. We don't make much likker. But, by Jiminy, what we do distill spends seven years coursin' through charcoal casks! You see, friend, we're jes a li'l ol' distillery."

Sometimes the ad. will consist of three men sitting on a white horse, gaily lapping up vodka martinis. Personally, I have trouble enough remaining on a horse without the additional responsibility of dangling a vodka martini in mid-air. Besides, it seems to me that the top of a horse isn't the most comfortable place to get drunk. Why don't those three bar-flies go to a saloon if they want to tie one on? It certainly would be less conspicuous.

I hate to admit it, but few of us can resist the power and pressure of modern, high-tension advertising. This particular ad. has softened me up to such a degree that I now find myself unwilling to drink a vodka martini unless I'm sitting with two other men on top of a white horse. Another thing that has always intrigued me about this ad. is: Who owns this animal? And what is its sex, if any? Is it owned by an advertising agency? Or is it just a stray white horse that happened to be roaming the countryside one day and, having nothing better to do, deliberately walked under these three drunks who were sitting in a tree, hoisting vodka martinis? Does each of the three men own a piece of the horse? If so, which piece? Or is it a co-operative horse, jointly owned in its entirety by the three men? Suppose one of them wants to go saddle-riding? What happens to the other two? Do they return to the tree? Or do they just hang there in mid-air until their companion gets back with the nag?

Some day, some kindly sage will answer these vital questions for us. In the meanwhile, we can only wonder.

I DON'T WANT TO mention any names, but some of my best and most talented friends died long before their time, thanks to Prohibition. The amount of damage wreaked on this country by the blue-noses who were responsible for this act can never be estimated. Prohibition created Al Capone, Dutch Schultz and hundreds of other "Little Caesars."

Well, enough social philosophy. To get back to Great Neck, many of those who couldn't afford to pay the overblown prices the bootleggers were charging, now decided to make their own joy juice. I had a friend (now dead) who used to mix orange juice with grenadine and then, as an added fillip, drop ten or fifteen drops of ethyl gasoline into the mixture.

One day, my father came to the house. When I offered him a drink he shook his head. "Groucho," he said, "why do you drink that rotten gin? Why don't you drink wine?"

"Look, Pop," I answered, "the wine you get nowadays is just as bad as the booze. I might just as well drink grain alcohol."

He smiled. "Listen, Groucho, you know I come from France. Not Paris or Marseilles, but from the wine country. I can make you a wine that's as good as any of the vintage wines you could get here before Prohibition."

"How are you going to make wine?" I asked. "You know grapes are out of season."

"I don't use grapes," he answered.

"You can make wine without grapes? That's a good trick, if you can do it!"

"Grapes are old-fashioned," he declared. "I use white raisins and malt. You get me three dozen wine bottles and corks and I'll make you a vintage wine in three weeks that will have such a bouquet you won't be able to keep your friends away from the house."

Pop's face lighted up. "Maybe we go in business together. Marx's wine, made with white raisins, malt and a secret formula. We'll have stores all over the world!"

This last statement had a familiar ring. "Pop," I said, "you may have stores all over the world, but you won't have them in the United States."

"Nonsense!" he replied. "They can't stop you from making a little wine. It's against the law? Nonsense! Anything you make in your own home is your own private business. And if they try to interfere with us," he added, "I'll sue the Government for every nickel they've got!" He looked at me craftily. "You know you can do that now under a new law that's just been passed. It's called the Mann Act."

THE NEXT MORNING Pop happily made his way down to the cellar, lugging along eight feet of rubber hose, assorted corks, bottles, raisins, malt and a large canvas bag.

"Pop," I asked, "what's in the bag?"

"Groucho," he answered, "even though you're my own son, I can't tell you that. That's my secret." Poking the bag significantly, he added, "That's the stuff that does the trick! Everyone else who makes wine just uses raisins and malt. But without this stuff"—he poked the bag again—"all they get is white dish-water. You wait. Marx's Wine Importers and Exporters. We'll make millions!"

About five o'clock that afternoon the mysterious concoction was finished and all the bottles were neatly stacked, cork down, against the wall. My father looked pretty beat when he came up out of the basement. "Groucho," he asked, "do you know you have rats down there?"

"Of course," I replied. "Where do you want me to have them—in the living-room?"

"Why don't you try getting rid of them?" he went on, completely unaware that I had just unloaded a terrific joke.

"I've tried getting rid of them, but it's a hopeless job. You see, Pop, our house is right near the corner, just a few feet away from a sewer. The rats evidently come up out of the sewer and get into our cellar through some subterranean passage. I've had exterminators from all parts of Long Island. They've set traps and they've sprinkled poison around. I don't think there's anything they haven't tried, but nothing has helped."

"You know," he said, "while I was filling the bottles a rat jumped over my knee."

"Yes, Pop, I know. He's one of the best jumpers we have down there. I've been thinking seriously of entering him in the Olympic Games next year."

Whenever I had to go downstairs to stoke the furnace, I always armed myself with a baseball bat. I once killed four rats in one day. I became pretty good at it. It was either them or me, and since I had paid for the house and the rats hadn't, it seemed only fair that my interests take precedence over theirs.

One night, about three weeks later, I had just gone to bed when there was a terrific roar and the house shook as though an earthquake had struck. Quickly putting on the bottom half of my pyjamas (and now you know how I sleep! . . . talk about your candid autobiographies!), I rushed downstairs and joined the rest of my family, who were making a mad dash for the front door.

There was no one else in the street. "That's odd," I thought. "This must be a private earthquake. Apparently mine was the only house visited."

We stood outside, quivering with cold and fright and fearful that the quake might play a return engagement. When day broke, we nervously crept back to our beds. Around noon my father arrived.

"What's the matter?" he asked. "You all look sick. Something happened?"

"Pop," I said, "at three o'clock this morning an earthquake struck our house and we haven't had any sleep."

"An earthquake? Hmmm. What you all need is a good, stiff drink of my wine," he said. "That's why I'm here. Today the three weeks is up and the wine is ready."

He should have come a day earlier. What we thought was an earthquake was just my father's wine exploding. Broken glass and corks were strewn all over the cellar and the wine was flowing as though it was New Year's Eve on an expense account. In addition to all the debris, a dozen rats were sleeping the sleep of the dead. At first I thought they were drunk, but there wasn't a hiccup in the group, so I assumed they were connoisseurs of wine and didn't care much for my father's vintage.

I never did get to drink that wine. But during the eight years we lived in the Great Neck house, we never saw a rat again. Although I have no way of knowing, I am now inclined to believe that the secret ingredient in my father's mysterious canvas bag was the first step towards the hydrogen bomb.

CHAPTER EIGHTEEN

THEY CALL IT THE GOLDEN STATE

At the end of our eight ratless years in Great Neck, my wife, the children and I moved to California, along with a large assortment of related Marxes of various sizes, shapes and sexes. *Animal Crackers* had closed after a two-year run on Broadway. The reason for our family gold-rush to the West was a picture contract that was balm to the wounds of '29.

We piled aboard the Santa Fe and set off to stake a tentative claim in movieland. The year was 1931. When we stepped off the train at Los Angeles the air was sweet with a heavy blend of orange and lemon blossoms. The rush to California had not yet begun, and Hollywood still had that quiet, pastoral air about it.

The talkies had just intruded on the movie industry and scared the hell out of most of its members. Gilbert, Garbo, Charlie Ray, Tom Mix, William S. Hart, Fairbanks and Pickford and a few others comprised the movie royalty. Taxes were still nominal, and Hollywood's kings and queens lived far more luxuriously than most of the reigning families in Europe. Most of them tossed their money around as though they manufactured it themselves in the cellar. They went in for solid gold bathtubs, chauffeur-driven Rolls Royces, champagne for breakfast and caviar every fifteen minutes. It was the kind of world that today only exists in the pages of movie magazines and for the sons of a few Latin American dictators.

There was plenty of talent in the top twenty, but the rest got by mostly on their faces and their figures. Some of the girls knew the producers much better than their wives did. In time, many of them became the wives and the ex-wives became agents or sold real estate.

This was a Never Never Land that hadn't been paralleled since the red-hot days of Rome. The parties were lush, and so were most of the guests. No party was considered a success unless a number of the survivors were tossed into the swimming pool in their evening clothes, and I don't mean pyjamas.

Today's movie star is of a different breed. He's as well

insulated against financial misfortune as the Rockefeller Foundation. He has an agent, a tax expert, a lawyer and a business manager. If he behaves himself, he is allowed to have as much as fifty dollars a week spending money. A good many of them are in oil, cattle and real estate. I know two stars who own a sheep ranch in Australia. One of my friends owns a bowling alley, and if he happens to be between pictures he spends his evenings setting up pins.

Maybe I'm just out of circulation, but Hollywood today is one of the stuffiest and most dignified communities in the United States. The few names who do step out sneak off to Las Vegas, New York or Europe. Most everyone hits the sack by midnight, either to be on the set bright and early the next morning, or to meet their tax man to learn the latest gimmick in capital gains. It's getting to be just like Philadelphia. Ben Franklin would feel right at home here these days.

WHEN WE FIRST arrived here nearly everyone still travelled on the Chief. This wasn't an Indian. The Chief was the crack train on the Santa Fe. Today, except for a few cowards, almost everyone flies. In those days it took seventeen hours to fly from New York to Los Angeles, and for an extra fee you could get a berth and two sleeping pills. The planes were tri-motor Fords, and at times they made as much as 125 miles an hour, unless an engine flew off. When that happened the company usually conceded that the trip had been a failure.

There was an actor who was one of the brightest stars at a major studio, and he appeared mainly in pictures about flying. He was always the hero and he always portrayed a fearless pilot who, in the last reel, ruthlessly mowed down dozens of the enemy planes. No one in all Hollywood was as brave as he was. It wasn't generally known, but he had never flown in a real plane. He was scared to death of them and around the studio he made no secret of it. When he flew in a movie, it was always a double who did the dirty work. In the close-up the audience was allowed to gaze upon our hero's grim profile, nonchalantly chewing gum as he contemptuously machine-gunned the Hun or the wily Oriental, depending on which war it was.

This star had a dame in New York, but unfortunately the dame had a husband in Europe who cabled that he was soon returning to his loved one. At this news, she immediately phoned our hero and told him that if he expected to hold her in his arms, he had better forget about those four long dreary days on the train and hop a plane. She said, "Look, if you fly all day at the studio for money—you can certainly fly one night for love." He had no answer to this. And I doubt if you have.

The thought of his girl-friend's husband having the effrontery to return from Europe just as he was about to visit the man's wife filled him with despair and rage. Rage eventually conquered despair and gave him the false courage he needed to embark on such a hazardous flight.

I happened to be travelling on the same plane, but (I regretfully add) not for the same reason. As soon as the plane left Burbank, our hero began to whimper like a toy poodle. Flying was moderately dangerous in those days, but the airlines were smart and had installed beautiful hostesses on each plane to keep the male passengers distracted. Our friend kept looking out of the window and, as the ground receded, beads of perspiration began trickling down his clammy brow.

"What's the matter, Delaney?" I asked. (By now you know why I use a pseudonym.) "Why do you keep looking out of the window and squirming in your seat? You're not afraid of the wild blue yonder, are you?"

He looked at me with glazed eyes. "What's the first stop?" I said, "Phoenix, Arizona."

"Well," he announced, "I don't know about you, but at Phoenix I'm getting the hell out of this crate!"

I decided the best way to handle this craven was to ring for the hostess, a real knockout, and have her turn on the charm. While she tried to soothe him with the airline's standard flirtatious line of dialogue, I tried to help her by shaming him back to manhood.

"I saw your latest movie," I said. "The one where you shot down seven of the enemy aircraft. You certainly were brave! You sure know your way around up in those clouds. Tell me, don't you ever get scared?"

He looked at me, he looked at the hostess, and then he asked, "How long before we land at Phoenix?"

As soon as we were directed to fasten our seat-belts for the landing, he collected his hand luggage and began heading for the exit. The hostess and I grabbed him. He was too weak with fright to offer much resistance, and after some scuffling we finally were able to shove him back into his seat. The moment the plane was aloft again he turned to me and asked, "What's the next stop?"

"Nashville, Tennessee," I answered.

"How long before we get there?"

"About four hours." I patted his shoulder reassuringly. "Unless, of course, we crash!"

He blanched. "Well, don't think we couldn't crash! Anyway, Nashville is my favourite town. I have a lot of friends there, and that's where I'm getting off, and there isn't a man or a woman on this death-trap who can stop me!"

As the plane hit the ground at Nashville, he again made a grab for his effects. But this time when they opened the door, I stood in front of him, blocking his passage. I now began shouting his name. (It was a famous one.)

"If you get off here," I yelled, "every newspaper in America will be carrying this story tomorrow on the front page. Listen, you dope, the world thinks of you as a great hero and you can't afford to let them find out otherwise. If the public gets wind of your yellow streak, it will kill you professionally. You'll be laughed out of show business! You might even have to go to work!"

At the mention of the word "work," he paled. It had been years since he had poured gas into an Essex. "I'd rather be back at that gas station than up in this heap of junk!" he yelled, trying desperately to push me out of the way.

H E WAS HALFWAY out of the plane when help arrived in the form of the new hostess, wiggling her way up the boarding ramp. The first one was pretty. Very pretty. This second one was almost beyond description. She was a combination of Garbo and Helen of Troy. I'm sure this embarrassing situation was an old story to her, for she immediately took over and began turning on all the oil, charm and sex she had—and she had plenty of all three—enough for every man on the plane, including the pilot, the navigator and two fellows she had just left at the airport.

Our hero slunk back to his seat, ashamed of his cowardly behaviour before this fabulous doll. As the plane took off again, he turned to me and whispered weakly, "Groucho, what's the next stop?"

I answered, "Washington, D.C."

"I'll get out there," he said. "I'll sneak out quietly and no one will notice it."

"Now just a minute," I said. "You've gone all this way. The other passengers all know you're on the plane. Don't tell me you haven't guts enough to go the rest of the way. It's only two hours' flight time from Washington to New York!"

"I don't care if it's only two minutes!" he whispered hoarsely. "Can't you see I'm a nervous wreck? I tell you, I can't take any more! I've got a gun on me and I'll kill the first one who tries to stop me!" He eyed me appraisingly.

The plane was now nearing Washington. The hostess had tried everything. She pulled out stops on her charm that, up to then, I'm sure she never knew she had. "Listen, fellah," she pleaded, "please don't leave. It will be a blot on my record. Please stay on board till we reach New York."

I may be mistaken, but I thought I heard her add, "Look, if you'll just stay on the plane, as soon as we leave Washington, I'll climb in the berth with you!" If she had made me this proposition I would have stayed on the plane for ever, at least as far as Siam, but neither this unbelievably attractive offer nor my added eloquence had any further effect on "Old Yeller." As soon as the plane grounded he quickly scooped up his bags and was out of there while the propellers were still turning.

A few days later I met him in New York. After the initial greetings, I asked, "Well, Lindbergh, how did you get here?"

"Easy," he replied. He was all smiles now. "I took the night train out of Washington and arrived here the following morning. Believe me, that's the only way to travel. And you can bet your last dollar that no one, but *no one*, will ever get me on a plane again!"

Our hero spent a week in New York with his girl-friend, seeing the shows and hitting the hot spots. On the seventh day an emissary arrived from the studio and regretfully informed him that he had to be back in Hollywood the very next day for some retakes. It seems the picture had an immediate release date and the shooting had to be done within the next thirty-six hours. The only possible way to meet this schedule was to fly back.

At this news, our friend threw a large-sized tantrum. He screamed, "I'll quit the business before I let anyone get me up in that lousy air again!"

The studio's representative, however, was a much smarter man than our hero—or your narrator. He didn't insist on anything. In fact, he said nothing. That night he took our friend on a tour of the night clubs and saloons and got him blind drunk. I don't mean just plain drunk; I mean unconscious! He then whisked him over to the airport and poured him on a plane bound for Los Angeles.

By the time the hostess brought him to, with the aid of cold compresses, smelling salts and a few cartons of black coffee, the plane was landing at Los Angeles. A studio car met our friend at the airport and rushed him directly to the set. The dresser stuffed him back into his pilot's outfit, the director dumped him into the prop plane and, as the cameras started grinding, there he sat, once more the flying dare-devil that all America knew and loved.

WHEN *Animal Crackers* closed and we went west for Paramount, our first movie was to be *Cocoanuts*. Soon after we arrived I was called into a conference and informed that I would have to discard the black, painted moustache. When I asked why, they explained, "Well, nobody's ever worn a black painted moustache on the screen. The audience isn't accustomed to anything as phony as that and just won't believe it."

"The audience doesn't believe us, anyhow," I answered. "All they do is laugh at us and, after all, isn't that what we're getting paid for?"

Talk about sticklers for tradition! We finally had to compromise with them. We agreed to shoot an experimental scene with the painted moustache and run it at a local theatre. The reaction was the same as it had been at the Fifth Avenue Theatre back in our vaudeville days. The audience didn't seem to care what kind of a moustache I wore so long as the jokes were funny.

On the stage I frequently stepped out of character and spoke directly to the audience. After the first day's shooting on *Cocoanuts*, the producer (who has since retired from the movies for the good of the industry) said, "Groucho, you can't step out of character and talk to the audience."

Like all people who are glued to tradition, he was wrong. I spoke to them in every picture I appeared in. (Sometimes they answered back. This I found rather disconcerting.) Nevertheless, the movie industry went on just the same, turning out its share of good and bad pictures, and nobody seemed to care whether I stepped out of character.

THERE ARE PEOPLE who do nothing all their lives but fight progress or change. I'm sure it was their ancestors who hooted at the first self-starter and laughed loudly at the Wright brothers and their foolish attempts to get that contraption off the ground.

I'm equally sure that farmers were pretty sceptical when it was patiently explained to them that plumbing didn't necessarily have to be out in the back-yard near the pigsty but could be brought right into the house where they lived. And many cows must have been indignant and outraged when the farmer's familiar horny hand disappeared and was replaced with an electrical device tied to their udders.

Imagine how chagrined the barbers must have been when men first started using electric razors. (Incidentally, if this beatnik trend towards the wearing of beards continues, it won't be long before both sexes will be sporting foliage. When that day comes, I predict there will be only one barber left in the whole world—and he will be in Seville, shaving peaches.)

To GET ABOUT twenty years ahead of my story, I had somewhat the same experience when *You Bet Your Life* was first going to go on television, after having been a radio show for several seasons. The first thing they asked me was how I would dress. I told them I would wear a regular suit of clothes, sit on a high stool and question people about their lives just as I had been doing on radio.

A blood brother of all the other obstructionists bobbed up and said, "Mr. Marx, you realize this isn't radio. This is television, and television is just the movies on a smaller screen. You've got to give them action. You can't just sit there like a bump on a log." (This chap was a real wit.) "You've got to give them that funny walk and leap around the stage," he insisted.

"Rubbish," I said.

"Rubbish! Rubbish!" he exclaimed, as he jumped up and down. "What kind of an answer is that?"

"Not a very good one," I conceded, "but then you're no Ring Lardner yourself."

"You mean you're just going to sit on a stool and not move at all?" he demanded.

"Not a muscle," I replied.

"But you can't do that," he insisted.

"Now listen, you Brooks Brothers radical," I said. "I saw Sam Levenson the other night on TV. He wore a regular suit of clothes, stood in one spot and delivered a monologue. And when he finished, the audience yelled for more."

He had no answer to that. He just reached into his charcoal-grey coat pocket, pulled out two dry martinis, drained them and silently walked away, a beaten man.

A word about sponsors. I have heard all of the tales and most of the jokes about interference and how some of their wives are the dominant voice in deciding what goes into a show. This may have been true during the early days of radio and TV, but most of the current sponsors are mighty sharp cookies. If the show's ratings are high enough, you never hear from them. If the show doesn't succeed after a reasonable length of time—let's say one week—it's goodbye, Charlie.

RETURNING TO THE subject of this chapter, if any, an audience sitting in a movie theatre has no idea of the many curious and difficult problems that confront the director. For example, when we shot *A Day at the Circus* we had an important scene that required a gorilla. I know this will be argued, but there are very few live gorillas roaming the streets of Hollywood. The fact is, there were only two in the entire industry and they were booked up for years. It was definitely a simian monopoly, and I suggest that when the Government gets through investigating the footsie-footsie relationship that exists between du Pont and General Motors, they might (with great benefit to the amusement industry) take a long look at the gorilla situation.

Since we had neither the time nor the equipment to capture and train a live gorilla, we were obliged to engage an actor who specialized in playing these roles. Show business is the only profession extant where a man can earn a moderate fortune merely by standing inside a gorilla skin.

The complications were many. It seems the actor we had engaged to play the gorilla had an agent, but he had no gorilla skin. We then discovered that the gorilla pelt also had an agent. The day the scene was to be shot, both agents were on the set to protect their interests and also to make sure they collected their commissions. It was an extremely hot day and the intense lights on the set helped to make it even hotter. Mother Nature, with her customary slipshod design, had neglected to equip the gorilla with a window or any other form of ventilation. If she had, the gent inside the skin would have been able to survive indefinitely. But since he had no means of getting fresh air—or any other kind—he took the easy way out and solved his problem by fainting.

The two agents, alarmed over the possible loss of their commissions, immediately rushed over to their twin meal-tickets and frantically unbuttoned the hairy pelt. They quickly dragged the inner man out and doused him back to consciousness. When he finally came to, he whined that he had spent a good part of his career inside a gorilla skin, but, he angrily pointed out, this was the first one he'd ever inhabited where no provision had been made for ventilation. The two agents and the gorilla man then exchanged all the customary four-letter words they knew. The skin, on the other hand, not having spoken since it had been captured years ago in the jungle, just lay there on the floor, an inert, hairy mess.

The director, shocked by the agents' profanity, and having none of the wisdom of King Solomon, finally quelled the rhubarb by suddenly announcing, "Lunch!"

All during lunch, above the din of the circus strong man

munching celery, the gorilla man could be heard vehemently arguing with his agent. He flatly stated that he had no intention of stepping back into that skin unless some way could be found to provide him with a minimum amount of fresh air. The pelt's agent sat quietly all during lunch. However, he did warn the director that any attempt to tamper with his gorilla skin would be met with immediate legal reprisals from the Screen Gorillas Guild.

The ape man having dined elaborately on peanut butter and yoghurt, excused himself from the table, saying it was time for him to go to the men's room. (Apparently he went there only on schedule.) Doubling back on his tracks, he went to the kitchen and borrowed an ice-pick from the chef. Hurrying back to the temporarily deserted set, he hung the pelt on a nail and quickly jabbed a number of holes into his unventilated friend.

AFTER LUNCH the shooting resumed. Everybody seemed happy. The director resumed making passes at the ingénue, the gorilla was behaving like any other self-respecting working ape, and the two agents were now as thick as thieves, which, oddly enough, they were. They sat side by side, happily swapping animal reminiscences. They even decided that, the following year, they might go to Africa together on a *safari* and bring back some new skins for the ape man. They were so friendly that, at one point, the pelt's agent volunteered to go to the studio commissary and see if he could round up a coconut or two for the actor inside the skin.

Unlike the way it works with real actors, practically everything was shot in one take with this *ersatz* gorilla. Around 4 P.M. the ape man was working so smoothly that the pelt's agent began to grow suspicious. He finally walked over to the director and asked him to stop the cameras.

"There's something screwy going on here," he said. "He's been in that skin for almost three hours and he hasn't fainted yet! My experience has been that the man inside the skin always faints inside of two hours."

The ape man's agent immediately jumped up and yelled, "My man never faints unless he's wearing a second-rate skin!"

The first agent purpled. "There won't be any more shooting," he announced, "until I examine my property!"

This was the first time he had referred to the skin as "property," and I must say it sounded impressive. The cameras stopped grinding, the agent unbuttoned the skin, peeked in, curtly ordered the ape man out and took his place inside. After a minute or two he emerged in a rage. "Somebody stuck some holes in my gorilla!" he yelled. "I'll sue MGM for every nickel they've got!" (This was before TV, and MGM still had a lot of nickels.) Without another word he flung his pelt over his shoulder and, looking somewhat like D'Artagnan, stalked angrily from the set.

Three days passed. Not a camera was grinding and the costs were mounting while the studio executive frantically combed the town for another gorilla skin. Alas, there were none to be had. There were only two in all of Hollywood, and we later discovered that they were under contract to the same agent.

On the third day, the ape man, ill at ease outside a furry pelt, tracked down a man in San Diego who had an orangutan pelt. Even a child knows that an orang-utan is much smaller than a gorilla, but strangely enough the ape man didn't and he impetuously bought it without first trying it on. We gave him every opportunity to squeeze himself into the skin, but it was hopeless. When he finally realized he was too big for the pelt he broke down and cried like a baby. This was no time for sentiment. We were faced with reality, and also with the head of the studio. There was a picture to be finished and we were obliged to engage a smaller monkey man who specialized in impersonating orang-utans in and around San Diego. Moreover, because of the demands of the union, we had to pay the original ape man a standby salary, plus portal to portal, and psychiatric treatment.

At the first preview nobody mentioned us. Our gifted performances went for naught. The audience had eyes only for the gorilla. But overcritical viewers complained that the gorilla in some scenes seemed to be larger than he was in others, and that this had definitely weakened the credibility of the story. In the lobby I explained to an irate group (most

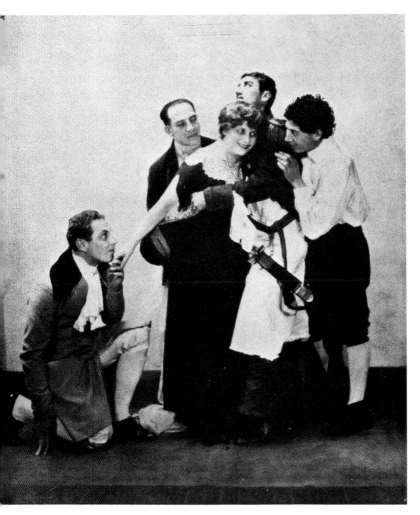

9. Gag picture taken with my mother when we played the Casino Theatre in New York. You'll notice Zeppo is on one knee. He thought he was in a crap game.

IOA. The Marx Brothers—Harpo, me and Chico—valiantly attempting to amuse Irving Thalberg.

IOB. This picture appeared as a *Time* magazine cover. The receptacle we're standing in is not our home.

11A. The Marx Brothers in *A Night in Casablanca*, the picture that made me realize I was no longer a boy.

11B. Me, Harpo and Chico successfully reliving the past.

12. The Marx Brothers' idea of golf. Me, Harpo and Gummo.

13A. A night at a night-club with my wife, Eden, an all-round good fellow. (You figure out what that means.)

13B. Eden, Melinda and me. It's fairly evident, from the expression on the face of the lady behind me, that the home team was taking quite a beating.

14. Melinda and me. The one without the teeth is Melinda.

15. Mr. Fenneman is presenting my daughter with a trophy of some kind. We tried to hock it, but it turned out to be worthless.

16A. The Groucho Marxes at home. Melinda is practising setting fire to the house.

16B. *Groucho* and *Me*. An intimate scene in the N.B.C. dressing-room, smiling after a magnificent performance.

of whom were in on passes) that years ago this gorilla had worked in one of the early Tarzan pictures in Africa, and, Blue Cross being unknown then, he had contracted a rare tropical disease. This virus, which had been lying dormant for years, had suddenly sprung back to life halfway through the picture and had shrunk all of his vital hormones. Thus the discrepancy in the gorilla's size. Like all glib explanations, this account seemed to satisfy nobody. Later, however, when the picture went into general release, the theatres were obliged to refund the price of admission to gorilla *aficionados* who complained that they had paid to see a full-sized gorilla, and instead had been slipped a shrunken ape.

CHAPTER NINETEEN

INSIDE HOLLYWOOD

BEFORE THE ADVENT of television, the word *genius* was tossed around the movie industry with all the careless abandon of a cooch dancer wiggling her muscles at a carnival side show. I presume there were a number of them out there at that time, but I met only one. His name was Irving Thalberg. He was so gifted they even named a building after him at MGM. Like all big talents, he didn't need a building to perpetuate his memory. He died at the age of thirty-seven and in the seventeen years he worked in pictures he cut a wide path for himself through the industry. If you think the word *genius* was an exaggeration, here are some of the pictures he made:

The Big Parade	*Trader Horn*
Ben Hur	*The Divorcee*
Merry Widow	*The Big House*
He Who Gets Slapped	*Barretts of Wimpole Street*
The Hunchback of Notre Dame	*Madame X*
Broadway Melody	*Mutiny on the Bounty*
Grand Hotel	*Good Earth*
Anna Christie	*Camille*
Min and Bill	*Romeo and Juliet*

And you can add to the list the two pictures Thalberg made with us: *A Night at the Opera* and *A Day at the Races*. During our years in the movies we made fourteen pictures. Two were far above average. Some of the others were pretty good. Some were deplorable. The best two were made by Thalberg.

I remember the first time we met Irving Thalberg. Chico, as usual, had arranged the meeting over a bridge game. Thalberg said, "I would like to make some pictures with you fellows. I mean *real* pictures."

I flared up. "What's the matter with *Cocoanuts*, *Animal Crackers* and *Duck Soup*? Are you going to sit there and tell me those weren't funny?"

"Of course they were funny," he said, "but they weren't movies. They weren't *about* anything."

"People laughed, didn't they?" asked Harpo. "*Duck Soup* had as many laughs as any comedy ever made, including Chaplin's."

"That's true," he agreed; "it was a very funny picture, but you don't need that many laughs in a movie. I'll make a picture with you fellows with half as many laughs—but I'll put a legitimate story in it and I'll bet it will gross twice as much as *Duck Soup*."

After we had signed the contract, he asked us whom we wanted for writers. Naturally we said, "Kaufman and Ryskind." That's the last advice we gave him.

It's a good thing we didn't bet. Our first picture was *A Night at the Opera*, and it doubled *Duck Soup*'s gross.

THALBERG WAS a difficult man to see. He would arrive at the studio at noon and leave around midnight. Most everyone in his employ was afraid of him. Perhaps afraid is too strong a word; let's say deeply respectful. But we had been successful in vaudeville too long to be impressed by this aura of cathedral atmosphere, and in his presence we deliberately behaved like the Katzenjammer Kids. He wasn't accustomed to this rowdy familiarity from his hirelings, and I believe that was why he was fond of us. We amused him.

The social side of Hollywood didn't interest Thalberg. He never had time for croquet or polo, and except for an occasional game of bridge, his burning interest was the movies. He never allowed his name to be used on the screen. He didn't care anything about that kind of publicity. He said, "If the picture is good they'll know who produced it. If it's bad, no one cares."

We once asked him why he didn't want his name up there. He said, "I don't want my name on the screen because credit is something that should be given to others. If you are in a position to give credit to yourself, then you don't need it."

He always had three or four story conferences going at the same time in adjoining offices. He would pop in and out, lending a hand here, offering a suggestion there.

We had just started discussing a comedy scene one afternoon in his office when he said, "Hold it, boys. I'll be back in a minute." The minute stretched to two hours. A few days later he repeated this trick. The third time, we got angry. We rolled all the steel filing cabinets against the two doors and wouldn't allow him back in his office until he promised he wouldn't walk out on us again.

Two days passed. We had just begun another conference when he again excused himself. We weren't fooled. We knew he was walking out to attend some other story meeting. In his absence we lit the logs in the fireplace and sent to the studio commissary for baking potatoes. When Thalberg returned he found us all sitting naked in front of a roaring fire, busily roasting mickeys over the flames. He laughed and said, "Wait a minute, boys!" He then phoned the commissary and asked them to send up some butter for the potatoes. He never walked out on us again.

ANOTHER FAMOUS producer whose name, oddly enough, is Delaney, was hosting a croquet game on his lawn. They were playing for pretty high stakes, and at one point the host announced that he was going for the fourth wicket. One of the more courageous guests present said, "I beg your pardon, but you're going for the third wicket."

The host shouted, "I tell you I'm going for the fourth wicket!"

The guest calmly replied, "If you persist in deliberately cheating, I'm bowing out of the game and going home."

The host, shaking a menacing mallet at him, retorted, "Whatsamatter? You for Stevenson, or something?"

This particular producer has a fine picture mind, and is one of the few remaining living legends of the motion picture industry, but outside the studio his brain wanders into all sorts of illogical conclusions. The fact that in the middle of a harmless croquet game he could charge a guest with voting for Stevenson, and make it sound like a political accusation, seemed to him to make sense. If you knew him as well as I do, you would know that in this charge there was a veiled implication that his friend was either a borderline Red or perhaps, for all he knew, even a card-carrying Communist.

My personal relationship with this famous producer has

always been an extremely casual and sketchy one. We have met at parties, at restaurants and at previews for more than thirty years. His greeting has never varied. He always tees off with, "How's Harpo, that brother of yours? He sure is a fine fellow."

After thirty years of this wandering and absent-minded rudeness, my patience finally wore thin. "Look," I once said to him, "I am just as fond of Harpo as you are, and probably a great deal more, but why, after thirty years, do you still persist in asking me how Harpo is? Just for a change, why don't you ask me how I am?"

"Groucho," he replied, putting a reassuring hand on my shoulder, "some day I will ask how you are. But right now I'd like to know, how's Harpo?"

WE HAD SOME pretty interesting directors in the movie business. In describing one of them, a friend of mine, a writer who had been in his employ, once bitterly remarked that he was the asbestos curtain between the audience and entertainment.

We had one director, a very successful one, whose only stage direction to the actors was as follows: "Now, baby, in this scene I want you to go in there and sell 'em a load of clams." He didn't care what the scene was about. It could be a love scene, a dramatic scene, a comedy scene. It made no difference. His instructions never varied. The actors always sold clams.

After three weeks of this brilliant and comprehensive stage instruction, Morrie Ryskind, one of the better writers we've worked with, sidled over to me before the beginning of a scene and whispered, "Groucho, I'm puzzled. Are we in show business or are we in the fish business?"

It is unquestionably true that the past ten years have seen the movie industry seriously injured by the obvious advantages television has to offer the public. On the other hand, because of financial desperation, TV gave the movie industry an opportunity to shake itself loose from the hundreds of deeply integrated incompetents who worked ceaselessly, day and night, ruining all the pictures they had a hand in.

Some of our producers were dillies. We had one (let's call

him Delaney) who loved to gamble, and so did the gent who was head of the studio. (We'll call him Delaney, too.) At one time this particular producer was out of work and none of the studios wanted his services. To make it worse, he owed the top dog of our studio around thirty thousand dollars in gambling debts. The head man, being no fool (except when it came to producing movies) realized there was very little chance of his ever collecting this debt unless he gave the unemployed producer a job at his studio. The next thing we knew, the head man engaged his gambling friend to produce one of our movies.

I will now briefly give you a day in the life of this producer. But first I had better describe him. He was a large, soggy man with a drooping belly, which he constantly kept pushing up with both hands as though fearful it might fall on the floor and get stepped on. He had a large, loud, angry voice which he only employed when he was absolutely certain he didn't know what he was talking about. He had a classic ignorance of the importance of a story, but he had a notion that if he bellowed instead of talking in a story conference, the sounds escaping from his face would surely make sense to someone in the room.

Working on the picture were three talented, timid writers who had only recently arrived from the East. Whenever they were summoned to the producer's office for a story conference, not only did their knees shake, but all the rest of their equipment trembled in sympathy.

Once long ago, this producer had had a fine mind, but by the time they slipped him to us he had dissipated it and was now just a huge, hollow shell. He ate like a pig, guzzled his booze and played the dames relentlessly. (Fortunately for the girls, in most cases unsuccessfully.)

It was the custom for the studio employees to arrive at nine in the morning. Our hero would roll in around eleven, complete with a jumbo hang-over. On arriving, he would immediately pick up the phone and call his wife. She would then relate, in detail, whatever juicy tidbits of scandal she might have garnered since he left that morning. After having been apprised of all the loose dirt around town, he would rise, push his stomach back into place and head over to the top man's office for a few hands of gin rummy behind locked doors. By the time he returned to his office it would be close to one o'clock and time for lunch.

The studio commissary's excellent cuisine didn't please this porcine epicure, so he usually repaired to a very expensive restaurant some miles away. Here he would belt a small seidel of martinis, a plate of *hors d'œuvres*, two different kinds of meat, assorted vegetables, coffee and a brace of brandies. He would then climb into his unpaid-for Cadillac and return to his office, full of indigestion, gas and malice. Around two-thirty, his insides rebelling, he would drain a beaker of bicarbonate. His belches would now begin to resemble the sounds of a large oil well that had just come in. By the time the various noises had subsided, it would be three o'clock and time for a siesta.

Around four he would wake up and bellow for his three timid writers, who had been sitting in the outer office for the past two hours, apprehensively awaiting his call. They would be ushered in by a very pretty young secretary, with whom our friend hoped soon to have an affair. He would then reluctantly read whatever dialogue the writers had sweated out that morning. After he had read the scenes he would shake his head, look at the three writers pityingly and resume shaking his head. Then there would be ten minutes of ominous silence followed by ten minutes of shouting and pounding on the desk with both hands. When he had all the objects on the desk dancing up and down in unison he would cry, "It stinks! It stinks!" Then he would put his head in his hands and just sit there, quietly glaring at the three Eastern writers who had come all the way to California to find happiness.

When the silence became unbearable, the writers would look at each other and then, as though on signal, they would rise, pick up their rejected scenes, and silently slink back to their hutches. Naturally, they were unhappy with their producer's reaction, but the knowledge that they had escaped with their lives gave them the strength they needed to survive another day. I hasten to add that this monster was not the average Hollywood producer. He stood alone in his field.

THERE WAS A producer at another studio who was getting two thousand dollars a week, but, unlike the one I just described, this one was a gentleman and a student, but, unfortunately, not of the movies.

He had no vices. He didn't drink, he didn't smoke and he

was true to his wife. His only claim to fame and his job was the fact that he had read all of the biographies of Lincoln and had a large oil painting of him hanging in his office. He knew more about the Great Emancipator than Ida Tarbell, Carl Sandberg, Raymond Massey and Mrs. Lincoln combined.

In a story conference, no matter what the problem, he would patiently listen to all the writers' suggestions and solutions. After everyone had said his piece he would silence the meeting, stand up, and then gravely deliver a long, windy discourse on some trivial incident in Lincoln's life. While he spoke, a slight smile would steal across his face. This was to show his listeners that he had many of the qualities of Honest Abe—patience, fortitude and a quiet sense of humour.

His homely little anecdote finished, the conference would disperse in an orgy of admiration for this quiet little man who could talk so interestingly and intimately about our saintly President. As they trooped out, completely forgetting what they had originally come to his office for, you could hear them saying, "What a wonderful man . . . so interesting. You know, in a way he reminds you a lot of Lincoln."

This faker was at the same studio for many years. He made all kinds of movies, all of them indifferent. But how could you fire a man who reminded you so much of our martyred President? Whenever his name came up somebody was sure to say, "It's true, he does make lousy movies, but, boy, doesn't he remind you of Lincoln?"

Incidentally, in all his years at the studio, the one movie he never made was the life of the Great Emancipator. That picture was made by another studio. It was a magnificent job, but financially it turned out to be a colossal failure.

If you must have a moral, remember that when your back is against the wall and you're in deep trouble, just drag out some obscure subject you've secretly been boning up on for years and let everyone have it right between the ears.

NOT ALL THE movie people in this chapter need to be nameless. There were the Delaney brothers, for example, whom I will call Warner for the sake of brevity. Some years ago I received a letter from my attorney. It was addressed to me, but sent to him. You see, in Hollywood no one gets his own mail. It's always sent to one's attorney, doctor, business manager or agent. If you get any mail from your dentist you don't even answer it. You just send him your few remaining cavities, and he plugs them up and sends them to your lawyer. It's all very confusing.

The letter I started to tell you about was from the Warner Brothers' legal department. They were pretty angry. It seems we were about to start a movie called *A Night in Casablanca*. Five years earlier, the Warner Brothers had made a picture with Humphrey Bogart and Lauren Bacall called, simply, *Casablanca*, and they threatened us with a lawsuit if we persisted in using a title which they claimed was too close to the original.

Since my attorney was out of town (he was playing *chemin de fer* in French Lick), I wrote them the following letter:

DEAR WARNER BROTHERS:

Apparently there is more than one way of conquering a city and holding it as your own. For example, up to the time that we contemplated making this picture, I had no idea that the city of Casablanca belonged exclusively to Warner Brothers. However, it was only a few days after our announcement appeared that we received your long, ominous legal document warning us not to use the name, Casablanca. It seems that in 1471, Ferdinand Balboa Warner, your great-great-grandfather, while looking for a short cut to the city of Burbank, had stumbled on the shores of Africa and, raising his alpenstock (which he later turned in for a hundred shares of the common), named it Casablanca.

I just don't understand your attitude. Even if you plan on re-releasing your picture, I am sure that the average movie fan could learn in time to distinguish between Ingrid Bergman and Harpo. I don't know whether I could, but I certainly would like to try.

You claim you own Casablanca and that no one else can use that name without your permission. What about "Warner Brothers"? Do you own that, too? You probably have the right to use the name Warner but what about Brothers? Professionally, we were brothers long before you were. We were touring the sticks as The Marx Brothers when Vitaphone was still a gleam in the inventor's eye, and even before us there had been other brothers—the Smith Brothers; the Brothers Karamazov; Dan Brothers, an outfielder with Detroit, and "Brother, can You Spare a Dime?" This was originally, "Brothers, can You Spare a Dime?" but this was spreading a dime pretty thin, so they threw out one brother, gave all the money to the other brother and whittled it down to, "Brother, can You Spare a Dime?"

Now, Jack, how about you? Do you maintain that yours is an original name? Well, it's not. It was used long before you were born. Offhand,

I can think of two Jacks—there was Jack of *Jack and the Beanstalk* and Jack the Ripper, who cut quite a figure in his day.

As for you, Harry, you probably sign your cheques, sure in the belief that you are the first Harry of all time and that all other Harrys are impostors. I can think of two Harrys that preceded you. There was Lighthorse Harry of Revolutionary fame and a Harry Appelbaum who lived on the corner of 93rd Street and Lexington Avenue. Unfortunately, Appelbaum wasn't too well known. The last I heard of him, he was selling neckties at Weber and Heilbroner.

Now about the Burbank studio. I believe this is what you brothers call your place. Old man Burbank is gone. Perhaps you remember him. He was a great man in a garden. His wife often said Luther had ten green thumbs. What a witty woman she must have been. Burbank was the wizard who crossed all those fruits and vegetables until he had the poor plants in such a confused and jittery condition that they could never decide whether to enter the dining-room on the meat platter or the dessert dish.

This is pure conjecture, of course, but who knows—perhaps Burbank's survivors aren't too happy with the fact that a plant that grinds out pictures on a quota settled in their town, appropriated Burbank's name and uses it as a front for their films. It is even possible that the Burbank family is prouder of the potato produced by the old man than they are of the fact that from your studio emerged *Casablanca* or even *Gold Diggers of 1931*. This all seems to add up to a pretty bitter tirade, but I assure you it's not meant to. I love Warners. Some of my best friends are Warner Brothers. It is even possible that I am doing you an injustice and that you, yourselves, know nothing at all about this dog-in-the-Wanger attitude. It wouldn't surprise me at all to discover that the heads of your legal department are unaware of this absurd dispute, for I am acquainted with many of them and they are fine fellows with curly black hair, double-breasted suits and a love for their fellow man that out-Saroyans Saroyan.

I have a hunch that this attempt to prevent us from using the title is the brain-child of some ferret-faced shyster, serving a brief apprenticeship in your legal department. I know the type well—hot out of law school, hungry for success and too ambitious to follow the natural laws of promotion. This bar sinister probably needled your attorneys, most of whom are fine fellows with curly black hair, double-breasted suits, etc., in attempting to enjoin us. Well, he won't get away with it! We'll fight him to the highest court! No pasty-faced legal adventurer is going to cause bad blood between the Warners and the Marxes. We are all brothers under the skin and we'll remain friends till the last reel of *A Night in Casablanca* goes tumbling over the spool.

Sincerely,
GROUCHO MARX.

For some curious reason, this letter seemed to puzzle the Warner Brothers. They wrote me—in all seriousness, as I live and breathe—and asked if I could give them some idea of what our story was about. They felt we might be able to work this thing out. I answered with the following:

DEAR WARNERS:

There isn't much I can tell you about the story. In it I play a Doctor of Divinity who ministers to the natives and, as a sideline, hawks can-openers and pea-jackets to the natives along the Gold Coast of Africa.

When I first meet Chico, he is working in a saloon, selling sponges to bar-flies who are unable to carry their liquor. Harpo is an Arabian caddie who lives in a small Grecian urn on the outskirts of the city.

As the picture opens, Porridge, a mealy-mouthed native girl, is sharpening some arrows for the hunt. Paul Hangover, our hero, is constantly lighting two cigarettes simultaneously. He apparently is un-aware of the cigarette shortage.

There are many scenes of splendour and fierce antagonisms, and Colour, an Abyssinian messenger boy, runs Riot. Riot, in case you have never been there, is a small night-club on the edge of town.

There's a lot more I could tell you, but I don't want to spoil it for you. All this has been okayed by the Hays Office, *Good Housekeeping* and the survivors of the Haymarket Riots, and if the times are ripe, this picture can be the opening gun in a new world-wide disaster.

Cordially,

GROUCHO MARX.

Instead of mollifying them, this note seemed to puzzle them even more, for they wrote back and said they still didn't under-stand the story line. And, believe it or not, they would appre-ciate it if I explained the plot in more detail. I naturally obliged with a much clearer synopsis of the picture:

DEAR BROTHERS:

Since I last wrote you, I regret to say there have been some changes in the plot of our new picture, *A Night in Casablanca*. In the new version I play Bordello, the sweetheart of Humphrey Bogart. Harpo and Chico are itinerant rug-pedlars who are weary of laying rugs and enter a monastery just for a lark. This is a good joke on them, as there hasn't been a lark in the place for fifteen years.

Across from this monastery, hard by a jetty, is a waterfront hotel, chock full of apple-cheeked damsels, most of whom have been barred by the Hays Office for soliciting. In the fifth reel, Gladstone makes a speech that sets the House of Commons in an uproar and the King promptly asks for his resignation. Harpo marries a hotel detective; Chico operates an ostrich farm. Humphrey Bogart's girl, Bordello, spends her last years in a Bacall house.

This, as you can see, is a very skimpy outline. The only thing that can save us from extinction is a continuation of the film shortage.

Fondly,

GROUCHO MARX.

That did it. Oddly enough, I never heard from the Warner brothers again. I later learned that two of them had gone to French Lick and joined my attorney at the *chemin de fer* table.

AFTER THALBERG'S DEATH my interest in the movies waned. I continued to appear in them, but my heart was in the Highlands. The fun had gone out of picture-making. I was like an old pug, still going through the motions, but now doing it solely for the money.

My swan-song was *A Night in Casablanca*. This was an independent venture, and we were to get a percentage of the profits. The name of the producer eludes me, but since he was a very nice man let's call him Delaney. Unfortunately, being a nice man isn't the only qualification required for making a good picture. It may have been just a coincidence, but shortly after the movie was released he retired and went into a less conspicuous line of work.

I know it sounds like an exaggeration, but during the shooting Harpo claimed he could hear my bones creaking, even above the sound of the dialogue. One day, after a particularly tough siege, we decided we were coming down the stretch, and that it was high time we quit while we were still partially alive.

There were many scenes that were better suited for acrobats (I mean *young* acrobats) than for three spavined comics, but we gamely submitted to all the violence. We had to. To begin with, we liked the producer. Second, and more important, we owned a piece of the picture. If it flopped we wouldn't wind up with enough money to pay a bone-setter for repairing our frames.

The most difficult kind of picture to make is a comedy. If you don't believe it, look around and see how many are made. They're as scarce as hen's teeth. (Why do people still insist on using this silly simile when even the rooster knows that the hen hasn't any teeth . . . and very little of anything else?)

NOW LET ME give you a typical day in the life of a movie comedian. You are ordered to be on the set at 8 A.M., bright and funny. This is a large-sized order. In fact, it would be tough even at three in the afternoon. Crawling out of bed at 6 A.M., you take a wet towel and slap yourself back to consciousness. Then, bolting a hearty breakfast of cold cereal and yoghurt, you reluctantly drive, with half-slit eyes, to the studio. At each stop light you take a hasty look at the script lying on the seat beside you. This distraction sometimes enables you to hit the car in front of you. But that isn't important; you're getting that deathless dialogue deeply embedded in your head, dialogue that is sure to flee from your memory as soon as the director yells "Action!"

The sound stage, where you're scheduled to be hilariously funny, is a dimly lit warehouse designed along the lines of an ancient mausoleum. On the floor are hundreds of cables and wires, all of which are deliberately placed in strategic positions for you to trip over as you drag your weary body to the dressing-room that the cleaning woman forgot to clean.

There are no toilet facilities on the sound stage—on *any* sound stage any place in the world. This vital omission has always been a source of wonder to me. Was this planned only for reasons of economy, or are we to conclude that architects never regarded actors as human beings and, therefore, saw no reason for this necessity? In my twenty years in the movies I've walked hundreds of miles in all kinds of weather, through make-believe streets, through towers of Babylon, waterfronts in Marseilles, desert sands on the road to Mecca, subway kiosks—movie sets, all of them—frantically looking, not for love, but for just a little old comfort station, so cosy and warm.

About a quarter to nine, the stage-hands drop their gin rummy cards and the actors are called to the set. After three rehearsals and seventeen takes, the director reluctantly concedes that perhaps he has what he wants "in the can." This is in no way related to the lavatory lack I was just discussing.

THE SHOOTING continues from nine to six, with time out for a hasty lunch. Afterwards, everyone returns to the set testy and querulous, except the stage-hands, who regard the whole production as a personal intrusion on their gin rummy game.

If you're lucky enough not to be in the first shot, you go to your dressing-room, which still hasn't been cleaned, and brush up on the afternoon's dialogue. Having mastered this, you decide to lie down for a few hasty winks. You have just dropped off and are now dreaming that you are under a coconut tree on the island of Bali-Ha'i, with Shirley MacLaine dancing the dance of love just for you, when the head of the publicity department bursts into your bower accompanied by two syndicated columnists. All they want from you is about forty minutes of sparkling monologue. If they can get this, they'll have enough copy for their next day's columns, which will leave them free to spend the afternoon at Santa Anita.

The unit manager now informs you that they are ready for you on the set. The director orders you to have your face freshened. The make-up man then proceeds to slap you with a wet sponge. This is particularly pleasant on those many days when you're running a temperature.

The afternoon grinds on, and by six o'clock no one cares any more what's been shot, or how. All the cast wants is to clear out of there, go home, eat dinner and drug themselves for the next day's shooting.

At six everyone rushes for the exit—everyone except the stars, the producer and the director. This weary group now drags itself up two flights of iron stairs to a projection-room to view the scenes the director massacred the previous day. (It is an unwritten law in the movie industry that the projection-room must always be two flights up an iron stairway.) The first scene we look at isn't too bad. In fact, it's quite good. It has only one defect. Chico's head is missing. It seems the cameraman who covered Chico had a hang-over and couldn't get his big Brownie focused on the spot he was aiming at—namely, Chico's head.

When all the scenes have been shown, the lights go up and everyone looks at everyone else accusingly, except the producer, who has silently crept out long ago to finalize his plans for going into some other business.

AND NOW BACK to reality and *A Night in Casablanca*. It was the last week of shooting. To complete the picture on schedule (otherwise we were told it would run far over budget), it was decided to shoot each night until ten. This made the stage-hands very happy, because this meant they were now on golden time. In case you've never been a stage-hand, "golden time" means that the crew now gets four times what they're worth instead of only twice as much.

We were to finish on a Saturday. They showed us some mysterious financial figures which none of us understood, and we were told that if we could kill the picture that night (which, incidentally, we had been doing rather successfully since the beginning), we would save a veritable fortune.

Perhaps I had better explain the last scene. There was a large prop aeroplane on the set, and extending from the door on one side of it was a ladder. It was sticking straight out, about twenty feet from the ground. We three boys were perched on this ladder, trying to climb into the plane. Inside were three husky "heavies," trying to prevent us from boarding it. Harpo and Chico had reached the door, but your correspondent hadn't progressed that far and was still hanging upside down by his knees.

At 1 A.M. the scene still hadn't been licked. While I swayed back and forth with a large wind machine blowing on me to create the illusion of flight—and to make it easier for me to fall on my head—I made the decision that, for better or for worse, changed the course of my life. As I hung there like a plucked turkey, I said to myself, "Groucho, old boy—and believe me, you *are* an old boy—don't you think this is rather a ridiculous way for you to be spending your few remaining years?"

We finished shooting at two, shook hands all around, and to neither Chico's nor Harpo's surprise I announced that I was retiring from the cinema.

CHAPTER TWENTY

COME BACK NEXT THURSDAY WITH A SPECIMEN OF YOUR MONEY

As I GET FURTHER along with this chronicle of trivia, it's beginning to dawn on me that writing is an extremely tough racket. In my day, I've written many allegedly comic pieces for magazines and newspapers, but to keep going for enough pages to fill a book is a new experience for me. I used to play golf daily and badly, take long walks with two expensive, flea-bitten poodles and even ride a horse occasionally. It seems to me that I don't do anything now but write. And anybody who has ever written knows that writing requires thinking. And everyone knows that thinking is easily the most distasteful way of spending the day. But I keep plugging along. I must say the subject of this book has never seemed to me the most entrancing topic in the world. I'm just curious now to learn whether I have the stamina and will power to see it through to the end.

Some time ago I read Stefan Zweig's *Life of Balzac*. The only way Balzac sustained himself through his lifetime of writing was to have his valet chain him to the bedpost at night and unchain him in the morning. To keep himself awake, he would drink twenty or thirty cups of coffee. Benzedrine and the other more potent stimulants had not yet been discovered. He finally died of coffee poisoning. There is a medical name for this, but I don't remember what it is, and I'm not going to phone and ask my doctor about it. If I do, he'll charge me for a visit.

I don't know how it is in the hinterlands, but in Beverly Hills the old country doctor with his horse and buggy and his little black bag has gone the way of the horse and buggy. I saw a man leaving my country club yesterday in a chauffeur-driven El Dorado Cadillac. As he rode away, I asked the parking attendant what business this man was in. I knew he must be a rich man, because a Cadillac and a chauffeur in these days of virtual tax confiscation can be a very expensive mode of travel. The attendant said the man was a doctor.

"A doctor!" I exclaimed. "And he can afford a Cadillac and a chauffeur? What kind of a doctor is he?"

"He's an allergist," the boy answered.

I GUESS MOST of you know what an allergist is. If not, I'll describe one to you briefly. Let's say, for example, that your skin turns slightly blue when you eat cucumbers. You, being the average man (or jerk, as the case may be), wake up one morning, look in the mirror and discover that your entire carcass is covered in blue patches. A pretty picture, I must say.

Naturally, you have no idea what's wrong with you. All you know is, this is not the way Mother Nature intended you to look. Alarmed, you feverishly call up your family physician. He is busy taking X-rays of his nurse, who by an odd coincidence turns out to be a very beautiful girl with precisely the same measurements as Sophia Loren. You say, "Doctor, what shall I do? I'm turning blue all over."

"Hmmm," he answers. "Blue, eh?"

While phoning, you're shivering in the cold bedroom. You know you should get your clothes on, but the sight of your blue body fascinates you.

You repeat, "Well, Doc, what should I do?"

The doctor says, "Drop by tomorrow."

You say, "Doc, you don't understand. I told you I'm turning blue. I must see you immediately. I'll be over there in twenty minutes. Is that okay?"

The doctor is not crazy about this impending intrusion, for he isn't through taking the nurse's X-rays. Also, he has to move fast because his wife has promised to look in on him some time that morning. You're still standing there naked, and now in addition to turning blue, your body is beginning to acquire ridges. You're beginning to look like a relief map of northern Greece. The doctor, meanwhile, anxious to get back to his X-rays, has solved his side of the problem by hanging up. Not only by hanging up, but by leaving the receiver off the hook.

You quickly get dressed, and after a hasty breakfast of nothing, you rush to your doctor's office, hoping against hope that you will arive there before you croak. As you enter the office, the nurse is putting the receiver back on the hook. The doctor is pretty annoyed at your showing up so quickly, and the fact that you still owe him eighty-five dollars from last month doesn't help bridge the gulf between you.

"What's the matter with you?" he asks querously.

"Oh nothing much," you reply sarcastically. "I'm just turning blue all over."

"Blue, eh? Well, take off your clothes and we'll have a look at you."

The "we" puzzles you. Does he mean you and the doctor, you and the nurse or the doctor and the nurse?

"Sit up!" he orders. After eyeing you for a few minutes he proceeds to tap you sharply with a small hammer. Sitting on a cold bench, naked, with basic low blood pressure—this is not the easiest way to keep warm. "Hmmm," he says. "Something is definitely the matter with you. You're blue all over."

Now there's a hot piece of news! Your gardener (to whom you also owe money) could have told you that.

Meanwhile, the nurse is getting pretty impatient, and at a nod from her the doctor says, "I'll get right to the point. I can't do anything for you. What you need is an allergist."

"An allergist? I thought *you* were a doctor," you reply.

"I *am* a doctor, but this is not my field. Let me explain it to you. There is evidently something that doesn't agree with you."

You say, "Let's keep my wife out of this." (This isn't much of a joke; but you must remember, he isn't much of a doctor.)

"No," he shakes his head impatiently. "I mean there's something you *eat* that doesn't agree with you."

"There is nothing I eat that agrees with me—but what's that got to do with my turning blue?"

"We'll have to take some tests to find out what you should avoid."

You think to yourself, "What I should avoid is this quack." But since you're naked you are obviously in no position to defend yourself, so you decide to let sleeping docs lie.

As soon as you get your clothes on, the doctor hands you a card. It reads, DR. HUGO SCHMALTZ, ALLERGIST.

"Doctor Schmaltz is a leader in his field," he says. "A good man . . . world-famous . . . Vienna, you know. Oh, by the way, be sure to tell him I sent you." You know what that means. It means he's getting a cut of whatever Schmaltz soaks you.

Sophia Loren then makes an immediate appointment for you to see Dr. Schmaltz.

TEN MINUTES LATER you're over at Schmaltz's Allergy Emporium. The doc is about five feet three, and his Adam's apple is almost the same size as his head. From his looks, you're sure he's wanted in Vienna. Not by his former patients, but by the police.

"Well, Mr. Marx," he says, "what brings you here?" (I forgot to tell you—your name is Marx. So is mine, by the way.)

Now there's a great beginning for a world-famous allergist!

"Why don't you take off your clothes and we'll have a look at you." To idle away the time while you're undressing, he asks, "What seems to be the trouble?"

"Oh, nothing much," you chuckle. "I'm just turning blue all over."

"Blue? Hmmmm."

This news seems to unsettle him. Apparently some of his past experiences with blue patients haven't been happy ones. Then he fools you. You thought he was going to bring out the little hammer. Not Schmaltz. He's from Vienna. He brings out a stethoscope. He doesn't use it on you. He just hangs it around his neck. He probably thinks this makes him look more like a doctor. "What have you been eating?" he asks.

"Well," you begin, "I had nothing for breakfast . . ."

"What did you have for dinner last night?" he interrupts.

"Let's see now. There was Norman Krasna and his wife, Mr. and Mrs. Nunnally Johnson and the Sheekmans," you reply.

His tone grows sharper. "Maybe I don't make myself clear," he says. "Tell me everything you *ate* last night."

"Oh," you say. "Well, I had spaghetti and meat-balls, some frozen fish-sticks and a cucumber salad."

"And how often do you have cucumber salad?" he inquires. But before you can answer, he starts walking around the room, humming to himself, "Cucumbers and fish-sticks. Cucumbers and fish-sticks." He's probably thinking it's not a bad idea for a Calypso song. He wheels on you sharply. "When can you come again?"

"When can I come *again*?" you exclaim. "I'm here right now!"

"*Ja*," he says. Apparently this is the first time he realizes you are in his office.

"Why can't you tell me what's wrong with me?" you insist.

He looks at you pityingly. "Mr. Marx, it don't go that fast. Already first we're going to have to take some allergy tests. You may have to come every day for a month."

"Every day!" you repeat. "Didn't you tell me it was cucumbers?"

"Not at all," he replies. "*You* said you ate cucumbers, but that don't mean that from cucumbers you are turning blue."

This makes sense to you. Everyone knows that cucumbers are green. But you continue hopefully, "Well, I'll just cut out cucumbers."

"No," he says patiently. "You do not understand. It could be the cucumbers. On the other hand, it could be also the meat-balls." Then he laughs heartily. "It could even the fish-sticks be. So! You see what we are up against?"

It's always embarrassing to ask a doctor what his fee is, but if you are going to have to make daily visits to Joe Allergy, you'd better find out how much you're going to be rooked. You decide that if it's going to be more than twenty-five bucks a day, you'll just have to remain blue. In your mind you rapidly multiply thirty days by twenty-five dollars a throw. Seven hundred and fifty dollars a month! The price of a pretty good second-hand car. Clearing your throat and averting your gaze, you ask, "Doc, what do you get for each visit?"

"Well," he says, "my regular fee is fifty dollars, but since you have to come every day for a month, we'll make it twenty-five dollars."

"Now just a moment," you say. "Suppose you find out by the third day what's wrong with me? Why do I have to come every day for a month?"

"Don't you worry," he replies happily. "It'll take a month all right!"

I hope this will explain why Dr. Schmaltz was seen leaving the country club in his chauffeur-driven El Dorado Brougham Cadillac.

HAVING NEATLY demolished the medical profession, I would now like to set it up again for one last job. Are you, dear readers, beginning to get as tired as I am of all those fancy four-bit names that doctors call themselves?

To be sure, doctors are by no means the sole offenders in that respect. Like it or not, today we all live in a world of euphemisms and shabby concealments. The only one left with courage enough to face life is Portia, and I don't mean Shakespeare's girl-friend. For example, the man who buries you now calls himself a mortician. Everyone, except possibly the corpse, knows that he's an undertaker, but this fancy title helps to convince the mourners that their loved one isn't really dead, he's just going away for a few million years.

The creep who sticks you with a tract bungalow that is sure to fall apart by the time you've made the last instalment on the piano doesn't call himself a real estate agent any more. He now bills himself as a realtor. The janitor who sweeps his way through life now refers to himself as a sanitary engineer.

But this is bush-league sophistry. When it comes to real obscurantism, no group has been as successful in concealing its shady activities as the medical profession. For one reason or another, they've *all* discarded their original titles. It took me some years before I knew what kind of a doctor I was about to visit. The pediatrician used to be called a baby doctor. The foot doctor is now a chiropodist (not to be confused with a chiropractor).

A chiropractor is a sadist who spends a half-hour twisting your spine out of shape and the next half-hour hoping he can get it back to its original position. To add insult to injury, he persists in laughing while he's thumping the hell out of you. I'm not sure if he's laughing at the shape you're in, or whether he's laughing at the fee he plans on soaking you, but, boy, does he have fun! Apparently this is an occupational disease that they are unable to control. However, when cornered, to a man they will hotly deny this allegation and maintain they are as glum with their ministrations as the grim reaper himself. Pay no attention to them. I've watched them all closely for years and I know what I'm talking about. Any doctor or chiropractor worthy of the name who laughs while he's mangling your bones isn't worth the massage table on which he's crippling you.

Incidentally, as a piece of useless information but something you may want to use at a dinner party (instead of the catsup), the only difference between a chiropractor and an osteopath is that the chiropractor's title is longer. This gives the osteopath a decided advantage. Having the shorter name enables him to share his office with another osteopath, thereby splitting both the rent and your spine.

I'd hate to tell you how old I was before I found out that a gynaecologist is a medic who does mysterious things with women. (There are people in other walks of life who also do mysterious things with women, but as yet I haven't found out what they're called publicly.)

Do you, dear reader, know what a proctologist is? Well, I do. Let's not explore *that* subject.

The dentist now bills himself (and you) as an orthodontist. He, too, is of the "happy Joe" breed. Unlike the chiropractor, he doesn't laugh out loud. He just looks at you and smiles pityingly as you sit there helpless, with your mouth full of his tools, any one of which could pierce the hide of a rhinoceros.

While gaily drilling his way through to the back of your head (I always imagine he's looking for a short-cut to India), he tells you a whole series of jokes which he's forgotten you told him the last time you were there. Before you leave, he informs you that your breath is none too good. To remedy this, he suggests you do what he's doing—try eating nothing but whole-wheat bread and raw vegetables for the next three months. As you turn to say goodbye, three of his teeth fall out.

It's rather ironic, but the most important doctor, the one who has prevented more shotgun marriages than all the irate fathers in the world combined, is the abortionist. Unlike all the other medical charlatans, he doesn't stoop to sail under false colours. He proudly waves his banner on high. His profession may be a furtive one, but he has the courage of his convictions and, believe me, the one I'm referring to has had a number of those.

What is it about medicine that makes all medical practitioners so ashamed of their work? Why do they insist on plying their trade under baffling pseudonyms? Why don't they revert to the names they originally used? In those dear, dead, simple days of yore, I knew that if I was getting a pedicure I was having my toe-nails clipped by a foot doctor. From a foot doctor to the subject of love is quite a jump, but watch how easily I do it in the next chapter.

CHAPTER TWENTY-ONE

WHY DO THEY CALL IT LOVE WHEN THEY MEAN SEX?

I HATE TO START talking about matrimony, love and courtship. (I believe I've got them in the reverse order, but it really doesn't make too much difference unless you're in love.) Since I have three children, it's fair for you to assume that I have been married—although I have heard of exceptions to this rule.

I'm not crazy about embarking upon this subject. There's no other topic in the history of mankind that has been raked over, ploughed under and beaten to death as steadily as the holy bonds, not to mention the unholy ones. No magazine worth its editor has ever appeared on the news-stands without at least two definitive articles on marriage and courtship (frequently written by a group of celibates or virgins, if any). No daily newspaper can survive without an Advice to the Lovelorn column, next to the comics probably the paper's most important feature. At least half the movies that are made for the gum-and-popcorn crowd deal with boy meets girl, and the ultimate noose that the audience has been conditioned to expect in the last reel. Every afternoon on TV there are three hours of variations on "Life can be Ecstatic," and about as many hours of this gruel spewing from the radio.

There are now two divorced men on television, both admittedly experts, who make a fat living glibly advising people about their marital problems. The issues they wrestle with are varied and complicated, but nothing fazes these electronic Solomons.

I, on the other hand, am willing to concede that anything I have to say on the subject of marriage is worthless. (Cries of "Hear! Hear!" from the reader, the publisher and the editor.) I have neither the equipment nor the experience to discuss this subject intelligently. If you want the real lowdown, hot from the paddock, I suggest you go to the public library and bone up on Shakespeare, Ovid, Casanova and Freud.

However, if you can't wait, skip all the experts and just dig deep into the heart of Krafft-Ebing.

My FIRST MARRIAGE took place in Chicago. We had the licence and two dollars, and we could have been married quickly and unobtrusively at the City Hall, but my bride insisted on some sort of a religious atmosphere. Anybody who's ever been married knows that, at that stage of a romance, the groom, feverish with desire, is willing to concede anything.

I don't know if Chicago has changed for the better, but we were grilled by five men of the cloth before we found one who would consent to perform the ceremony. It seemed the five who turned us down had religious objections because we weren't of the same faith. Moreover, when they discovered we were both in show business, they hastily steered us to the front door.

Most people speak disparagingly of marriage. It is constantly held up to ridicule on television and radio. At stag and bachelor dinners the language hurled at the groom would shock the madam of a call-house.

I don't want to be irreverent, but I think you will all agree that whoever created sex certainly knew his business. Though everyone is crazy about it (those who are not are beneath contempt and will bear watching), the word itself, small as it is, seems to frighten more people than antidisestablishment-arianism, which, as you all know, is the longest word in the English language. Lyric-writers, in particular, always delete that lovely little word and replace it with "love." No singer (even a tenor) would dare sing "Sex is a Many-splendoured Thing." With this title the song would sell in the millions, but the singer would be tossed in the clink by some morals committee. The charge? Inciting the public into doing what comes naturally.

Love covers a multitude of emotions and attitudes. I believe you can love God, a child, your next-door neighbour (or his wife—choice of one), or even a poodle. But love in marriage is never clearly defined.

When people see a young couple aimlessly strolling arm in arm, oblivious to the whole world and as close together as two bananas on the same stalk, they invariably exclaim, "My, what a charming pair!" or "Oh, what a darling couple! Just look how in love they are. Isn't that sweet?"

Well, here's where good old Groucho, the expert on nothing, sticks his foot in his mouth and bares his soul to a hostile world. They call it love, but to be honest about it, in most cases it isn't. It's just two people who find each other sexually attractive and hope, with luck, to soon be lying in each other's arms.

I wonder how crazy this particular Romeo would be about this particular Juliet if she were bowlegged, knock-kneed and had her bust manufactured in Akron, Ohio.* Let's say she had crow's feet under her eyes and he had crow's feet. I wonder how strong their love would be then—unless, of course, they both happened to be crows, in which case they would be irresistibly attracted to each other.

I don't deny that even ugly people get married (take me, for example), but most youngsters get married because they're eager for that sublime sexual experience that's been dinned into their subconscious since grammar school by their friends, records, movies and cheap novels.

In *Cat on a Hot Tin Roof*, Tennessee Williams has Big Mama point to a bed and say, "That's where marriages are decided." If Mr. Williams thinks there's nothing to marriage but that bed, I suggest he take another look at the script and start re-writing.

There's no question that sex is the force responsible for the perpetuation of the human race. If it didn't exist, life would disappear in a few decades, which might not be such a bad idea. I believe, however, that real love only appears when the early fires of passion have cooled off and the embers just lie there smouldering. This is true love. This relationship has only a bowing acquaintance with sex. Its component parts are patience, forgiveness, mutual understanding and a high tolerance for each other's faults. This, I believe, is a much firmer base for the perpetuation of a happy and successful marriage. But why should I babble on like this? Let's turn the whole thing over to the master, G.B.S. (Shaw to you), and I quote.

* More rubber is manufactured in Akron, Ohio, than in any other city in the world.

"When two people are under the influence of the most violent, most insane, most delusive and most transient of passions, they are required to swear they will remain in that excited, abnormal and exhausting condition continuously until death do them part."

Now that Mr. Shaw and I have defined "love" and wrapped it up in a small, neat, inaccurate package, let's proceed. I believe that loneliness is responsible for more marriages than that old come-on, sex. I've read ever so many biographies describing the velvet-lined life of the lucky bachelor, but don't you believe it. A friend of mine named Devlin (a blood brother of Delaney) once told me rather regretfully that had television and frozen dinners been around during the days of his courtship, he would never have married. There is just enough truth in his statement to lead me to believe that he wishes he had never been hooked.

Silly boy, he doesn't realize that no matter how many frozen dinners he downed or how many TV sets he had in his apartment, he would still be lonely. Frozen dinners are a wonderful invention, but they hardly take the place of an understanding woman at your side, clutching you hungrily. If I had to reduce it all to one sentence, maybe this would be it: the best meal in the world isn't worth eating unless there is someone there to share it with you. And the same thing goes for all shared experiences. Half the fun of watching TV at home is in turning to your companion and commenting, in good old Elizabethan English, on the tripe that the networks are deliberately aiming at you. There is nothing more ghastly than sitting alone in a movie theatre with no one to talk to. During my reprieve from the marital state I frequently endured this dismal experience.

I may be one of the unusual ones, but I find it almost impossible to watch a movie unless I can hurl at my companion, male or female, questions like, "Didn't we see that heavy last year in *Puberty is Here to Stay*?" or "I forgot who directed this stinker—what's his name?" or "Do you think she's really guilty?" I realize that this sort of idiotic twittering can be maddening to my companion, not to mention the surrounding movie-goers, but it's a compulsion that unfortunately I cannot control. And thereby hangs a ghastly tale.

ONE GLOOMY week-end, bent on romance, I journeyed to Palm Springs. It was raining when I arrived. I had engaged a suite of one room at a prominent tennis club and, as is my wont, was on the prowl for female companionship. The weather had been unusually bad that year (according to the Chamber of Commerce), and the inn was almost devoid of the opposite sex. I dined alone. Except for my deep breathing, the only other distraction in the large dining-room was the fearful sound generated by an old gentleman in the far corner. He was breaking Melba toast into his clam chowder in the hopeful notion that this additive would make the mess palatable.

Wolfing my dinner, I casually cased the premises for young, or even middle-aged, female society. I finally came upon four elderly women in the card-room (and when I say elderly, I'm referring to Grandma Moses and her contemporaries), who were sitting there cheating each other at canasta. Luckily I had brought a good book with me (*Dead Souls*), and concluded that if this was the best the club had to offer I would return to my room and read.

It was a damp, chilly night, so I threw a few logs into the fireplace. Apparently there was something wrong with the flue, for instead of those warm, cheery flames leaping upwards towards the chimney, the room and I both began to fill with smoke.

Donning my Homburg and shifting my ulcer a little to leeward, I decided that rather than wind up as a piece of jerked beef I would journey to the local movie emporium. I don't remember what was playing. I was only attracted to this theatre because their advertisement said, "Smoking permitted in the balcony."

As I entered, the manager greeted me with all the deference due a great star. He said, "Hi, Groucho! Plenty of good seats left. Ha! Ha!" His laughter turned to sobs as I groped my way up the dark stairs.

The balcony was empty except for a lone, elderly man sitting on the centre aisle, deeply engrossed in what was taking place on the screen. I headed straight for him. Since I had come in after the picture began, I had no idea what it was about or who was in the cast. I therefore fired a series of questions at him in rapid succession. In return he gave me a series of curt and guttural answers. Waiting a few minutes, I asked him another question. At this point he deliberately picked up his raincoat and moved to the far side of the balcony. Since there was no one else to talk to, I soon left the theatre and returned to my smoky abattoir.

Quickly opening all the windows, I leaped into bed. As I lay there shivering, a terrifying thought occurred to me. Just suppose that man in the balcony had gone to the manager of the theatre and complained that some eccentric character, who had hastily disappeared, had attempted to molest him! What a fine headline that would have made: GROUCHO MARX ARRESTED FOR MOLESTING ELDERLY MAN IN LOCAL THEATRE!

I SUPPOSE, IF YOU are young and single, dating can be loads of fun. But the last time I was single I was middle-aged and between marriages. In case you've never been in that awkward position, I can tell you it's not quite the same thing.

Let me give you a specific example. One day I met an attractive girl. She had blue eyes, red hair, white skin, black stockings and was at the age where everything had grown into its proper location. She looked like a beauty-contest winner who, in a large field, had snared third prize. After some preliminary conversation, some heavy-handed levity and hocus-pocus, we arranged a date for that evening. "Seven-thirty all right?" I asked.

She said, "That'll be ducky." I hoped her clever reply wasn't a harbinger of what the evening was to offer. But I said nothing and bided my time.

Having spent a lifetime in show business, I have always had an awesome respect for the clock and the virtues of punctuality. In the entertainment world, despite all the nonsense about fidelity to the theatre, if you're not there when they ring up the curtain, the show goes on without you. Moreover, they frequently discover that, without you, the show is considerably improved. So when the current lulu agreed on seven-thirty, I was there on time, reeking of "a man's lotion." (A lotion that, according to the ads., was guaranteed with one application to convert a female stone statue into a raging tigress. This isn't bad for a buck and a quarter. In my time I've paid as much as five dollars without being able to achieve that effect.)

Seething with immoral intentions, though outwardly calm, I was ushered in by an overweight, over-aged harridan encased in a frowsy outfit that was the height of fashion during the Boer War. She quickly introduced herself as "Daisy's mother," which proved conclusively that Daisy was a bit of a stupe. A bright girl bent on matrimony is usually cagey enough to hide her old lady until she has had time to gouge a Buick and an engagement ring out of her intended victim.

I don't know where they got the furniture, but a decorator would describe it as Early Hideous. They were all large pieces, and they were upholstered in imitation velvet, partially concealed by flowered cretonne. You wouldn't have been at all surprised if, upon entering, you had discovered General Grant sitting in one of the chairs.

A peculiar odour permeated the apartment. It's an odour I have encountered often in my search for romance. It seems to be an integral part of this type of layout. I can't describe it precisely, but it was as though some unseen form of decomposition was occurring in the immediate vicinity. I would call it a general essence of despair, bad liquor and fried foods.

Waving me towards one of the overstuffed monstrosities, Mrs. Frowsy bounced off to inform her meal-ticket of my arrival. She returned in a few minutes and trilled that Daisy would be down "in two shakes of a lamb's tail." Then, eager to further the romance, Molly Pitcher asked if I would care for a drink.

"Why, thanks, I sure would," I said. "Bourbon on the rocks will be fine."

"I'm sorry, Mr. Ritz. . . ."

"Marx, if you don't mind!"

". . . but we don't have any hard liquor in the house. You see, I'm a charter member of the Rosicrucians and, as you know, they're violently opposed to strong drink." She quickly added, "My little girl does drink a little, but only if she's out in public in a night club. She says it makes her look more sophisticated." (What she didn't know, and what I found out later that evening, was that her "little girl" was a pretty fair lush who could have matched drinks with W. C. Fields in his heyday.)

"I'm sorry we don't have any bourbon," she went on, "but could I offer you a bottle of root beer?"

Having had smoked whitefish for lunch, I was thirsty enough to drink brown gravy. "Okay," I said, "bring on the root beer."

"Well," she replied doubtfully, "I don't know if you'll like it. The ice-box is on the bum and it's still warm."

"In that case I'll take plain water."

"I think you're just as well off," she confided. "You know, root beer is just loaded with sugar. My doctor told me if I don't stop drinking soda pop, I'll be a diabetic before you can say Jack Robinson."

During this spirited dialogue, Mama kept leaping in and out of the room, assuring me that Daisy would be ready in a jiffy. The "jiffy" coalesced into three-quarters of an hour. Finally, my date appeared. She looked adorable, and when her perfume struck mine, sparks began to fly. At the moment I was sorry I was thirty years older than she was. (In fact, I was sorry I was thirty years older than anybody, but this was no time for regrets.)

As we walked towards the door, her mater gave her a last-ditch warning. "Watch him, Daisy. You know what a terrible reputation show people have!" This remark broke the mother up and, as we departed, the cackling of this weather-beaten battle-axe could be heard all the way to the car.

We soon arrived at the night-club, where the *maître d'* escorted us to a front table with all the bowing and scraping due one in my position. To make sure this phony deference didn't evaporate too quickly, I grudgingly slipped him three bucks.

Before the waiter could open his mouth to say good evening, Daisy ordered a straight Mickey—no ice, no water, no soda, no twist of lemon—just whisky. "And make it a double," she added. I had a bourbon highball.

After the second double shot, my charming companion opened up and began to regale me with the story of her life.

It seemed she originally hailed from Moline, Illinois. After arriving in Hollywood, she had worked as a car-hop, but the third week the proprietor fired her.

"He told me that I wore my Capri pants so tight that the male customers lost all interest in his cheeseburgers," she explained. "Besides, he was on the make."

She had told her boss that she was only trying to look attractive, but he pointed out that there was a place for that kind of pants, and the place wasn't a drive-in. Subsequently she worked in two other drive-ins, but because of her insistence on wearing the Capri pants she always got fired. She finally decided that the only profession where they didn't care what kind of pants you wore was show business. Apparently she knew more about show business than I did.

Bending over a trifle, she went on, "You know, not long ago I met an assistant casting director from one of the big studios. He was a real nice man. While we drove to the motel he told me that with just a tiny bit of training I could be the next Kim Novak." Turning her big blue lamps on me and brushing back a lock of her hair, she burst out, "Tell me, honey. What has Kim Novak got that I haven't got?"

"Frankly," I said, "I don't know. But I'll promise you this. If I'm ever out with Miss Novak, I'll try to find out and let you know. Now look," I went on, "you say you want to be in show business. Have you had any theatrical experience?"

"Well, no-o, not professionally, that is." Then she smiled brightly. "But when I was in grammar school I played the lead in *Rumpelstiltskin* for two successive years!"

I must have given her a look, for she hastily added, "Oh, I realize I need more training than that to be a great star. But you must admit it's a beginning. Besides, everyone says all I need is a little push. And I think if you got behind me," she leaned even closer, "I could deliver the goods."

There were a number of obvious answers to this statement, but I decided to keep my trap shut. I sat there, stupefied by the numbing effect of her childish prattle. As she rattled on and on, I found myself thinking, "What the hell am I doing here listening to this when I could be playing poker at some friend's house, watching a ball-game or even taking a mud bath at White Sulphur Springs? Why, at my age, do I persist in jockeying myself into these untenable situations?"

The time passed slowly. Oh, how slowly! Talk about leaden

feet, time was now crawling on its hands and knees! I wasn't a boy any longer, and after the second bourbon highball, I was getting sleepy. No matter what subject I carefully opened up, it took Daisy but a few minutes to switch the conversation back to her career. You've heard about variations on a theme by Haydn? Well, this kid threw in variations that Haydn never dreamed of.

Three long, deadly hours were consumed while my eardrums slowly petrified. I guess it was just my imagination, but it seemed to me that even her looks were beginning to fade. Her face was growing as dull as her dialogue, and as far as I was concerned sex had taken a holiday . . . a long holiday! All I could think of now was getting to bed. I don't mean with her—just by myself. Daisy had rung up a record that would last for some time. In three hours, she had talked me into celibacy!

Don't think that this episode with Daisy was an unusual experience. It happened to me all the time. Other men met well-educated, rich girls whose fathers owned department stores, oil wells or factories. These daughters of the rich seemingly had no interest in theatrical careers. All they wanted was marriage, a family and a reasonable percentage of their father's income. But as for me, I always picked the Daisies.

CHAPTER TWENTY-TWO

MELINDA AND ME

Ever since I began this illiterate chronology, my editor (a well-known sadist) has been pressing me (pressing me? goading me!) to disclose some intimate details of my private life. "Look," he said, "up to now you've written 80,000 words." (This will give you an idea of the sleaziness of this man . . . he counts each and every word as though they were pearls.) "And," he went on, pursuing the subject to the point of nausea, "your readers still don't know a damned thing about you."

Bristling at his determination to invade my privacy, I said to this throw-back to Captain Bligh, "Sir, I don't think my private life is any of the public's business. I'm not writing true confessions for one of these magazines that carry nine different ads. for acne cures and nineteen for electric belts, nor am I writing one of these 'as told to someone else' books where the leading character is blind drunk for thirty years and then tells how he found God, the A.A. or both." (I have a hunch that when these characters first start boozing it up they have already planned the collaborative autobiography that they eventually hope to sell to a movie studio.)

To those of my readers who insist on prying into my private life I'll admit this much . . . I am married and I have three children. Two of them are grown up. The third is a female moppet named Melinda, who is twelve and a half and whose word is law.

A few weeks ago Melinda ordered me to her room. "Daddy" (she calls me that when I'm within earshot), "I have to have a party."

"Okay," I agreed, "invite a couple of kids over some night."

"No," she said, "I don't think you understand. I have to have a *real* party."

"All right, invite four kids over," I said genially.

She shook her head. "Four kids are no good."

"Melinda," I replied, "*no* kids are any good. But tell me, just what are you after?"

"Well, Daddy, I want to have twenty-two kids over next Friday, and you have to stay in your room until they all go home."

"To begin with," I said, "let's separate those two commands. Let's do it slow and easy. Now then, why do you have to have twenty-two kids over to my house?"

"*Our* house," she corrected.

"What's wrong with having four kids? And would you mind turning that radio down before I kick it to shreds?" (During this discussion Melinda was doing her homework, the radio was going full blast and the TV set was on without the sound. She was also stroking a young cat which had just finished spilling ink on her new and expensive carpet.)

"Daddy!" She gave me an injured look. "You know I can't do my homework without the radio on."

"Melinda," I replied, "you can't do your homework *with* the radio on—but we'll discuss that later. Now then, why do you have to have twenty-two kids?"

"Because I haven't been to a party in over a month."

"Neither have I," I replied, "but you'll notice there's no ink on my carpet. Now then, why haven't you been to a party in over a month? Do you have one of those loathsome diseases that the television announcers are constantly screaming about? Are you anti-social in the cafeteria? What major deficiencies do you have that make you a marked girl in your school?"

"Oh, Daddy," she said, "you know there's nothing the matter with me. It's just that if *you* don't give a party now and then, the kids don't invite you to *their* parties."

The ink on the carpet now having settled into a stiff blue frieze, I proceeded to take the offensive. "What will this party entail in the way of preparations?"

"Really nothing," she smiled brightly. "Just some little old potato chips, Coca-Cola and Seven-Up."

At the mention of the menu my tongue started to coat. "Okay," I said, "I'll go for that."

AFTER SCHOOL the following day (the radio still blasting), Melinda came home and called out, "Daddy, are you ready? We have to go to the toy-shop now."

"Toy-shop? Why do we have to go to the toy-shop?"

"To get things for the party," she explained patiently.

"Melinda," I said, "I realize you're only twelve and a half, but don't you know you don't buy potato chips, Coca-Cola and Seven-Up at a toy-store?"

"Oh, I know that, Daddy, but we have to get bunting and some flags, otherwise the whole party will droop. And after that we have to go to the hardware store for the charcoal for the barbecue."

"Charcoal for the barbecue!" I interrupted. "What's that for?"

"Well, Daddy, I figured that we'll all be hungry after dancing. But don't worry, we won't have anything elaborate—just hot dogs and hamburgers and a three-layer cake filled with ice-cream and maybe some small sandwiches and fruit."

"Just a moment," I said, "you forgot cigarettes."

"No, I didn't," she answered, "but we won't need many. Very few of the kids smoke."

"Well," I asked hopefully, "is that it?"

"Daddy!" she said reproachfully, rolling one eye at me and the other at a boy who was just crossing the street. "We have to have records."

"Records!" I yelled. "You've got a roomful of records. I bought you the top ten just last week!"

She now rolled her other eye at the boy. "Those records are all old stuff. All the kids have heard them. A new list comes out every week, and the kids just won't dance unless they have the latest records."

As we left the record shop, partly asphyxiated from the leaden air in the small booth where we had been confined for the past two hours, I suddenly realized I now had over forty bucks tied up in a shindig that had started with just some little old potato chips, Coca-Cola and Seven-Up.

THE DAY OF the party dawned bright and clear. My wife, no fool, left at 7 P.M., hurriedly shouting that she had to go to a P.T.A. meeting. A half-hour before the semi-bandits were due to descend upon us, Melinda came to my room and asked, "Daddy, how do I look?"

"You look just great," I said. "And don't forget, everybody out by ten-thirty."

"Okay," she nodded. Then eyeing me speculatively, she announced, "I think I told you before, Daddy, but please don't come out of your room until all the kids have left."

"What's your problem?" I asked. "Are you ashamed of your dear old Dad?" Then, cribbing a line from *Iolanthe*, I said, "You may not be aware of it, but I'm generally admired."

Melinda shook her head. "Of course I'm not ashamed of you, Daddy, but if the kids know there are grown-ups in the house—except the maid, of course—the party will be a flop."

"Now let me get this straight," I said. "You mean to tell me I have to stay locked up in my room in my own house, just because twenty-two of your scavenger friends are going to be out there bolting the non-deductible grub that I paid for?"

She came over and gave me a big kiss. That is always her answer when she doesn't have an answer. As she started to leave the room, I said, "Wouldn't the kids feel more secure if I slipped into a strait-jacket?"

"Oh, Daddy," she replied, "that won't be necessary." She went out, closed the door behind her and carefully turned the key in the lock.

Being of a literary bent, I now picked up the *Wall Street Journal*. I had no sooner read the third editorial on the dangers of inflation when the two almost-house-broken poodles began yelping, announcing the arrival of the first guests. Eight o'clock ticked by and all was well. Things were still pretty quiet in the old corral. I sat there, happy in the thought that my little daughter was out in the midst of a social whirlpool, the cynosure of all eyes.

Suddenly the record-player began blasting at a pitch that is seldom heard outside of Cape Canaveral or the Straits of China. Intermingled with this were childish screams and the duller sounds of scuffling and wrestling. Stuffing cotton-wool in my ears, I resolutely picked up a book determined to concentrate and ignore the twenty-two bulls in my china shop.

The Donnybrook now became louder and wilder. When I finally realized I had read the same paragraph four times, I threw the book on the desk, got up and sneaked warily out of the door of my study (which Melinda had fortunately overlooked), and down the corridor to the living-room. I arrived just in time. Three of the larger boys were carrying one of the smaller ones over to the fireplace, apparently with intent to barbecue. I rescued the medium-rare victim and then delivered a short, stern speech, pointing out that the interior of an expensive living-room was hardly the ideal locale for re-enacting the last days of Joan of Arc.

Melinda rushed over to me and said, "Daddy! Get back to your room! The kids all resent you."

"Well, I resent them, too," I said. "And, furthermore, if I hear any more rough-house out here, I'll throw them all out!"

With that I strode back to my room and began reading Kafka's *Life of Camus* (or maybe it was the other way around . . . by this time it really didn't make much difference). Every once in a while I peeked through the keyhole and tried to visualize what was taking place in the living-room. I guess my stern speech had put the fear of God into the juvenile Mafia, for suddenly all was quiet.

BY NINE-THIRTY the comparative silence began to get on my nerves. I crept out again to see how young America on the march was making out. On one side of the room the girls were dancing with each other. On the other side of the room the boys were engaged in a very interesting contest. They were throwing lighted matches under the sofa. It seemed the one whose match burned the longest was to collect ten cents from each of the losers. I suppose there was also a bonus for anyone who set fire to the sofa.

Again I rushed into the room and made practically the same speech I had made before. But this time I was smarter. I persuaded the ringleader to come out in the hall and promised him a box of cigars for his father if he'd take over and keep the orgy under control. I then returned to my room, sat down and stared at the clock. At the stroke of ten-thirty I ran out and shouted, "Okay, party's over! Everybody out!"

A few of the more gentlemanly ones thanked me for a pleasant evening. Two of the boys kicked me in the shins as they left. Soon the house was quiet again and Melinda was in her room. I went in.

"Melinda," I began apologetically, "I'm sorry I had to

break my promise and horn in on your party. I hope I didn't offend any of your guests."

She turned to me with a big smile. "Oh, no, Daddy. They didn't mind your coming in. They all see you on TV and they know you're always kidding. It was a wonderful party, and I know now I'll get a lot of invitations from the other kids."

Melinda ran over and gave me a big hug. She looked up smiling and said, "Daddy, next year can I have another party? Nothing elaborate—just potato chips, Coca-Cola and Seven-Up."

"Okay, Melinda," I said. "Turn off the record-player, brush your teeth, go to bed. And by the way, good night, dear."

CHAPTER TWENTY-THREE

MY PERSONAL DECATHLON

THE SOCIAL SIDE of my life (what there is of it) hasn't been touched upon by this poor man's Pepys. Perhaps it's just as well. My private life has had none of the glamour or excitement of Elsa Maxwell, Grace Kelly or Rubirosa. To achieve that kind of distinction you either have to be very rich, have ancestors who fought at the Battle of Lexington (it doesn't matter which side), be a six-goal polo player with your own string of ponies, or occasionally get bounced out of the Stork Club or El Morocco. You're certainly not going to hit the society columns getting booted out of Lindy's or the Seventh Avenue Delicatessen.

In my younger days, I thought I would make it as one of America's outstanding athletes. You know, the burly type like Jim Thorpe or Bob Mathias. Since I only weighed 120, stripped, I put my clothes on again and abandoned the notion.

First I tried swimming. I don't mean the English Channel or the Hellespont, like Leander. The fact is, until I was twelve I couldn't swim at all. I could float for hours, but the minute I turned over on my other side I'd start to drown. When I was seventeen, we were playing Poli's Theatre in Bridgeport, and there I learned to swim at the local YMCA. As soon as I learned how to swim, for some curious reason I no longer could float. Every time I turned over on my back I started going under again.

I have a swimming pool now, and also a young daughter to go with it. When Melinda's little friends come over I watch their antics in the pool. It's frightening! They swim under water for what seems to me like hours. They do jack-knives, back-flips off the diving-board and stand on their heads in the water. Sometimes you don't see anything but feet for ten minutes at a stretch. It's getting so I'm ashamed to go into the pool at all.

I still use the (if you'll pardon the vulgarity) breast stroke. It was all the rage during the Spanish-American War. Don't blame me. That's what they taught me at the YMCA in Bridgeport. I must say, it's not a very swift stroke. I have a forty-foot pool and the other day I timed myself. It took me three minutes to get from one end to the other. This was at top speed. I was so exhausted from this effort that it took the combined strength of the gardener, the mailman and the upstairs maid to drag me from the pool.

WHEN MY SON Arthur (who is now around eighty) was twelve, I took him to Forest Hills to see Tilden play Cochet. The following day he forced me to buy him a racket. Fortunately, I was able to get him one wholesale. In no time at all he could knock off the average opponent. At one time he had about a fifteen rating nationally, which means he was the fifteenth best player in America, and in the two years he played at Forest Hills, he clobbered many a seeded player. Although he was never as good as Vines, Tilden, Budge or Kramer, he was the only athlete our family had ever produced and we were all very proud of him.

When Arthur took up tennis in a big way I, too, bought a racket wholesale. With this weapon I decided I could spend more time with him. You know, "togetherness" and all that jazz. However, this long preamble is only to set the stage for what followed.

At the age of thirteen, Arthur used to play doubles with another kid who played about as well as he did. I frequently played against them with whatever partner I could pick up around the club. There were some pretty good players there, but no matter whom I teamed with we always lost.

At that time Ellsworth Vines was the U.S. Champion and Fred Perry was the British champ. One day I said to Perry, "Fred, I'd give anything to beat those kids. Boy, are they cocky! Would you play with me against them?" Since he had only recently won at Wimbledon, I didn't anticipate much of a contest.

Well, the boys beat us in straight sets. I'd rush the net and they would lob one over my head. No matter where I stood, the ball wasn't there. Their tactics were simple, but effective. They just hit everything to me. Fred scrambled, but he couldn't cover the whole court.

I still wouldn't admit defeat and decided that Perry didn't have the right kind of a game to help me demolish these kids. I knew Vines had a bigger serve and could hit harder, so a few days later, I explained my plight to Ellsworth and he consented to play with me against the boys. We did a little better, but Arthur and his friend had caught on. They used the same tactics they used against Perry. They just kept playing me. I never saw so many tennis balls whizz by. They knocked us off neatly and swiftly.

I had now had as partners both the American and British champions, and had lost with both. It wasn't too long afterwards that I threw in my racket and retired. I played only one more match—Charlie Chaplin and Fred Perry against the American team of Ellsworth Vines and Groucho Marx. Word of this match had got around, and a fairly large crowd showed up. Charlie played pretty good tennis on his private court, but he wasn't accustomed to playing before a crowd. Besides, I kept talking and needling him until he finally sat down on the concrete on his side of the net, completely unhinged. Not wishing to strain international relations, I sat down on my side of the net and we watched Perry and Vines fight it out between themselves. I don't remember who won.

Those were my tennis years.

THEN CAME GOLF. Actually, golf is not a game at all. In addition to being a curse, it's a way of life. Golf has broken up more homes than the legendary "other woman." It is probably the only pastime that a wife will accept as a plausible excuse for her husband's remaining away from the old homestead.

If you swim, you usually do it with your family. You can play three sets of tennis in an hour. However, by playing eighteen holes of golf instead of nine, a husband can manage to remain away from home most of the day. And if he's one of the many duffers and hooks or slices a great deal, he can spend most of the day in the rough, where it's impossible for his wife to find him.

But staying away from home isn't all there is to golf. It's not even the most important part. The locker-room is where the game really begins. Here's where the boys booze it up, far away from the watchful gimlet eye of the wife. Here's where they lie about their scores, brag about their sexual exploits, tell dirty (and usually very old) stories and consummate business deals. I have no figures to prove it, but I'll wager that there are more contracts negotiated and sealed by firm handshakes within the sound of the club showers than in any of the steel-and-aluminium office buildings that stretch across the country.

But the grassy fairway is where man really reverts to boy again. Here he wears all the brightly coloured Christmas sweaters, funny hats and trick trousers that he doesn't dare wear in any other public place. Here is where he kicks his ball out of the rough. Not always, just often enough to beat the president of some rival corporation out of two bucks. Here he bawls out the caddie and pulls all the snide tricks that, in any other environment, would brand him for life as a social leper.

My first attempt at golf was on a Sunday morning at Van Cortlandt Park in New York. I was just a youngster then, with a lot of time at my disposal, and I disposed of it all right! I had heard about the congestion there and was advised that if I expected to play, I had better show up early in the morning. I arrived at five. After standing in line for six hours, I finally teed off at eleven. I never saw such a crowd. There must have been five hundred players on each hole.

My score for the first hole was pretty good. Four golf balls whizzed past me and two got me. One hit me in the groin and another knocked my hat off. I finished the one hole and fled. I had read about Flanders Field during the First World War, but I never knew what it meant until I played that one hole at Van Cortlandt Park.

YEARS LATER, I decided to take up golf in earnest. I bought a set of second-hand clubs, a canvas bag and three balls. We were appearing at the Orpheum Theatre in San Francisco. On the bill was a singer by the name of Frank Crummit. He shot in the middle seventies and, one day, invited me to join him in a game. We didn't belong to any club, so we went to the Lincoln Park Municipal Course. I was sixty-four for the first six holes. We then proceeded to play the seventh. On this hole the tee is high on a hill: the green, completely surrounded by murderous traps, is nestled below. It was a pitch of 154 yards, and Crummit advised me to use a five-iron. I took a swipe at the ball. It hit the green and rolled into the cup.

The next morning the sports pages of the San Francisco

Chronicle and the *Examiner* carried my picture. In fact, there were three pictures. On one side of me was a photo of Bobby Jones, on the other side was a picture of Walter Hagen. The caption was simplicity itself: GROUCHO MARX JOINS THE IMMORTALS.

That evening, two newspapers called up and asked if I planned on playing the following morning. And would I mind if a few photographers accompanied me on the round? "Of course not," I replied. Then they asked, "Would you object if we sent a few reporters along? We are all curious to see how you play that seventh hole."

I didn't tell them what my score was on the first six holes. I just said, rather modestly, "You realize I don't get a hole in one every time I play a short hole." But suddenly overcoming my modesty, I added, "But it's not nearly as difficult as so many mediocre golfers claim it is."

Well, there was quite a crowd there the next morning to watch me tee off. It was obvious that my reputation had preceded me. For a duffer, I didn't do too badly on the first six holes. On the seventh they had set up cameras on the sides of the green. Oddly enough, I wasn't a bit nervous. I'm more or less made of steel, as many a bruiser who has crossed my path will ruefully attest. To my surprise, I made a fairly good shot. The ball hit the green, hesitated, and rolled off into a sand trap. I then hit it a savage blow with my sand wedge. It came out—and very neatly plopped into a trap on the other side of the green. This continued for quite some time. Well, dear reader, there's no point in keeping you in a fever of suspense. I had a twenty-one on the hole—and that was only because I was putting unusually well! Home once more from the hills, I realized that there was more to golf than meets the eye.

SHORTLY AFTER THAT, I was living on Long Island and appearing on Broadway. This was during the Prohibition era, and the gangsters were riding high. Having forgotten what happened to me at Van Cortlandt Park, I started to play at another municipal golf course. This one was called the Queensborough Club and it was a grim-looking layout. I didn't know that this was where all the hoodlums congregated. Dutch Schultz and his boys used to play there every day. This was their hang-out, but since I didn't regularly move in their circle I knew them only by reputation.

I was still a duffer, but by this time I played well enough to keep the ball rolling towards the next hole. One morning, playing alone, I teed off and hit a fairly long drive. As I started to hit my second shot, I heard cries of "Fore!" coming from the first tee. The shouts continued, "Fore! Fore! Fore!"

" 'Fore'?" I said to myself. "They must be beginners. Don't they know they're not supposed to tee off until the player ahead of them has had his second shot? As soon as I finish this game," I decided, "I'll tell them a thing or two! Somebody ought to teach those gents a few things about golf etiquette and manners, and I'm just the boy to do it!"

It was a foursome, and they now shouted, almost in unison, "Hey, you! You with that canvas bag! Get the hell outta there or we're gonna shoot!"

By now I was seething. I angrily waved my club at them and yelled, "What's the matter with you guys? Are you blind? Can't you see I haven't had my second shot? Why don't you shut up?"

My tirade didn't have the slightest influence on them. They shot, all right—but not in the way I thought they meant. Suddenly a bullet flew past me. Then three more bullets in rapid succession. It began to dawn on me that these thugs were out to get me. I decided that this was not the time to stop and figure out why. I hurriedly picked up my golf-bag, dashed to the parking lot, hopped in my car and drove off at such a speed that a few minutes later I was stopped by a state trooper and arrested for doing eighty miles an hour in a fifteen-mile zone. This was my farewell to Hoodlum Hall.

I now came to the conclusion that if I was going to play golf I had better abandon the municipal links, spend some money and join a country club. There was a very swank one in Great Neck called the Lakeville Club. It was a real snobbish rendezvous and they were very picky about who was to enter their sacred portals and tread their hallowed greens. Before becoming a member I had to submit to both a blood and saliva test. Once these had proven satisfactory, they grudgingly accepted my membership cheque for five thousand five hundred dollars. Three months later, the cheque cleared, and soon after that I was reluctantly admitted to the club-house.

The second week, my brother Gummo invited himself to play with me. "Gummo," I asked, "have you ever played golf before?"

He looked at me in astonishment. "Groucho, are you kidding? I just finished twelve lessons in a gymnasium, under the personal instruction of one of the most famous golf pros. in America! He was formerly at St. Andrews in Scotland. Of *course* I can play!"

"Now look, Gummo," I persisted, "are you *sure* you can play? This isn't some municipal dump, you know. This is probably the classiest country club on Long Island. I've only been a member for a few weeks and we don't want to go out there and make ourselves look ridiculous."

"Don't you worry about me," assured Gummo. "My golf pro. told me I'm a natural golfer, and that with my swing I can hold my own on any golf-course in America."

I t was a lovely Sunday morning in May. Gummo arrived, resplendent in his golf garb. His attire was something to behold. He was wearing English shoes with tassels, peppermint-striped stockings, very large and overblown plus fours and the type of headgear that Zulus wear when they are performing one of their traditional ceremonial war dances.

When it came our turn to tee off there was still a big crowd waiting to shoot. The parking lot at Lakeville parallels the first green. "Gummo," I whispered, "since you shoot so well, you tee off first. That will create a good impression with the crowd."

Disdaining the wooden tee, he did what the real pros do. He took a pinch of wet sand and confidently teed up the ball. After a few preliminary waggles and a long professional look to the green, he took a hefty swipe at his target. The ball sailed off beautifully—and instantly smashed two of the windows in the club President's Cadillac.

With a hollow laugh I turned to the crowd and said, "Tough luck. . . . But you know, this could have happened to anybody."

There were no answers. Some of them turned the other way and others began shuffling their feet impatiently.

I turned back to my brother. "Gummo," I said, "that was really tough luck. Tee up another ball, big boy (he happens to be an inch taller than I am) and away we'll go."

Gummo didn't seem a bit disturbed by the window-shattering incident. As a matter of fact, he acted as if this was a regular part of his game. He nonchalantly took another pinch of wet sand and teed up again. Again he waggled. Again he peered down the fairway. Then he took careful aim, hit the ball a resounding smack and stood back to admire its flight. The ball immediately hooked to the left and crashed through a window in the ladies' dining-room. It just barely missed decapitating the woman whose husband was head of the Membership Committee.

I then decided that we were both over-golfed. Taking our bags from the hysterical caddies, we made a hasty exit. I vowed never to play at the club again until the snow fell . . . and Gummo had departed to some remote caravanserai.

MOST OF US are egotistical enough to believe that when we do something badly it's really not our fault. This is especially true of golf. The tendency is to blame it on the equipment, an incompetent caddie, your wife's mother (who came to visit one night and stayed three months), or the fact that your clubs are out of alignment or the grounds-keeper hasn't been putting enough manure on the putting greens.

I've been playing golf now for a bad thirty years. With cheating, I usually shoot around ninety-five. However, if my opponent is smart enough to count my strokes, I invariably shoot a hundred and one. This puzzles me. I see old gaffers on the fairway, so creaky with arthritis that their bones can be heard a full brassie shot away, regularly posting scores in the low or middle eighties.

Don't think I haven't taken lessons at five dollars per half-hour. I have. I've stood on practice tees and belted balls until I ached clear down to my toes. At various times I've been instructed to put my weight on my left foot, on my right foot, to squat down in the Ben Hogan manner, to keep my chin pressed to my left shoulder, keep my head down, my left knee pointing towards my right knee. What makes these lessons interesting (and baffling) is that every pro. has a theory all his own. Nevertheless, as soon as I leave the practice tee and start playing, my game is always the same as it was before I wasted the five dollars.

Talk about Dr. Eliot and his five-foot shelf, I have a six-foot shelf. It's all about golf. Through these books I have been instructed by Henry Cotton, lectured by Sam Snead and advised by Walter Hagen, Ben Hogan and all the other greats. Tommy Armour, for example, writes (with uncalled-for familiarity): "Hey, you! Forget about your left hand. Grab the club tightly in your right hand and belt it!" MacDonald Smith patiently advises: "Swing the club—pretend there's no ball there at all." Henry Cotton assures you that the right hand has no place in golf. "Imagine you've left the right hand at home." (Presumably in the closet.) "Just swing smoothly with the left." Ernest Jones tells you, "Pretend you have a long piece of string with a stone at the bottom of it, and just swing it back and forth as though it were a pendulum."

Your club pro., who was born in McKeesport, Pennsylvania, tells you with a rich Scottish burr (which he acquired for twenty-five dollars from a Scotch dialect comedian) that the trouble with your game is that you're not using the right clubs. "I make all my own clubs," he boasts. "I get my woods from a rare species of briar tree that grows only in the north of Scotland. Listen, laddie," he croaks, "you buy a set of these woods and my own special set of irons, which are forged for me in Manchester, and laddie boy, you'll cut ten strokes off your game before you can say Bobby Burns." You don't find out till the end of the month that this new hardware has also cut five hundred and fifty dollars off your bank-roll.

To sum it up, it doesn't make any difference where I play or what equipment I use. At the end of eighteen holes, my score is always a hundred and one!

While we're on this golf bit, I have to tell you one story. It's about the late Jesse Lasky, who, at one time, was President of Paramount Pictures. Despite that, he was one of the nicest men I ever knew. Some years ago, we were playing golf at Hillcrest Country Club, which is directly across from the Rancho Gold Club. In those days there was no fence between them to restrain the rabble from invading either Hillcrest or Rancho. At some holes, the fairways adjoined each other. On this particular hole, Jesse hit a long, beautiful drive off the tee. The ball drifted off into a semi-parabola and, unknown to Lasky, landed on the Rancho fairway. "Caddie," he said, "what club shall I use from here?"

The caddie, with all the contempt of a professional, replied, "Mr. Lasky, you tell me what club you belong to and I'll tell you what club to use!"

CHAPTER TWENTY-FOUR

YO HEAVE HO, AND OVER THE RAIL

I HAVE NEVER BEEN one for life on the ocean wave. To begin with, I don't understand the theory of *mal de mer*, or seasickness, as it is euphemistically called in our country. What causes it? Is it some dislocation in the inner ear? Does the retching come from fried foods and unripe watermelon balls? All I know is that this curse has afflicted me ever since I first sailed a boat in a bath-tub.

I have flown all over the United States and Europe. I flew in the first tri-motor Fords that limped uncertainly across the country. I flew in open cockpit Army and Navy planes. I was never sick. But the minute I step on anything that floats on water, I'm a goner.

I have been sick on the Clyde Line out of Jacksonville, bound for New York with a cargo of cotton. I have also been sick on the *Mauretania*, the S.S. *Paris*, the *Cedric*, the *Europa* and the Albany night boat. Ah, what a night that was! They gave you a girl with each cabin. If you were poor and could only afford a small upper berth, they loaned you a nymphet as far as Poughkeepsie.

Any bark that sails the seven seas or its tributaries can make a shambles out of my insides. I have tried Dramamine, codeine, aspirin, Bonamine, champagne and raw eggs. I have tried them separately and together. All the fabled remedies just go in one inner ear and out the other. I have tried spending the entire voyage in bed, in a chair, walking briskly around the deck, breathing deeply and not breathing at all. The way love laughs at locksmiths is the way the sea laughs at me, and my efforts to outwit it are futile and tragic.

My last joust with Father Neptune took place on the S.S. *Malola* headed for Hawaii, gardenias, *luaus* and outrigger canoes. We were instructed by the passenger agent (the gent who sucked us into going) to be sure to get to Wilmington (not the one in Delaware, but the one in California) at least two hours before the boat sailed. I remember his exact words.

"I promise you, Mr. Marx, there will be fun galore. The

minute you set foot on that dream boat, all your cares and troubles will disappear into thin air. There will be music and streamers and confetti. You'll never see a happier throng. Even the friends and relatives who come down to the pier to see their loved ones off, have almost as much fun as the lucky nine hundred who sail into the setting sun. And, Mr. Marx," he continued, "it's not only fun galore at the pier, but it never lets up. There's something going on every minute. We proudly boast that all our ships are happy ships."

He hitched his chair close and whispered confidentially, "I wouldn't want the company officials to get wind of this, because I'm up for a better job, but of the entire fleet, my favourite ship has always been the *Malola*. People say the food is as good as that served at the Tour d'Argent in Paris." At the mention of food, I immediately began to feel queasy.

"We particularly pride ourselves on our *smorgasbord*," he rattled on. "The *Malola* is the only ship sailing the Pacific that serves sixteen different kinds of cold herring!"

Although I was still on dry land, the thought of sixteen kinds of cold herring on a boat quickly put me in condition for the old heave-ho. The passenger agent raved on. "Wait'll you smack your lips over our pickled eel! You know, on my last trip on the *Malola* I ate so many pickled eels that my missus said I would soon look like one."

His wife was wrong. He already looked like one. However, it wasn't worth arguing about, so I paid for the tickets and left while I was still able to navigate.

As I staggered from his office, he said, "Oh, by the way, have you ever been to the Mardi Gras in New Orleans?"

I was a bit puzzled by this question because, off hand, I didn't see any connection between New Orleans and a pickled eel. Suspiciously, I said, "Yes, I've played there a number of times."

"Well, forget it!" he said. "The Mardi Gras is nothing compared to a trip on the *Malola*."

"Have you ever been there?" I asked.

"Well, no," he replied, "but I've seen it in the newsreels many times, and I can tell you that the *Malola* is more fun than the New Orleans Mardi Gras. It's much healthier, too, because you're getting that bracing salt air in your lungs from morning till night."

Although he had told us to be at the dock by eight, we

didn't arrive until eleven. You see, we had only been planning this trip for three months, and our sailing date came as a complete surprise to my wife. It took her three hours to get dressed, fix her hair, polish her nails, paint her toes and pack, before she finally announced that she was ready. I then put into my one suitcase all the stuff she couldn't force into two steamer trunks and three handbags, and before I knew it we silently headed for Wilmington and paradise.

We arrived about an hour before the boat sailed, and virtually everything the passenger agent had told us was true. It really was fun galore. The pier was crowded with friends and relatives and the din was ear-shattering. Most of the passengers were lined along the railing on one side of the top deck. Streamers and confetti were flying through the air. Laughter and jolly admonitions were being hurled back and forth. To my relief, the sea was as smooth as glass, and the good ship stood staunch and steady as she rode there at anchor.

The "All ashore" finally sounded, the ship's horn began tooting its farewell and the band began playing "Aloha." As they began to haul up the anchor, on the far side of the top deck, elegantly accoutred in a vicuña coat and yellow beret, stood a lonely figure. That figure was I, leaning over the rail into dat ol' debbil sea and, as has been a tradition for many years, vomiting.

SPEAKING OF seasickness (as I usually am), I knew a character who started off in life as a street-car conductor. By pocketing most of the fares, he eventually manœuvred himself into the position of top dog at a major movie studio. He decided that, now he was the head of a studio, he should have a yacht. J. P. Morgan had one. Vanderbilt had one. Sir Thomas Lipton had one. Even Columbus had one—and he certainly had more money than Columbus. In fact, if it hadn't been for Queen Isabella, Columbus would have been a bum. (Sometimes I wonder what actually *was* the relationship between Columbus and Isabella. One of these days I'm going to get the real low-down from Hedda and Louella. Those girls are up on everything.)

Well, back to our friend, the head of the studio. Not long

after he had made this decision, he became the proud owner of a large yacht and a large crew. He now had three hundred thousand dollars less in the bank: but this didn't worry him because he had many millions. He then ordered his tailor to run up a complete wardrobe of yachting outfits—white suits, blue suits, uniforms for all occasions, and all with gold braid.

He had never been on a boat before. On his maiden voyage, attired in an outfit that would have done credit to Admiral Dewey, he instructed his captain to sail him from Los Angeles to San Diego. The ship was fully equipped with vintage wines, booze, Beluga caviar and a couple of starlets (in case he couldn't find anything to read).

Two hours out of the home port he began feeding the fishes. By the time they sailed into the harbour at San Diego, this top dog was a mighty sick dog, and I don't mean a sea dog. He then went to a hotel and remained in bed for forty-eight hours. Shortly afterwards, he was notified by his first officer that the sea was calm again, and he prepared to return to the yacht.

The ship rode peacefully at anchor in the San Diego harbour, and our friend, determined to be a yachtsman, vowed to conquer this silly weakness. For the next seven days he paced the deck like a true sailor. He strode back and forth with all the authority of Charles Laughton in *Mutiny on the Bounty*. On the seventh day he got an urgent call from his studio. One of his stars had got stewed the night before at a fancy party, and kicked a valuable camera out of the hands of an Associated Press reporter. Then, ripping off all her clothes, she threw them in his face and dived into the swimming pool. Our hero was told that a large lawsuit was in the offing, and he had better get back to Hollywood and straighten it out.

He ordered, "Full steam ahead!" He didn't know quite what this meant, but he remembered the line from one of the sea pictures his studio had made. Fifteen minutes out of San Diego he took to his bed again and remained there, cursing his fate, until they arrived back in Los Angeles, where he was carried off the ship in a deep daze from an overdose of Dramamine tablets. It was apparent that life on the ocean wave was not for him.

The yacht now presented quite a problem. He loved his sea-going white elephant and he loved wearing the uniforms, but it seemed he could only remain on the ship while it was lying at anchor in a harbour. Here was a fine dilemma! He had three hundred thousand dollars tied up in the boat and another two grand tied up in the uniforms. He had never had any class, but now, as the owner of an ocean-going yacht, he was beginning to acquire some social distinction. Yet the thought of another trip on this bark filled him with terror.

However, he was a resourceful man and he finally solved his problem, though not entirely to his satisfaction. It was a compromise, but isn't life a series of compromises?

He instructed his captain to take the boat again to San Diego. Dressed in one of his naval outfits, Lord Nelson the Second then had his chauffeur drive him there. Upon arrival, he was piped aboard with homage and deference. While the ship lay at anchor he strode the deck, fiercely scowling into the wind and peering with his bifocals through the binoculars, as though he were about to engage the entire Japanese fleet in battle.

When he finally wearied of this marine monotony, he ordered the ship back to its home port and, as it slipped over the horizon, he was piped into his Rolls Royce. Comfortably settled, and still in full regalia, he then ordered the chauffeur to drive him back to Beverly Hills.

Tired of looking at San Diego and its environs, he eventually sold all his uniforms to the Western Costume Company, stuck some sucker with the yacht, bought a trailer and spent the rest of his days commuting to Palm Springs.

CHAPTER TWENTY-FIVE

GO FISH

FISHING ALWAYS BRINGS to mind ex-President Hoover, sitting in a dumpy row-boat on some placid lake deep in the heart of the wilderness, or Hemingway strapped in an office chair on the back of a sixty-foot launch, spearing a marlin.

Fishing is big business. I read somewhere that the amount of money wasted on this finny pastime could, in a reasonable length of time, wipe out the national debt. It's supposed to be good for the nerves—all the babbling brooks, the mountain streams and the picturesque waterfalls (which, in many states, rival power companies are fighting to get their hands on).

The ivory-tower egghead boys are now unanimous in declaring that man originally emerged from the ocean disguised as an amoeba, a one-legged frog or some similarly nauseating species of marine low life. I go along with this theory. Personally, I've been just as eager as my ancestors to get out of the water and on to dry land.

I don't understand the craze for fishing. In my time I, too, have taken a fling at the Izaak Walton stuff. I have fished off the pier in Atlantic City with a drop-line and a condemned piece of meat dangling from the end of it. I still shudder with horror when I think of the repulsive-looking things I pulled up with that bait.

I have fished in mountain streams wearing high rubber boots, a yellow hat, four sweaters and a windbreaker. This kind of fishing requires no bait at all. You just tie a red, whirling object on the end of your line, close your eyes and cast. Casting means whipping your line away out into the running stream—where the hook immediately sinks into the rear of your host's trousers. To put it briefly, very little love is lost between our finny friends and me.

AN OVER-ENTHUSIASTIC friend of mine is the typical nut. I have a theory about men who are crazy about fishing.

It's the same theory I have about ardent golfers. It's one of the few valid excuses left to get a man away from the wife and kiddies. My guess is that this friend of mine (to be on the safe side, let's call him Delaney, although his name happens to be Irving Brecher) is unhappy about something and tries to forget his problem by fishing in far-away places. He nailed me one day with, "Groucho. I know you don't like fishing, but you know there is fishing—and fishing."

"You're so right," I nodded as I edged away from him.

But Delaney is a very eloquent, persuasive gent and can't be brushed aside that easily. "How would you like to catch a trout as long as your arm?" he continued.

"I don't like trout," I replied. "I don't even like my arm. What I'm crazy about is Kansas City T-bone steaks with hash brown potatoes, home-made apple pie and a good-sized chunk of Cheddar cheese—and if the waitress is good-looking, I'd like her marital status and phone number."

He shook his head sadly. "I can't understand your not liking trout. You could smoke it and have enough for the whole winter."

"When I smoke," I answered, "I prefer a good cigar."

He chose to ignore this feeble joke, and continued, "We'll get two other buddies of mine, princes, both of them. We'll rent a car and drive up to Jackson Hole, Wyoming. An Indian guide told a friend of mine that there's a lake up there that's never been fished, and he said the air is like wine. It'll be an unforgettable experience. Something you can tell your grandchildren."

I later tried telling this story to my grandchildren, but it didn't work. You see, the minute they spy me they always run away and, unfortunately, I can't run fast enough to catch them.

Meanwhile, back to mine host, Delaney. "How's about it?" he persisted. "Will you come along? We'll pack some booze, beer, sandwiches—and, Groucho, I'll promise you a million laughs." This was a few years ago. He still owes me 999,999 laughs.

ANOTHER THING ABOUT this piscatorial racket is the rigid rule that requires you to get up at the crack of dawn.

This is one of those silly legends that I suppose will live forever. If there are fish in a lake or stream at 5 a.m., unless they are caught during the day, they certainly must be there at 5 p.m. If not, where did they go? Besides, how do they know when it's five in the morning?

At any rate, one grim and smoggy morning we all dragged ourselves into the car, fortified with bicarbonate, Band-aids, booze, cigars and funny clothes. Two hours out of Los Angeles, miles from a gas station, we discovered we had no gas in the car. We tried flagging other cars, but one look at us and they pressed harder on the accelerator. Well, everyone is familiar with this bit. It happens all the time. One of us was elected to walk back three miles to a station and return with a tin can full of gasoline. Since I was the oldest one in the group and could hardly walk at all, this distinction was conferred upon me.

Mr. Delaney, the alleged host, had decided not to risk driving his expensive car up through the wilderness, so at his suggestion we all chipped in and rented an old Buick. (I later discovered he had rented this wreck from his uncle, who had been trying for two years to trade it in on a '37 Chevrolet.) If you think the Buick was old, you should have seen the tyres. Four hours out of Los Angeles we had a blow-out. I don't mean a party: I mean a hole in the tyre large enough to stuff a shrunken head into. Luckily, this time we were only a half-mile from a garage, and in less time than it takes to tell (three hours, to be exact), the garage man decided that this old piece of rubber was beyond repair. The host, with his customary generosity, then invited us all to chip in and pay for the new tyre.

We had many other gay adventures along the highway. At sundown the first night out, one of Delaney's chums became car-sick from the rolling and lurching of the ancient limousine over the hump-backed roads, and passed out. We carried him out of the car, gently laid him on the ground near a polluted stream and threw water in his face until he returned to consciousness. Apparently he enjoyed this attention, for after that he became car-sick every few hours, and this constant carrying him in and out of the car slowed us up considerably. At one point we seriously considered burying him along the wayside, but we were playing Ghost at the time and we couldn't afford to lose

him. He was the only one in the car who could spell words
with more than four letters.

SOME DAYS LATER we arrived at Jackson Hole, none the
worse for wear except that we could hardly walk, thanks to
the cramped quarters in the Buick. We looked up the Indian
guide whom Delaney had engaged, and he immediately warned
us to keep our eyes straight ahead and not give the local
womenfolk the once-over. "Men up here real men," he grunted.
"No like stranger from Hollywood."

To avoid any trouble, we had our dinner in a private dining-
room at the lodge. We then quickly rushed to our bedrooms
and locked ourselves in until the following morning. Having
nothing to read but an old copy of *Confidential* and two of my
daughter's comic books (*Porky Pig* and *Donald Duck*), I decided
to turn in early and get a good night's rest. Taking three
Seconals and a generous amount of phenobarbitone, in less than
three hours I drifted off into nature's oldest remedy—slumber-
land.

Fifteen minutes later (or so it seemed), the Indian pounded
on my door and yelled, "You fellahs ready? Fish no wait.
We go now!"

"Ugh!" I hollered back at him, but he had disappeared.
Rousing my fellow-sufferers, and still groggy from the sleeping pills, I quickly swallowed a handful of thyroid tablets to
prepare me for the death-trail.

Rubbing our eyes and stumbling over each other in the
darkness, we climbed into the ancient Buick and immediately
began playing Ghost. Up to now I hadn't caught any fish,
but I was getting a hell of an education.

We had driven sixty miles when our guide stopped the car.
A few feet away stood four saddle horses, much more alert
than we were. Apparently they had had a good night's rest,
for they were prancing, dancing and snorting like prize bulls
at stud.

The Indian helped us all into our saddles, then slap-
ping the horses on the rump he shouted, "Go!" Shaking
with fright and clutching the pommels with both hands, we
galloped the next fifteen miles. The trail then became

impassable. The guide told us to dismount and he would equip us for the final trek. He explained why the horses couldn't go any farther. "Swamp ahead. Horses sink in. No get-um out."

Ahead of us, as far as the eye could see, loomed a greenish-grey, gooey mess. In addition to my toilet articles, I was now festooned with a frying-pan, a fishing-rod, a ten-pound sack of buckwheat flour and a can of bait. All the others were similarly loaded. Our guide, Son of Cochise, carried nothing.

IT WAS NOW five o'clock and the sun made its usual appearance. I hadn't walked a hundred yards before I sank half-way to my knees in the ooze. My three companions hauled me out and the guide warned us that we'd have to be careful where we stepped. "Get in line. All of you," he said. "Follow guide!" He was quite a conversationalist. Unadorned with any equipment, the Indian took long, rapid, confident strides. Behind him stumbled the four merry fishermen, slipping and sloshing through the slime.

As we straggled towards the lake, we encountered a new hazard. The guide said they were deer-flies. This was an appropriate name for them, for they were almost the size of a small deer. They charged at us like locusts devouring a corn-field and, encumbered as we were with all the hardware we were lugging, it was virtually impossible to shake them off. Within ten minutes my face looked like a piece of rejected meat in a Mexican butcher's shop, and I was happy to see that my three companions were all in the same condition. There wasn't a fly on the Indian.

Four hours later, decorated with bites, bumps and bandages, we arrived at the lake. It was too early for dinner and too late for lunch. Except for a few deer-flies, I hadn't eaten a thing all day. Sinking to the ground in relief, we divested ourselves of our paraphernalia. Our friend, Dizzy David, the All-American hypochondriac, who had been car-sick on the way up, suddenly decided this would be a good time to faint. Before we knew it, he was stretched out again. After thumping him back to consciousness, the guide told us where to pitch our tents. We were to rest in sleeping-bags, two to a tent.

THE LAKE SPARKLED in the late afternoon sun, and except for the fact that we knew we had to make the same journey back, we all felt pretty good. The Indian then ordered us to collect some twigs and logs, and in less than two hours he had a roaring fire going. I finally spoke up. "Ugh! How about eating?" (I think it's always wise, when one is in a foreign country, to speak their language.)

"Chum," he said, "fire no good. Fire not ready. Logs wet. Fire take long time. Fire go out. Ashes come. Then chow." (In Italian, chow means "goodbye," but there was no point in telling him this. The fact is, there was no point in telling him anything. He was fully content to spend the rest of the afternoon collecting hot ashes.)

I said, "Ugh!" (I found out later that this was his name.) "Why do you need such a big fire?"

"Mountain lion! Timber wolf! No like fire!" he grunted.

This certainly was a cheery way to start the evening. There was now a good chance of my being eaten by a wild beast, just to catch something I didn't want in the first place! I had always hoped to die at home, surrounded by my family and friends and uttering some earth-shaking last statement that would make all the front pages the following morning. I now had to worry about winding up as a mountain lion's *hors d'œuvre*.

It was growing chilly. Chilly is hardly the word for it. It was getting cold. Ice cold! I guess it must have been the unaccustomed exercise, for by this time we were all starving. Eventually the fire died down into glowing ashes and our friend, the redskin (actually he was whiter than Delaney), began to prepare dinner. On top of the fire he placed a griddle, and on the griddle he rubbed some odd-looking grease. I don't know what kind of grease it was, but it smelled like something he had drained from the crank-case of the Buick. Nevertheless, we watched hungrily as he placed some sausages in the hot grease. As soon as they were done to a crisp, black turn, he poured a yellowish concoction on the griddle which, to my surprise (and probably his) turned out to be flapjacks. We were ravenous, and we ate flapjacks and sausages as fast as he could dish them out.

In most Western pictures, after the cowboys have had their chow they usually sit around the camp-fire, plucking at a guitar and singing "Buffalo Gal," "Home on the Range," and "Git Along, Li'l Dogie." We had no guitar and none of us could sing. So, logy from the heavy food and utterly bored with one another, we all decided to turn in.

MR. DELANEY (*né* Brecher), the louse who had got me into this fix, was my tent-mate. Rapidly undressing in the freezing air, and wearing nothing but our shorts, we crept into our sleeping-bags. I guess parts of the sleeping-pills I had taken the night before were still circulating inside of me, for I fell asleep almost immediately. It was then around 11 P.M.

I woke up two hours later. My stomach was jumping up and down and rumbling like a laundromat gone berserk. I realized that I wasn't accustomed to eating flapjacks and greasy sausages just before going to bed, but I had never felt like this before. I later discovered that it wasn't just the food. It seems that after we had retired for the night, our Indian guide, Ugh, his motherly instincts aroused, had silently crept into our tents and, being a veteran woodsman, he had rubbed creosote on the top of each sleeping-bag to ward off the deer-flies. Well, son, between the smell of that creosote and the greasy garbage I had recently consumed, I was in great shape!

By this time it was really freezing, and for all I knew there was a mountain lion crouching in the shrubbery, licking his chops and waiting for his dinner. I didn't care. I had to throw up or die. My first impulse was to throw up on Delaney, my genial host, but he looked bad enough without any additional desecration. I looked at him. He was sleeping like a papoose. I finally decided I had to get out of that bag and give my all . . . or else.

The lake was only twenty feet away, and I stood there in my shorts in the bitter night air, violently and eagerly relinquishing all I had eaten to the fishes. (Assuming that there were any.) Once the debris was disposed of, I raced back to the tent. Here I got another whiff of the creosote and quickly leaped back to the lake. The constant sprinting back and forth, and bounding in and out of the tent, finally awakened Delaney. He blinked his eyes, sat up and asked, "You fishing already?"

"Fishing!" I moaned. "I'm deathly ill!"

"You're probably hungry," he said. "Why don't you ask the guide to fix you some hot cakes and sausages?"

"Hot cakes and sausages! I tell you I'm dying, Father Abraham. I'm *dying*!"

"Relax, my boy," he soothed. "Just relax. Let old Doctor Delaney fix you up. In ten minutes you'll be a new man."

At the moment I was a very old man, but I was in no condition to bandy words.

Delaney whipped out a large bottle of salts, which apparently he always took to bed with him, poured a generous amount into a tin cup and said, "Here. Take this cup down to the lake. Fill it with that cool, clear mountain water and drink it. In a little while you'll have the strength of ten men." He then said, "Selah," and soon was fast asleep again.

I had made many trips to the lake that night, but this was the first time I had carried a cup. Shivering in my shorts, I quickly swallowed the swill and crept back to our igloo.

JUST AS I CLOSED my eyes, Ugh shook our sleeping-bags and announced, "Hurry, men. Fish bite now!" Bright and groggy, I quickly slipped into my clothes. Our Indian friend started to prepare breakfast, and when I saw him pouring the same yellow mixture on the griddle and spotted the sausages awaiting their turn, I decided I would skip that course for ever and dine on something light, like deer-flies and creosote.

Now if you will remember, dear reader, my sleeping companion of the night before had slipped me an abundant dose of salts. I hope this doesn't sound too gross, but Dame Nature is a relentless taskmaster.

Not wishing to appear vulgar, I asked Ugh where the powder-room was. He looked up in astonishment. "You go hunting?" he asked. "You want powder?"

"No, you don't understand," I answered, hopping up and down impatiently. "I mean, where does a man go when he has to *go*!"

Ugh pointed towards the sky, a beatific smile on his kisser.

"White man go same place Indian go. Happy hunting ground."

"At the moment," I pointed out, "this is not practical. That's a long trip, and to be honest with you, I'm in no condition to wait that long!"

I couldn't wait around to hear his answer, because it was later than he knew. I dashed into the woods and took my stance, cursing Delaney, the Indian and the whole miserable expedition. At that moment someone waved at me. It was a peculiar wave. I couldn't see too clearly, for in my haste to commune with nature, I had left my glasses behind in the tent. He waved again. His hands looked strange. He must be wearing gloves, I decided. If he wasn't, those were certainly the hairiest fingers since the Neanderthal man.

Anyone who knows me will agree that I'm always willing to meet a friendly figure halfway, so when he waved at me I waved back. As he advanced, I suddenly noticed that he was completely covered with fur. That was when I stopped waving and started running!

It is very difficult to run with your clothing at half-mast. Besides, I was in my bare feet. I reached my tent inches ahead of the bear and dived, head first, into the only opening I could see—my sleeping-bag. I decided that if he was planning to have me for breakfast, he would have to start with my feet. They were expendable.

He stuck his hairy head into the tent, and whether it was because of me or the creosote I never found out, but he took one sniff, turned away and lumbered down towards the lake. For his sake, I hope that grizzly wasn't as sick as I was!

WELL, THAT'S ABOUT all there is to this saga of the great outdoors. I know now why we heard that the lake had never been fished before. There weren't any fish in it. My friends fished steadily for three days, while I played canasta with Sitting Bull. My companions never caught a fish, and as a fitting climax, Ugh beat me out of eighty-three dollars! On the return trip through the swamp, the Indian confessed he had once been a croupier in Las Vegas.

Our fainting companion fainted only once more. That was when we were safely back in Los Angeles and Delaney slipped him the bill for his share of the expedition and the rental of the Buick.

CHAPTER TWENTY-SIX

FOOT-IN-MOUTH DISEASE

WHENEVER A MONOLOGIST walked out on a stage you could safely bet he would open with that old standard, "A funny thing happened to me on my way to the theatre." This was once a fairly effective way of introducing a monologue, but actually I doubt if anything funny ever happened to any monologist on his way to any theatre. (On his way back to the hotel—well, that's something else again.)

What the monologist was trying to do was get into his act without too much preparation, and what I'm reluctantly doing now is going into a subject that, over the years, has created all kinds of trouble for me. I guess it could be called a nervous compulsion, an automatic reflex or just a basic perverseness. But whatever it is, it has caused me many uncomfortable moments. Perhaps an analyst would describe it as foot-in-mouth disease. I'll cite a few examples just to show you how easy it is to talk yourself, or write yourself, into trouble, once you fall into the habit.

I'm not a particularly gregarious fellow. If anything, I suppose I'm a bit on the misanthropic side. I've tried being a jolly good club member, but after a month or so my mouth aches from baring my teeth in a false smile. The pseudo-friendliness, the limp handshake and the extra firm handshake (both of which should be abolished by the Health Department) are not for me. This also goes for the hearty slapper-on-the-back and the all-around, general claptrap that you are subjected to from the All-American bores, characters you would instantly flee from if you weren't trapped in a club-house.

Some years ago, after considerable urging, I consented to join a prominent theatrical organization. By an odd coincidence, it was called the Delaney Club. Here, I thought, within these hallowed walls of Thespis, we would sit of an evening with our Napoleon brandies and long-stemmed pipes and discuss Chaucer, Charles Lamb, Ruskin, Voltaire, Booth, the Barrymores, Duse, Shakespeare, Bernhardt and all the other legendary figures of the theatre and literature. The first night I went there, I found thirty-two fellows playing gin rummy with marked cards, five members shooting loaded dice on a suspiciously bumpy carpet and four members in separate phone booths calling women who were other men's wives.

A few nights later the club had a banquet. I don't clearly remember what the occasion was. I think it was to honour one of the members who had successfully managed to evade the police for more than a year. The dining tables were long and narrow, and unless you arrived around three in the afternoon you had no control over who your dinner companion was going to be. That particular night I was sitting next to a barber who had cut me many times, both socially and with a razor. At one point he looked slowly around the room, then turned to me and said, "Groucho, we're certainly getting a lousy batch of new members!"

I chose to ignore this remark and tried talking to him about Chaucer, Ruskin and Shakespeare, but he had switched to denouncing electric razors as a death-blow to the tonsorial arts, so I dried up and resumed drinking. The following morning I sent the club a wire stating, PLEASE ACCEPT MY RESIGNATION. I DON'T WANT TO BELONG TO ANY CLUB THAT WILL ACCEPT ME AS A MEMBER.

BEFORE *Confidential* magazine had trouble with the postal authorities, the police and Hollywood, not to mention vice versa, they published two pieces about me. They weren't particularly vicious, but I must admit I was annoyed even to see my name in that scrofulous sheet.

In the first article, they accused me of liking young girls. I would be the last one to deny this. The second article said my TV show was crooked. This was nonsense and hardly worth denying. However, my patience exhausted, I wrote a letter to the Editor wherein I said, "Gentlemen? If you continue to write nasty pieces about me, I shall be obliged to cancel my subscription."

LAST YEAR I went to Europe. Having been there before, I remembered how dreadful the cigars were on the Continent, particularly in Italy. So along with my hot-water bottle, Baedeker Guide, Band-aids, codeine, passport and two pounds of Instant Postum, I tucked a hundred cigars into my portmanteau.

I was staying at the Hassler Hotel in Rome, and I had just finished polishing off a magnificent dinner. Lighting one of my costly stogies, I decided to take a leisurely stroll along the Via Sistina. As I reached the corner someone bumped into me, and my expensive cheroot fell to the sidewalk. Having eighty-five cents tied up in this cigar, and being basically a miser, I stooped to retrieve the weed.

As I bent down to pick it up, I angrily muttered, "Oh, hell!" Then, sticking the cigar back in my mouth, I turned to see who the clumsy oaf was who had bumped into me. I paled as I looked at two priests in full regalia, looking straight through me. I was embarrassed. Here I was, a visitor from a strange land, profaning a holy city and cursing like an infidel! To make matters worse, I knew they had heard me say "hell."

At this point one of them beckoned to me. I walked over, fully expecting to be admonished for my crudeness and vulgarity. But I realized I had it coming and I was prepared to accept a dressing-down. As I approached them, one of the priests reached into the folds of his cassock, pulled out two cigars, handed them to me and said, "Mr. Marx, you just said the secret word!"

I was astonished at their excellent English and even more astonished on talking to them to discover that they were from Cleveland, Ohio. They then told me that they had come to Rome to attend a religious convocation, and that back home in the States they always listened to my show. Incidentally, the cigars were first-rate. I'm sure they must have brought them with them from Cleveland.

A FEW YEARS AGO I was invited to visit Mexico on a goodwill tour. Since the whole trip was to be "on the cuff" and, since I have always been one of free-loading's staunchest disciples, I quickly accepted.

It was a movie festival honouring famous actors and actresses from all over the world. The first day in Mexico City, we were all herded into a large assembly room, where a representative of the government was explaining in endless detail where and what our activities were to be for the entire week. He rattled on rapidly in Spanish, but luckily he paused every few minutes to allow his aide to translate his remarks into French, German, Portuguese and English.

At one point he said, "I am deeply honoured to inform you that at four o'clock tomorrow afternoon you are all invited to meet the President at the palace."

I raised my hand. The translator noticed me and said, "Yes, what is it, Mr. Marx?"

I said, "What assurance have I got that he'll still be President by four o'clock tomorrow afternoon?"

From that moment on, for some strange reason, no one in the entire crowd spoke to me. Neither the group from Hollywood, the Latin contingent nor the European visitors thought it prudent to be seen in my company. One unfortunate remark and, overnight, I had become a skulking pariah in a strange land. South of the border I was the equivalent of Typhoid Mary—in spades!

Every night that week there was a banquet honouring something or other, but no matter what the event, I always found myself seated at a small single table at the far end of the dining-hall, far, far from the madding throng. They all had wine with their dinners. The best I ever got was bottled water and *tamales*.

My remark certainly was ill-advised and, I suppose, rather rude, but at that my prophecy was fairly accurate. Two days after my *faux pas*, they found one of the President's staff lying face down on his bed, a large-sized knife in his back. It seems he had been too attentive to the wife of one of his friends. It could just as well have happened to the President of Mexico. I believe his name was Delaney or Aleman or something.

ONE NIGHT, Paramount Studios invited me to attend a screening of *Samson and Delilah* starring Hedy Lamarr and Victor Mature. At the conclusion of the picture one of the heads of the studio came over to me and asked how I liked it.

"Well," I began, "there's just one glaring fault that——"

He immediately bristled. "Fault! Just what do you mean?"

I said, "No picture can hold my interest where the leading man's bust is larger than the leading lady's!"

Many years went by before Paramount invited me to another screening.

So FAR, none of the slipped quips I've quoted in this chapter led to the mayhem I so richly deserved. In fact, no one has clobbered me yet for putting my foot in their mouth. But I sure came awfully close to it at the ball-park one afternoon.

This was no ordinary ball-game. It was a deathless encounter between two girls' teams, and the gals were pretty good at that. But their skill with the bat and the glove was by no means their most outstanding attraction.

One dark-haired beauty stationed at third base was a particular stand-out in her tight blue jersey and white baseball pants. I was attending the game alone, but I've never been noted for my British reserve. Turning to the burly stranger in the next seat, I said, "You know, I never dreamed I'd be sitting in the grandstand of a ball-park and wishing I was in bed with the third baseman."

"Is that so?" snarled the stranger, half rising from his seat. "That third baseman happens to be my sister!"

By this time I was part way up the aisle. "I'm going to buy some peanuts," I shouted over my shoulder. "Want some?"

I never did hear his answer. In fact, I never even found the peanut stand. I hope this fellow isn't still sitting in the grandstand waiting for me to bring him his bag of peanuts.

But DON'T THINK I *always* put my foot in my mouth. Sometimes it's a pencil. At least, that's what I used to fill out a Customs manifesto when I returned from a trip to Europe some time ago. I should have used a pen—with disappearing ink.

One of the questions was "What is your occupation?" Without pausing for anything that might qualify as deep cerebration, I filled in "smuggler."

How I ever got out of Customs in less than five hours will for ever remain a mystery. But don't think that it was a dull, inactive afternoon. Have you, dear reader, ever had the more remote portions of your anatomy subjected to non-therapeutic X-rays? Have you ever stood by while they performed the same delicate operation on your luggage? Have you ever taken off your shoes and watched an expert carefully rip out their inner soles in a systematic search for hidden gems?

All of these experiences can easily be yours. Just go to Europe and, when you return, fill in your Customs manifesto with the same unhesitating honesty that I did.

WE NOW COME to the hand-in-mouth division of this little confessional. I was standing in the elevator of the Thalberg Building one day when Greta Garbo entered. She was then at the peak of her career, acknowledged by all as the greatest movie star of the day.

Miss Garbo was wearing a hat approximately the size of a large manhole cover. The rest of her was encased in slacks and a mannish-type coat. I was standing behind her and, being in a playful mood, I gently lifted the back of her hat.

Thinking back on the incident, I can see that the result of lifting the back of a woman's hat is inevitable: the front of the hat slides down over her face. At the time, however, I had not thoroughly worked out this problem in physics.

Miss Garbo turned on me in a rage, angrily pulling up the hat and revealing the classic features that are still admired by millions. "How *dare* you?" she exclaimed in icy tones.

"Oh, I beg your pardon," I replied. "I thought you were a fellow I knew from Kansas City."

No further words were exchanged. But it is pretty obvious to any student of the cinema that this is the real explanation of why Greta Garbo never appeared in any of The Marx Brothers pictures.

LAST YEAR I was invited to attend a May Day dance on the lawn of Melinda's school. The little girls, all twelve years old, looked beautiful, charming and innocent in their pastel pink, blue and yellow dresses. It was a merry festival and all the parents were there to watch their little ones dance gaily in the sun. I was very proud of Melinda, and, like every other parent, I thought *my* daughter was the prettiest.

During the dance, one of the heads of the school came over to me and said, "How do you like it?"

I turned to her and said, "Madam, do you realize that in twelve years fifty per cent. of these children will be getting alimony?"

She looked at me incredulously. As I slunk away into the distance, her eyes followed me with the gaze of a bird seeing its first snake.

I could cite many more examples of this impulsive (or repulsive) foot-in-mouth affliction of mine, but I think by now you've got the idea. Some day I'll learn to keep my big trap shut, maybe.

CHAPTER TWENTY-SEVEN

WHAT PRICE PUMPERNICKEL?

As I GREW SUCCESSFUL, the one thing that continually haunted me was the fear of being destitute in my old age. I realize that this is not an uncommon fear, but in my case the fright was embedded so deep in my psyche that no day passed without my being chilled at the mere thought of it.

My brothers and I had been big stars on the stage and in the movies, and over the years we had probably received far more money than we were worth. But I was always conscious of the fickleness of the profession and, except for a chosen few, how quickly well-known names appeared and disappeared.

I hadn't been poor in years, and I suppose if you've never had money it isn't too bad to die broke. But if you've lived high on the hog for a few decades, the thought of spending your declining years *sans* all the wonderful things you had when you were in the chips can give you the horrors. To be young without money is no great tragedy. Most of us have experienced this. But when your interests change from sex to a monthly check-up at your doctor's office, a large, juicy bank-roll is a wonderfully cushy bulwark against Father Time and the spavined carcass you are gradually acquiring.

I hope this doesen't sound as though I worship at the shrine of Fort Knox to the exclusion of life's other values, but to those who have never had any, I haven't the words to tell you what a lovely, reassuring, comforting thing money is. I've seen too many theatrical stars wind up supported by their guild, or reduced to extra work on a movie set, to ever sneer at the beauties of a healthy bank account.

In 1936 we were doing a picture called *A Day at the Races*, and that morning we were shooting a scene representing the lobby of a prosperous sanatorium. In strategic spots, posing as patients, were fourteen middle-aged women. Between takes Sam Wood, the director, wandered over to me and said,

"Groucho, you see those women over there? Well, ten years ago, twelve of the fourteen were stars and earned fifteen hundred dollars a week and more. Today they're extras, getting ten and a half dollars. Pity, isn't it?"

At this information I shook so with nervousness that I could hardly play the next scene. I don't know if I actually said, "There but for the grace of God go I," but its equivalent was certainly circulating through my morbid mind. When five o'clock came and we quit for the day, I rushed home and even before saying hello to my family, I called up my insurance agent.

"Suppose I was out of work and washed up," I asked, "how much money would I need a week to support myself and my family?"

"Well," he answered, "you'd certainly need a minimum of eighty dollars."

"And how big an annuity would I have to buy to get eighty dollars a week?" I asked.

He said, "If you pay twenty-five thousand dollars cash, and let it lay for twelve years, you would then have eighty dollars a week rolling in the rest of your life."

"Okay," I said, "send me the policy. I'll put a cheque in the mail tonight."

I REALIZE THAT eighty dollars a week doesn't seem like much of an income today, but remember this was twenty-four years ago, and a loaf of pumpernickel could still be purchased for eight cents. Please don't get the impression that my family lived exclusively on pumpernickel. We had many other things. We even owned a piano. It's just that I always measure the country's financial condition by the price of pumpernickel. It used to cost eight cents a loaf. Now it's thirty-three cents. If it ever climbs to fifty, take my advice and run for the hills.

As it happens, I've never been in need of the income from this annuity. But psychologically it was a wonderful investment, and it did wonders for me. For one thing, it helped to alleviate insomnia and, when I negotiated a deal, the mere thought of this eighty bucks standing by was enough to shake the jello from my spine and replace it with concrete. I've never told this to anyone, but, folks, deep down I've always been chicken.

Sometimes I regret my long years of success, for had I again been reduced to comparative poverty, I would have had the enjoyment from that annuity that I had always looked forward to. Unfortunately, good luck never deserted me again. And now in the twilight of my life, it doesn't seem as if I'll ever get a chance to reap the benefits of that psychological crutch I have been leaning on all these years.

THANKS TO THE bravery and derring-do that my eighty bucks ace-in-the-hole gave me, I've been able to take a flier in other branches of show business. For example, I tried radio a number of times. I don't mean listening to it, I mean appearing on it. First with Chico, for Standard Oil of New Jersey. Someone had talked them into having a different show for each week-day. We were one of the lucky five.

Chico and I enacted the deathless roles of two lawyers; the name of our firm was Flywheel, Shyster and Flywheel. The original name was Beagle, Shyster and Beagle, but some lawyer objected to the use of his name and informed our sponsor that if they didn't want to get involved in a big, juicy lawsuit they had better drop the name Beagle, and fast. He contended that strange people continually called him up and asked, "Is this Mr. Beagle?" When he answered, "Yes," the party at the other end would say, "How's your partner, Shyster?" At this point the clever funster would hang up. Beagle's complaint was that this was not only ruining his health, but his practice. Thus, Flywheel, Shyster and Flywheel.

We thought we were doing fine as comic lawyers, but one day a few of the Middle East countries decided they wanted a bigger cut of the oil profits, or else. When this news broke, the price of gasoline nervously dropped two cents a gallon, and Chico and I, along with the other four shows, were gently disentangled from the network.

After that, in swift succession, we were employed by the

American Oil Company and Kellogg's Cornflakes. If you're hungry some morning, you might try this combination.

HAVING FAILED signally with Chico (through no fault of his, I hasten to add, for we did some very funny shows together), I decided to fly solo. This didn't seem to help, for I continued to get bounced. The last ticket-of-leave was from the Delaney Brewing Company. I still think the show I did for them was a pretty good one, but, unfortunately, my opinion wasn't reflected in the ratings. Whether they were accurate or not is open to question, but at any rate they didn't seem to make the head of the company happy. After a year they replaced me with another comedian, Delaney by name. He fared even worse than I did.

I had a premonition that the Delaney Brewery people were going to give me the old heave-ho, for it was only two weeks before the *coup de grâce* that I received an embossed invitation to participate in their one hundredth anniversary celebration. The party was a real gala, and I must say I cut a noble figure that night as the President and I crossed cake-knives, doling out large hunks of lovely pastry to the major and minor executives of this magnificent brewery.

A word of warning to all executives earning twenty thousand dollars a year or more. Be on your guard! Watch yourself! If, during your association with a large company, you one day receive an invitation to attend an important celebration commemorating some milestone or other, immediately start looking for another job! If, in addition to this invitation, you receive word through underground channels that, because of your long years of faithful service, you and the President of the corporation will alternate in cutting the cake—hide! Start looking at the want ads.

Now back to me and that memorable night. As I sliced my way through the succulent goo, I had a premonition that I was in trouble. I suddenly felt a kinship for this once-beautiful cake, as the sharp knife cut relentlessly through its innards. I knew even then that my days were numbered, and that it was only a question of time until a knife similar to the one employed for the cake would be slicing across my professional jugular vein.

None of this is said in anger. The sponsor was a very pleasant, amiable employer. But alas, he was also a practical business-man. He was putting up the money and he certainly had the right to buy what he wanted. It was my misfortune that what he wanted wasn't me.

The preceding paragraph doesn't alter the fact that my advice to all executives is sound. Don't ever let the president or the chairman of the board of a large (or small) corporation invite you to cut the anniversary cake. Before the party, if word reaches you that you have been singled out for this honour, eliminate the middle-man. I mean the cake. In fact, don't even go to the party. Just stay home and cut your own throat!

BEING AN annual failure on radio wasn't doing much for my ego. I listened carefully to all the current shows, and it didn't strike me that they were much better than mine. It wasn't the money (remember, I still had that eighty dollars a week annuity), it was just a matter of pride and a desire to conquer a medium that had successfully rejected me for years.

Oh, I did a lot of guest shots, but that's not quite the same. A guest shot, in case you're a coal-miner in Pennsylvania and not familiar with the term, is an invitation from an advertising agency (with the sponsor's approval, of course) to do four or five minutes of fantastically convulsive banter with the head of the show. Once you have done your little bit, you are quickly shunted off the stage to give the star the rest of the half-hour to strut his talents. At the end of the performance, you are permitted to emerge with the rest of the nonentities and join in a chorus of "There's no Business like Show Business." This is a must. There are a few shows that wind up the proceedings with a religious hymn. The singing prayer, I presume, is to put the fear of God into the sponsor. However, if the show happens to fall on a patriotic holiday, let's say Washington's or Lincoln's birthday, they may vary this wind-up with "God Bless America."

At Christmas, at least fifteen different programmes will present fifteen different versions of Charles Dickens' *Christmas Carol*. You can also count on a dozen obnoxious children bleating the latest novelty Christmas song hit. A few years ago, it was that great ballad, "All I want for Christmas is My Two Front Teeth." As a man who loves children, I want to say publicly, here and now, that I uttered a silent but solemn vow that if those precocious tots ever got those two front teeth they were constantly wailing about, I'd be only too happy to kick 'em down their throats!

SPEAKING OF children, as we seem to be doing, TV is heavily populated with what are loosely termed "family situation comedies." Some of them are beautifully written and have ratings almost as high as the Westerns, but in most cases the writers have the children speaking as though they were forty years old. These tots knock off witticisms that would do credit to George S. Kaufman, Sid Perelman, Mark Twain or G. B. Shaw. As you know, I've raised three children, but I can assure you that this type of crackling dialogue has never been heard around my house. Over a period of thirty-five years I can remember only two jokes that came out of three children, and that's hardly a memorable average. When my son, Arthur, was ten, he wanted an air-gun. Putting on the stern father act, I told him he couldn't have one. "What do you want it for?" I asked.

"I want to go out in the back-yard and shoot bottles off the fence," he answered.

"That's fine!" I said. "Suppose you miss and hit some kid in the eye and blind him for life?"

"I'll be very careful," he insisted. "I'll just shoot at bottles."

"I'm sorry, Arthur, but that's too dangerous," I replied.

Like all kids, he kept pleading and insisting until, finally exasperated, I said, "Look here, son, as long as I'm the head of the house, you're not going to get a gun!"

Looking me straight in the eye, he said, "Dad, if I get a gun, you won't be the head of the house!"

The other deathless line came from my little daughter, Melinda. She was then attending nursery school. She left the house every morning at eight and returned at three in the afternoon. Being a fanatic about "togetherness," and terribly nosy about her activities, I would ask Melinda what she had done in school each day when she returned. She would invariably shrug her shoulders and say, "Nothing, Daddy." Again putting on the pompous padre act, I said, "See here, Melinda, you spend seven hours every day at that nursery school. What do you do there?"

"Oh, Daddy," she answered impatiently, "all we do is paint and go to the toilet!"

Which, by the way, is the most accurate description of a nursery school that's ever been uttered.

I have a theory that most TV writers don't come in contact with many children. Or maybe it's the children who avoid contact with the TV writers. At any rate, they certainly seem to inhabit two different worlds.

But to get back to my own somewhat more mature world, the clock was striking 1947, and radio and I still showed no signs of having been made for each other. And then one of those unpredictable coincidences reached a long arm into my life and waved a microphone in my face.

CHAPTER TWENTY-EIGHT

YOU BET MY LIFE

A VERY NICE MAN, who for some curious reason thought he was beholden to me (no, it wasn't Delaney), used to produce a show for the Walgreen Drug Company. They did this spectacle only once a year, and they didn't seem to care how much money they spent. The result was that each year this friend of mine engaged me at a fat salary to do a five-minute spot with a partner. On this particular show my partner turned out to be Bob Hope. We both started kidding around with the dialogue, ad-libbing and generally ignoring the script. Bob, by the way, can take care of himself in this department.

Now, I sound like a real ham, but the truth of it is that the routine was hilarious. When I came off the stage, a bulky, doubtful-looking man sidled over to me and asked if I would be interested in doing a quiz show.

"A quiz show?" I repeated rather superciliously. "Pardon me, suh, but do you live in a tree?"

He said, "No, but I have many branch offices!"

I waited until his hysterical laughter subsided, then I continued, "Well, suh" (I had been drinking Southern Comfort all morning, and it was creeping into my dialogue), "let me tell you-all something. A quiz show is the lowest form of animal life. Don't you know there are over fifty of them on the air this very minute, swindling the public in devious ways?"

[He hung his head in shame. I learned later that three of these shows were his.]

Here I had just done a brilliant five-minute spot with one of America's great comedians, and before me stood this rather venal-looking sneak, offering me a golden chance to disappear permanently from show business. In high dudgeon, I proudly stalked away to my dressing-room near the boiler-room in the cellar.

He was a persistent fellow and apparently immune to insult. Large and awkward though he was, he somehow scrambled downstairs and arrived in the cellar before me. "Mr. Marx,

I didn't mean to offend you," he whined apologetically as he offered me a cheap cigar which I quickly stepped on. "I realize that 'quiz show' is an ugly phrase, but I don't want you to do just another quiz show. Don't you see, Groucho? The quiz part would be just a device for you to engage in conversation with a lot of strange people and interrogate them about their lives and their loves. You see, I watched you ad-libbing with Bob Hope, and that's exactly what I would like you to do on my show, Grouch."

The character then took two pinches of snuff and began sneezing with such emphasis that all the dormant dust in the dressing-room began blowing about, half-concealing me from this baleful man. Ten minutes later, the grime having settled, I eyed him suspiciously and asked, "Suh, do you have a sponsor?"

"Grou," he replied (I found his increasing familiarity almost unbearable, but, having been reared carefully, I allowed old baggy pants to gabble on), "don't worry about that. Let me put this thing together and I predict that in a year the show will be a sensational success."

DESPITE HIS DUBIOUS appearance, he turned out to be a fairly accurate prophet. We first went on radio, and in addition to our commercial success we impressed the critics well enough to earn the Peabody Award, one of the few distinctive accolades in show business. The following year we moved over to TV. That was eleven years ago and, unless the sponsor watches my show some night, I am prepared to display myself publicly until I fall apart. (When this happens, please send any mucilage you can spare to Groucho Marx, care of the National Broadcasting Company.)

The success of the show proves what I've always maintained. Talent isn't enough. You have to be lucky. I think if I had my choice of one, I would choose luck. I was lucky to meet this mysterious gentleman, whose name, by the way, is not Delaney, but John Guedel, and who really doesn't deserve any of the libellous names I have called him. And I was lucky to get involved in the kind of show that just seemed to fit my particular talent, small or large as it may be.

Some of our contestants have gone on to success in show business. Most of them have disappeared into limbo. We have had scientists, musicians, singers, acrobats, an elevator jockey who sang three songs in Sanskrit, a woman who ran a hotel for cats, a man who blew up a large inner tube and then fainted just as the quiz started, an Italian widow whom we deliberately kept on for three successive weeks in hopes that she could snare a husband, and a woman who swam to Catalina and back without stopping. We've had admirals, generals, mayors, statesmen and tramps. (The tramps were very interesting.) We've had brilliant high school kids, far removed from the "beatnik" types. Here are just a few of the outstanding contestants who appeared on the show:

Anna Badovinac. She was born and raised in the town of Badovinac, Yugoslavia. Most everybody living in this town was named Badovinac. She married Pete Badovinac, who left her and came to America. She came here, too, looking for him. She never found him. But she did find Jim Badovinac, and married him! He died. She was on "You Bet Your Life" in search of another Badovinac.

Prince Monolulu, self-admitted Prince of Ethiopia. Monny is actually a well-known horse-race tout in London. A fine figure of a man, six feet two, he made quite an impression standing there in ostrich-feather headdress, lion's-claw necklace, purple-red-blue-and-silver pantaloons with the Star of David emblazoned on his back!

Aly Wassil, Pakistan's unofficial goodwill ambassador to the United States, a very bright and witty U.C.L.A. student now on lecture tour. His turban caused considerable comment. He said a woman attending one of his lectures in Beverly Hills asked what he kept under his hat. "A cobra," he answered. "Don't you worry about it?" she wanted to know. Aly's reply was: "No, I don't worry at all—you see, he's insured!"

We've had Mr. and Mrs. Story, of Bakersfield, mother and father (or sire and dam, and I think by this time the dam has burst) of twenty-three children. We also had *all* of the kids. We've had Joe Louis, General Bradley, Liberace and Fifi Dorsey. Then there was that "sheep-headed woman" from the circus, and the world's strongest man (three of them claimed to be, but unfortunately we couldn't get them together). Charles Goren, the bridge expert, made a big hit, as did John Charles Thomas; Rex, the smartest horse in the world, who has been married three times; and a woman with seventy-eight cats (and all seventy-eight were also on the show).

BILLY PEARSON, the jockey who went on to quiz fame, started his intellectual career on our show. We had a woman who told about the "woodpeckers in her cocoa palms," a man who "walked" across twenty-three miles of ocean on some floating shoes he built. (He had to be rescued about fifty feet from where he started.) Two real hoboes, recruited right off the wagons, joined our little entertainment. One of them won five hundred dollars, went on a five-day drunk and got thrown out of Alcoholics Anonymous.

Pedro Gonzalez-Gonzalez was the biggest thing we've had. He was a short, scrawny, Mexican comedian who had a provocative air about him, plus a lot of talent. He was very funny, and at the end of the spot, I said: "You know, you're a pretty funny fellow, Pedro; you and I could go into vaudeville together. What should we call ourselves?"

To which Pedro answered: "We could call ourselves 'Gonzalez-Gonzalez and Marx!'"

"Thirty-five years in show business," I cried, "and I'm playing third billing to two people!"

Greg Morton, founder and President of "Sodowo," the Society for the Domination of Women, appeared on "You Bet Your Life" and went on record with the cute notion that women should lose their vote, have higher entrance requirements to colleges and pay a dowry to their husbands. Mail poured in by the truckload. (As if we didn't know it would in advance. Why do you think we put him on?) Curiously enough, most of the female letter-writers indicated they'd fallen in love with him!

And we shouldn't forget Eve Samler, aged widow looking for a man; as she talked with me, she sent a stream of bubbles soaring upwards from her hat. And there was Zetta Wells, who had a "very talented myna bird" that could talk and sing, except it wouldn't on our show; then, in the middle of the quiz and squarely out of left field, the bird suddenly started whistling "The Star-spangled Banner," at which point the whole audience got up and stood at attention.

No one ever left the show angry, even those who didn't win any money. They always thanked me and said it was a wonderful experience. Altogether we've watched a parade of more than twenty-five hundred contestants.

The list is endless. Some gave their winnings to charity; most of them needed it and kept the money themselves. But they were all worth talking to. It's been twelve wonderful years and I've enjoyed every minute of it.

WHEN YOU CONSIDER that television grinds on for twelve or fourteen hours a day, you must concede it is a remarkable medium. If you have any criticism, please temper it with mercy. True, too many of its hours are given over to boredom and bilge, but despite its limitations and restrictions, over the year it gives the public many hours of satisfaction and enjoyment. At times—Sunday afternoons, for example—it is even educational.

To the actor it is Nirvana. No travelling, no squalid hotels, no snowbound trains in the hinterlands, no theatre managers fleeing with your salary. The money is good (what you can keep of it), and, what is even dearer to the actor's heart, you are admired and loved by millions of people.

I think I can best sum it up by relating what happened to me not so long ago. I was walking down State Street in Chicago when a middle-aged couple came up and began circling me. They went around two or three times, looking me over as though I were a creature from outer space. Then the wife hesitantly came over and asked, "You're him, aren't you? You're Groucho?"

I nodded.

She then touched me timidly on the arm and said, "Please don't die. Just keep on living."

Who could ask for anything more?

THE END